DYNAMIC ECONOMICS

DYNAMIC ECONOMICS

BURTON H. KLEIN

Harvard University Press
Cambridge, Massachusetts
London, England 1977

Printed in the United States of America

Library of Congress Cataloging in Publication Data

Klein, Burton H
Dynamic economics.

Includes bibliographical references and index.
1. Economics. 2. Statics and dynamics (Social sciences) 3. Equilibrium (Economics) 4. United States—Economic conditions—1945- I. Title.
HB171.K519 330 76-58550
ISBN 0-674-21866-3

To my wife

Preface

Twenty years ago economists were attempting to explain two paradoxes associated with America's splendid economic performance: the growth paradox and the trade paradox. In terms of orthodox economic doctrine the long-term growth of nations depends upon thrift and capital accumulation. But America's growth came about mainly in the form of productivity increases supported by the generation of new technological knowledge. And according to classical trade theory, as the most affluent country in the world the United States should have been exporting capital-intensive products (automobiles) and importing labor-intensive products (computers). However, as the technological leader of the world the United States exported both capital- and labor-intensive items, and the distinguishing feature of its trade was the exchange of recently pioneered technologies for raw materials and products whose pioneering had been more or less completed. In other words, the United States was exchanging goods created by imaginative entrepreneurs, who could deal with a high degree of uncertainty, for goods whose further development and production depended less upon dynamic than upon methodical organizations. Indeed, most impressive about its splendid economic performance is that it was accompanied by advances no one could have predicted and involved a high degree of dynamic behavior: behavior whose outcome cannot be predicted until entrepreneurs put their imaginations to work.

Within the past fifteen years, however, the American economy has become more predictable. Just as during the Victorian Age productivity advances slowed down in Britain, so has there recently been a productivity slowdown in the United States. And just as Britain's technological leadership eroded steadily during the Victorian Age so is this occurring now in the "New Victorian" United States.

Associated with these declines in dynamic behavior, first in Great Britain and then in the United States, has been an even more profound paradox for classical economic theory. According to equilibrium theory the concepts of stability and predictability go hand in hand. However, the slowdown of the British economy in the third quarter of the last century was succeeded by the appearance of economic instability in the form of an economy that was vulnerable simultaneously to both inflation and recession. And it is becoming more and more apparent that the American economy is acquiring a similar pattern of economic instability.

However, while the desire to explain these three mysteries was the principal motivation for writing this book, it is impossible to develop a theory without basing it upon economic reality. It is essential to start with a fairly typical representation of how progress comes about, and then devise a theory that is not only consistent with the observations, but can also make good predictions. And I feel confident that the dynamic theory to be presented provides a better understanding of economic reality than static theory does. Nevertheless, it would be naive to assume that this book can provide more than a beginning of our understanding of the microbehavior within firms that is associated with dynamic processes, and the incentives that favor or disfavor this microbehavior. Neither in chemistry nor in biology were the dynamic revolutions made in a day.

Of course I am not the first to introduce dynamic considerations into economics. However, previous attempts have closely resembled classical thermodynamics: economic theory has been made somewhat more realistic with the introduction of the element of time, but its basic flavor has not changed. In particular, dynamic considerations were introduced into economic theory without making it less deterministic.

By contrast, this book has been written more in the spirit of twentieth-century science. This is not to say, however, that the definition of a "dynamic process" to be found in this book closely matches the definitions contained in chemistry and biology books.

Moreover, any resemblance between my concept of dynamics and that employed in any physics book should be regarded as purely coincidental, and for good reason: the dynamic processes with which physicists deal contain no human beings.

The spirit of twentieth-century science requires that to better explain reality economists must adopt a less deterministic theory. To insist upon a high degree of determinism is, in effect, to impose pompous preconditions on our subject matter. And, while we can never hope to understand economic reality in all of its detail, to understand the plight of the American economy today, and the policy measures required to deal with it, it is imperative to adopt a more realistic theory.

To be sure, during the nineteenth-century age of pompous preconditions it was essential for any discipline to appear quite as deterministic as Newtonian celestial mechanics if it was to become established as a "science." However, the attitudes once required to provide economics with scientific respectability are not necessarily the attitudes that will enable it to evolve into a mature science that can better and better explain reality. And inasmuch as two hundred years have elapsed since Adam Smith wrote the *Wealth of Nations,* the infant-industries argument is not applicable today.

Adopting a new theory is almost like adopting a new religion. But one does not change his religion overnight. For much longer than he would like to believe, he desperately clings to both religions, and only succeeds in confusing himself. As a result this book has gone through two or three dozen drafts, and has been commented upon by at least two or three dozen people. Grateful as I am, however, I shall not try to list their names, because it would appear to be an exercise in name dropping. Nevertheless, there are several people who deserve special thanks. One of them is Paco Lagerstrom, who taught me that if science is what scientists do, my conception of science was entirely wrong. Three are former students who played an important role in the evolution of my ideas. They are Georg H. Küster, Ionnis Kessides, and Allan Coltry. Roger Klein supplied some very instructive comments, which helped me see a few key points more clearly. But most of all, I want to thank my wife and editor, Cecile, without whose encouragement and pertinacity this book never would have been completed.

Contents

DYNAMIC ECONOMICS

1. Three Mysteries

The purpose of this book is to demonstrate the utility of dynamic economic theory by showing how it can explain two older mysteries and a relatively new one. The two older mysteries are commonly known as the growth paradox and the trade paradox. The growth paradox was discovered in 1956 by Moses Abramovitz, who showed that during the period 1900-1950 increases in capital and labor inputs played a minor role in the economic growth of the United States.[1] According to Robert Solow's later calculations for the same period, one-eighth of the per capita GNP growth of the United States is to be attributed to a per capita increase in the capital stock and about seven-eighths to a pure productivity increase (increases in real GNP divided by the weighted inputs).[2] To resolve this mystery a theory is needed to explain the gain in rate of productivity.

The trade paradox, which was first discovered by Wassily Leontief in 1956, was restated ten years later by Raymond Vernon. Leontief found that classical trade theory failed to predict the pattern of trade of the United States; that is, he found that the United States did not export capital-intensive items and import labor-intensive items.[3] Vernon discovered an alternative pattern of trade when he found evidence of a "trade cycle" in which the United States exported newly pioneered products, whose large-scale production was later taken up in the more advanced countries, and which, at a still later stage in the cycle, the United States imported.[4] For example, just as today the United States is the leader in computers, in the 1930s it was the leader in commercial aircraft, and in the 1920s, the leader in automobiles. In other words, Vernon discovered that, as the technological leader of the world for roughly half a century, the United States traded newly pioneered products for older products and raw materials. To resolve this mystery it is essential to show which particular characteristics of the United States' economy resulted in its technological leadership. Why did entrepreneurship and risk-taking flourish more in America than in other countries?

The third mystery is why American technological leadership is declining in this century as Britain's declined in the last; why its productivity performance is worsening relative to other countries; and why the United States has developed an economy vulnerable simultaneously to inflation and recession. The third mystery can be described as an "economic stability paradox." As the United States economy has become more predictable and less dynamic, so has it become less capable of dealing with adversity and, hence, more unstable. To resolve this mystery it will be necessary to explain the difference between static and dynamic concepts of stability.

Since it is impossible to provide a good explanation for the third mystery without taking into account the solutions of the first two, it is important to observe at the outset that although the growth and the trade paradoxes are commonly discussed as if they were separate, they are in fact strongly related: becoming a technological leader was a necessary condition if the United States was to continue to improve its productivity. According to Simon Kuznets' calculations, shortly after the Civil War, when the rapid industrialization of the United States began, its productivity was as high as that of any other country in the world.[5] To be sure, it would have been nice if Britain had continued to be the leader, because productivity gains can be brought about less expensively if one is a technological follower rather than a leader. But the British Industrial Revolution was almost entirely focused on steam power—a technology that had been more or less fully exploited by the end of the century. Therefore, if productivity was to continue to improve in industry as well as in agriculture American entrepreneurs had no alternative other than to take over the task of pioneering new technologies.

Of course this is not to say that the American industrial revolutions began where the British Industrial Revolution ended, namely, by providing alternatives to steam power. Rather, the industrial revolutions that began in the United States around 1900 can be regarded as extensions of the British Industrial Revolution. Generally they consisted of the development of machinery and mass-production techniques. For example, when in about 1890 meat-packing firms introduced moving production lines to disassemble carcasses, the idea rapidly spread from industry to industry, quickly making America the world's leading exporter of industrial machinery.

For the United States to become a technological leader, it was not necessary that the crucial discoveries be made in the United States. In a number of cases, including the automobile, the jet engine, commercial aircraft and computers, the initial work was done in Europe. Nor did American technology have to be more sophisticated than European technology. Generally speaking, European technology is quite as sophisticated as American technology. What distinguishes, say, American commercial airplanes from those of Britain is their cost. The problem, therefore, is to explain why the United States had a relative advantage in bringing about rapid improvements in new technologies once the initial discoveries were made, and what motivated American firms to operate under tighter cost constraints than their European counterparts?

The United States' becoming a technological leader provided important benefits for other countries too. Advances in technology (for example, computerized machine tools) or ways to exploit technology from a consumer point of view (the concept of the Model T) enabled other countries to increase their productivity at quite as rapid a rate as the United States. Thus, according to Kuznets' estimates for the period 1920-1960, the annual rate of increase in output per worker for the United Kingdom, France, Germany, Sweden and Japan averaged 1.9 percent, as compared with 1.8 percent for the United States.[6] The best borrowers during the period were Japan and Sweden, where labor productivity increased more than 2.5 percent annually. And in the post-World War II period, Germany, Italy, and France had the highest increases in total factor productivity.[7] In fact, the only major industrial country that showed no significant improvement in its rate of productivity-increase was Britain, where during the postwar period total factor productivity increased at only about one-fourth of the rate achieved in Germany.

To explain what makes countries either good generators or good borrowers of technological ideas is a question that must be answered at the level of the firm. For example, Britain's unimpressive accomplishments certainly cannot be blamed on a lack of imaginative people. Rather, it must be explained by the inhospitality of British firms to imaginative people. For this reason British performance in bringing about productivity gains has been very unimpressive, though, ironically, a theory of the firm patterned on the basis of British experience is accepted by some economists as gospel. Marshall described the evolution of British firms in terms of a semi-closed system paradigm in which the external environment is taken more or less as a given. And in a country that has generated as low a rate of productivity as Britain, it can be assumed that firms do take their outside environments as a given and engage in highly predictable behavior. If all American firms had behaved like British firms the United States could not have become the technological leader that paved the way for productivity increases not only within its own borders, but in other countries as well.

One aspect of the third mystery is the recent disappointing performance of the American economy. The near-monopolistic position the United States once held in selling new technology to other countries is rapidly eroding. And relative to other countries its performance in bringing about productivity gains is declining. As Figure 1 shows, in 1972 the United States, by Michael Boretsky's calculations, was importing more than three-quarters as much of the technology-intensive commodities (commodities with a high ratio of scientists and engineers per dollar of sales) as it was exporting.[8] Moreover, American firms were much less competitive than before in older technologies.

To be sure, Boretsky's calculations involve a serious shortcoming: they assume that the larger the number of scientists and engineers involved, the more discoveries will be made. And it is by no means clear that becoming a technological leader is a research-and-development-intensive activity, as he assumes. Even more disconcerting is Boretsky's attempt to provide policy measures to stimulate research and development without any real analysis of why a downturn occurred. For example, he argues that because the entire social value of research and development cannot be captured in profits, incentives should be introduced to make it more profitable.[9] However, this leaves the question of why, if incentives were inadequate, American firms excelled in dynamic behavior—the behavior associated with pioneering new products and processes.

An even more serious question concerns the upturn in technology-

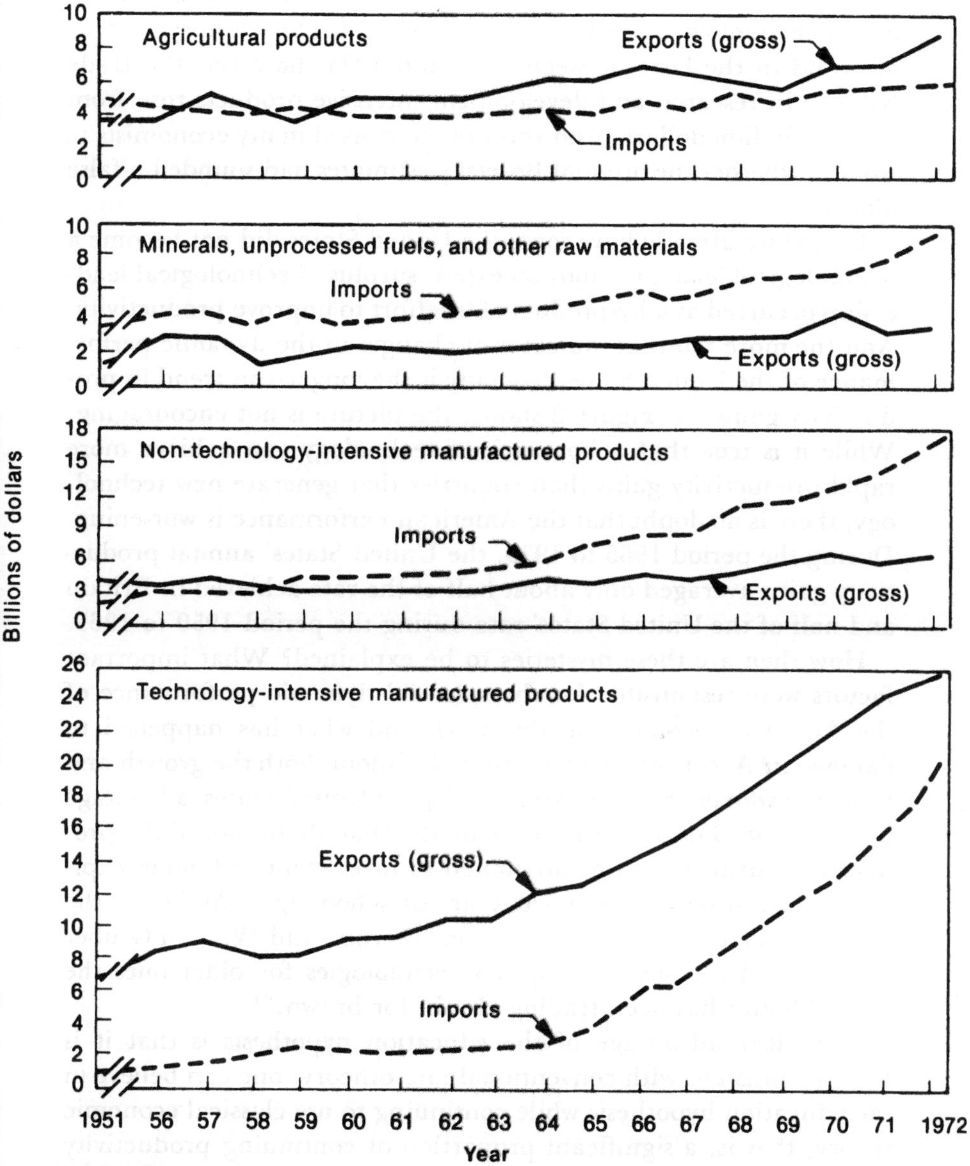

Figure 1. United States trade, 1951-1972. From Michael Boretsky, *U.S. Technology: Trends and Policy* (Washington, D.C.: United States Department of Commerce, 1973), p. 37.

intensive exports during 1973 and 1974. When the original Boretsky estimates appeared, a quite plausible inference was that the United States' technological leadership was eroding in this century as Britain's did in the last. Between 1972 and 1974, however, the trade balance in research-and-development-intensive products rose from 10 to 25 billion dollars. And this upturn caused many economists to wonder whether the original Boretsky estimates had sounded a false alarm.

But, as we already have seen, the United States did not become a technological leader to enjoy an export surplus. Technological leadership occurred as a by-product of its effort to improve productivity. And the more relevant indicator of changes in the dynamic performance of the United States economy is the longer-run trend in productivity gains. As Figure 2 shows, the picture is not encouraging. While it is true that a borrower of technology can achieve more rapid productivity gains than countries that generate new technology, there is no doubt that the American performance is worsening. During the period 1965 to 1975, the United States' annual productivity gains averaged only about half of the rate achieved in Britain and half of the United States' rate during the period 1950 to 1965.

How then are these mysteries to be explained? What important factors were responsible for the splendid dynamic performance of the American economy in the past? And what has happened to damage it? According to conventional wisdom, both the growth and trade paradoxes are to be explained by the United States' advantage in education. Edward Denison estimates that about half of the productivity advance is to be attributed to investment in human capital, as measured by increased years of schooling.[10] As far as the trade paradox is concerned, Raymond Vernon and William Gruber have argued that by trading new technologies for older ones the United States has been trading "brain for brawn."[11]

One clear advantage of the education hypothesis is that it is wholly consistent with conventional microtheory: one can believe in the education hypothesis while continuing to use classical economic theory; that is, a significant proportion of continuing productivity gains are "explained" by attributing them to a better and better educated labor force, in other words, by finding measurement errors in the stock of human capital. On the other hand, there are two reasons for being skeptical about the hypothesis. First, it is by no means clear whether increased investment in education, as mea-

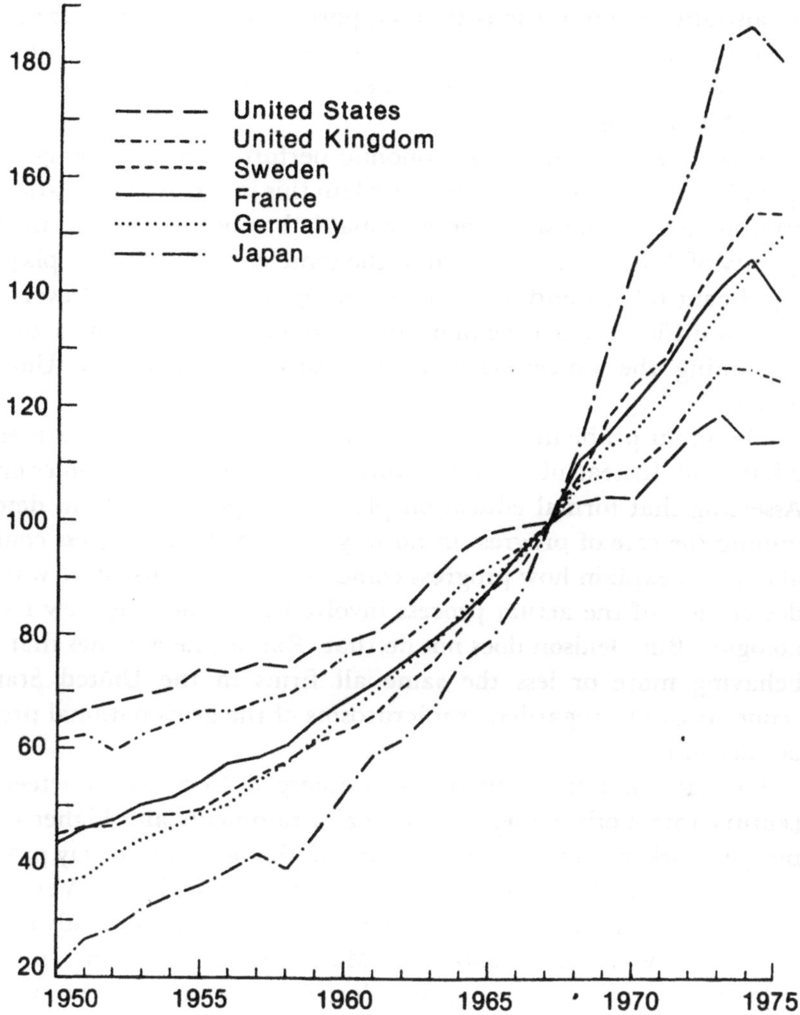

Figure 2. Output per man-hour in manufacturing (1967 = 100). Data from United States Department of Labor, Bureau of Labor Statistics, September 1976.

sured by the number of years of formal schooling, is to be regarded as a cause or an effect—an investment good that causes increases in productivity or a consumption good made possible by increases in productivity. If it is an investment good, we should be able to observe a high correlation between educational attainments within the United States, on the one hand, and advances in technology and organizational innovations that support productivity increases, on the other. But there seems to be no such correlation. For example, the automobile industry was pioneered by people who had little formal education.

Second, while America's economic performance is no longer so splendid, it would be difficult to explain this in terms of educational attainments. To be sure, there probably has been a decline in the quality of American education in the sense that it no longer plays a significant role in adding to the meaning of experience. Nevertheless it is difficult to believe that formal education is a major factor in explaining the worsening economic performance of the United States.

The main problem with Denison's argument, however, is methodological. Instead of demonstrating a relationship, he assumes one. Asserting that formal education plays an important role in determining the rate of progress in no way explains how progress comes about. To explain how progress comes about one must start with a description of the actual process involved in pioneering new technologies. But Denison does not do that. Rather, he assumes that by behaving more or less the same all firms in the United States economy can be regarded as microcosms of the gross national product accounts.

The fact that the United States emerged from the nineteenth century with both higher educational attainments and higher output per worker than any other country in the world in no way proves education was the responsible factor. In fact Denison's, Vernon's and Gruber's arguments are highly reminiscent of those advanced by British Victorian economists. Marshall, in particular, had a tendency to attribute the entire Industrial Revolution to the system of values that existed at the end of the nineteenth century.[12] But is it not conceivable that the British scientific and technological revolutions of the seventeenth and eighteenth centuries would never have come about if there had been the same love of order and predictability as prevailed in Victorian society?

Not all economists subscribe to the Denison argument. In fact, many believe that productivity gains are exogenous to the economic system: that they depend upon knowledge generated in some mysterious manner quite outside the economic system. Science has often been viewed as a pail of all-purpose knowledge that can be turned into useful technology at will. Again, the virtue of this argument is that it permits technological change and classical theory to coexist side by side. But the argument is incorrect because, while advances in science can increase the potential for advances in technology by providing hints, there is no mechanism for assuring that the potential will be exploited. In spite of the fact that Britain, for example, ranks among the leading countries of the world in scientific achievements—and except for the United States and Russia spends more on research and development than any other country[13]—its economic performance has been very disappointing. Actually a number of inventions brought about in British laboratories were exploited by United States firms before they were by British firms, which indicates that productivity gains are endogenous to an economic system—endogenous inasmuch as they must be explained at the level of the firm. Usually, the motivation for quickly adopting new ideas is rivalry between firms to obtain a larger share of the market. It is necessary, therefore, to appreciate the role of rivalry in determining the rate of economic progress, whether such progress is directed toward less expensive alternatives or improvements in quality. Furthermore, we should also understand the internal characteristics of firms that make them better or less able to engage in rivalry that results in significant and rapid improvements in a technology.

The classical theory of competition cannot explain how progress comes about, because it is premised on the assumption of a completely static world in which firms act on the basis of perfect knowledge. Indeed, if firms acted as if their knowledge were complete, no progress could ever occur! Therefore, to explain how progress does come about it is essential to turn to dynamic economic theory: a theory premised on the assumption of a world of imperfect knowledge. The dynamic theory to be developed in this book is composed of three major elements. First, it is based upon a dynamic concept of stability: the ability to make smooth progress in improving the performance of a technology (for example, automobile technology). The dynamic behavior associated with this stability is described as dynamic efficiency: the efficiency associated with producing a given output with fewer inputs (for example, reducing the cost of automobiles). Second, it is based on a dynamic concept of competition in which firms engage in rivalry to generate better or cheaper alternatives in order to increase their share of the market. In terms of static theory, the firm is regarded as an accounting department that confines its activities to making choices among well-defined alternatives. But according to dynamic theory, the firm is composed of people who are more than technically alive and who, when prodded by a competitor, often regard all of the existing alternatives as unsatisfactory. The third major element is the concept of an open system, without which it is impossible to explain how entrepreneurs generate new knowledge.

2. A Dynamic Process

To explain the growth, trade, and stability paradoxes it is essential to understand the main determinants of the rate of technological progress. If progress took the form of many isolated inventions with no apparent relationship between them, it probably would be impossible to devise a satisfactory theory. To be sure, it can be argued that inventors act like profit maximizers.[1] But such an assertion is tantamount to proclaiming that those inventions that have occurred were those destined to occur, which contributes little or nothing towards understanding how progress comes about.

However, progress in this century, if not in the last, can hardly be regarded as the result of inventors working in isolation from each other. The performance of a number of technologies has improved so regularly that the improvements seem almost to have been preordained. And if we do not believe in determinism, a theory must be found to explain such a phenomenon. The first step in devising a new theory is to describe the phenomenon to be explained in a manner that will capture its most important features. Following a description of the phenomenon of a dynamic process, it will be shown why neither classical microtheory nor Bayesian probability theory can be used to explain a dynamic process. A brief overview of dynamic theory will then show how it can be utilized to construct a predictive theory. The hints for developing a new theory can come from chemistry, from biology, or from the correspondence between

Jefferson and Madison. It really does not matter from where. The acid test of all theory is neither its ancestry nor its mathematical elegance but, rather, its ability to make predictions.

The Phenomenon to be Explained

Progress can take the form of reductions in cost (for example, reductions in the cost of air travel) or improvements in quality (for example, reduction in travel times). And as Kuznets and others have pointed out, whether measured in terms of reductions in cost or improvements in quality, progress typically takes the form of an S-shaped curve, with a period of rapid advance in the performance of a technology followed by a period of slower advance.[2] (See Figure 3.)

In addition to its overall shape, there is another noteworthy feature of the S-shaped curve. Though the advances can occur almost like clockwork, individual advances such as the DC-3 or the J-47 engine (as shown by the solid lines in Figure 3) are quite unpredictable. In other words, we are dealing with a phenomenon that exhibits a high degree of predictability when viewed on a macroscale and a high degree of unpredictability when viewed on a microscale: that steady progress will occur is fairly certain, but the specific form it will take is highly uncertain.

The distinction usually made between "static" and "dynamic" processes is that whereas a static process occurs at a point in time, a dynamic process takes place over a period of time. However, the inclusion of the element of time is a necessary but not a sufficient condition for a dynamic process. The key difference between static and dynamic processes is that whereas the former involves types of change that can be predicted on the basis of initial conditions, the latter involves quite unpredictable changes in initial conditions. An entrepreneurial organization discovering a way to produce a given output with fewer inputs changes initial conditions. And the change is quite unpredictable. Until entrepreneurs put their imaginations to work and discard many unsatisfactory hypotheses before discovering a satisfactory one, they cannot predict what form an advance will take. A related difference between static and dynamic processes is that whereas the former involve quite reversible changes that depend only upon factor prices, the latter are irreversible inasmuch as they change the knowledge of the world and the ideological

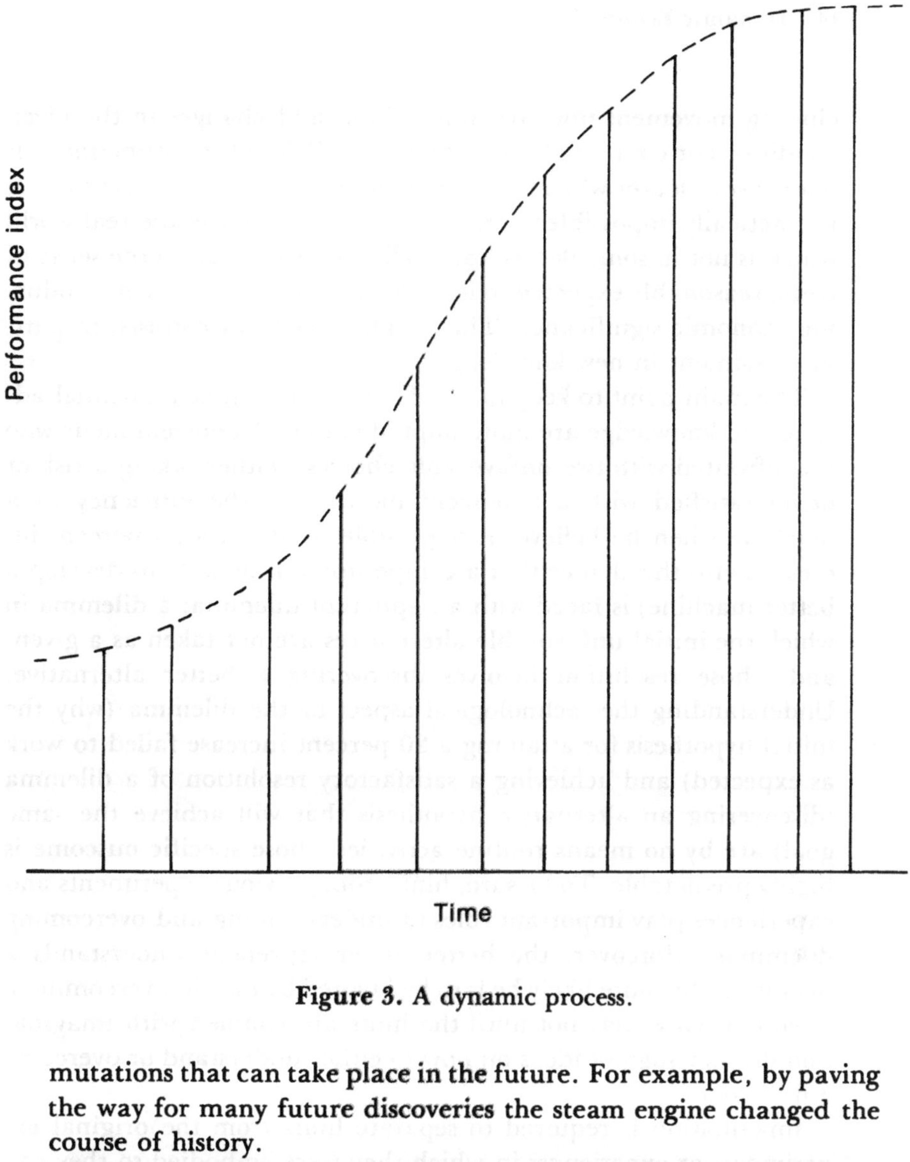

Figure 3. A dynamic process.

mutations that can take place in the future. For example, by paving the way for many future discoveries the steam engine changed the course of history.

Some economists tend to regard all changes in the economy as changes towards a predetermined equilibrium, almost as if the economy were more or less continuously involved in working out God's will. Not all economists, however, regard an economic system in such terms. In particular, in the preface to his *Risk, Uncertainty and Profit* (written in 1915) Frank Knight observed: "I must regard it as one of the major errors in the classical tradition that it failed, and still largely fails to make a sharp and correct theoretical distinction between the working of a system under given conditions, including movement towards equilibrium, and changes in the given conditions or content of the system itself."[3] And the distinction was made even clearer when he pointed out in his later writings that: "It is practically impossible to imagine any investment in the real world which is not in some degree rationally experimental, in the sense of being reasonably expected to lead to knowledge having some enduring economic significance. That is, all investment consists, in part, in investment in new knowledge."[4]

The main point to keep in mind, however, is that individual advances in knowledge are quite unpredictable. An entrepreneur who is confronted with two unfavorable choices—either taking a risk or being satisfied with a 5 percent increase in the efficiency of a machine when he believes it is possible to attain a 20 percent increase (with the chance that a competitor will be able to develop a better machine) is faced with an apparent dilemma: a dilemma in which the initial unfavorable alternatives are not taken as a given, and whose resolution involves discovering a better alternative. Understanding the technological aspect of the dilemma (why the initial hypothesis for attaining a 20 percent increase failed to work as expected) and achieving a satisfactory resolution of a dilemma (discovering an alternative hypothesis that will achieve the same goal) are by no means routine activities whose specific outcome is highly predictable. To be sure, hints from previous experiments and experiences play important roles in understanding and overcoming dilemmas. Moreover, the better an entrepreneur understands a dilemma, the more likely he is to be favored by luck in overcoming a dilemma. However, not until the hints are coupled with imagination do they suggest ideas on how to either understand or overcome a dilemma.

Imagination is required to separate hints from the original experiments or experiences in which they were embodied so they can be used in guessing at new hypotheses. For example, when Frank Whittle obtained an idea from an oil burner manufacturer to help solve his combustion problem, it may be assumed that he did not literally take the combustion scheme from an oil burner and mate it to a jet engine. If ideological coefficients were fixed, in the sense that hints could never be disembodied from particular applications for use in others, man could never have escaped from the Stone Age! It is impossible to make probabilistic predictions of the success likely to be achieved in resolving particular dilemmas because, until the entrepreneur puts his imagination to work, he cannot hope to know what hints will be useful for understanding, much less overcoming, a dilemma.[5] In other words, the very act of putting one's imagination to work changes the initial conditions!

To be sure, just as there is no sharp line between a "predictable" and an "unpredictable" event (make the variance large enough and an event will become unpredictable), there is no sharp line between a more and less unpredictable event. And in particular, it can be assumed that when the S-shaped curve is rapidly rising (that is, during fast history) the degree of unpredictability will be greater than when the S-shaped curve is rising slowly (during slow history). This means that when making fast history the hints required to generate new ideological mutations are likely to come from a wider diversity of experiments or experiences than when making slow history. Obviously, a wider diversity of hints is needed to suggest a new type of engine than a new type of spark plug. And given the fact that fast history is more unpredictable than slow history, we should expect to see fast history associated with more pronounced changes in business fortunes.

Why must entrepreneurs use their imaginations to make significant advances? Evidently God planned the world in such a way as to leave something to the imagination of man. The reasons are implicit in the laws of nature: "implicit" in the sense that nature imposes limits beyond which it is impossible to go without making new discoveries. To be more specific, consider Sadi Carnot's theory about the efficiency of machines, which paved the way for the second law of thermodynamics.[6] Carnot's theory tells us that the physical efficiency of a machine—the amount of work the engine can generate in relationship to the heat put into it—is proportional to the temperature difference that can be obtained, or:

$$\text{Physical efficiency} = \frac{W}{Q_1} = \frac{T_1 - T_2}{T_1}$$

where $\frac{W}{Q_1}$ is the output of work per unit of heat, and $\frac{T_1 - T_2}{T_1}$ is obtained by taking the difference between the highest and lowest temperatures at which the engine runs and dividing that difference by the highest temperature.

The temperature difference is in turn limited by (1) the best available fuels, (2) the best available materials, and (3) the engineering know-how to make the machine approximate an ideal reversible machine. To be sure, Carnot's theory applies to the physical efficiency of machines and not necessarily to their economic efficiency. For example, increasing the physical efficiency of a machine by using more expensive materials or fuels would not necessarily result in a gain in terms of economic efficiency. However, amending the theory to take into account the cost of achieving a higher degree of efficiency does not change its basic nature. Carnot's theory enables engineers to determine which way is "up"—which hypothesis, if successful, will result in a significant increase in physical efficiency. On the other hand, it cannot predict the success of particular hypotheses to increase the temperature difference.

In addition, technological progress takes the form of scaling machines to make them either larger or smaller so they can be used in new applications. For example, turbine engines were used in Swiss mines before they were developed for use in airplanes. However, because in the laws of nature and in materials there are constants that prevent scaling at will, typically difficult scaling problems are overcome only by the discovery of new materials. Galileo is usually credited with having discovered that limits exist with respect to scaling. Pondering in his *Two Sciences* the problem of how big a bone would be required to build a dog twice as high, he found it simply coud not be done without the invention of a stronger bone. Galileo, it is often said, discovered that engineers are needed to invent new kinds of bones! But it is important to note that progress in scaling does not only result in building bigger machines; it can also result in smaller machines. For example, the new electric process in steel can achieve the same economies as the oxygen process—but with much smaller plants.

Pioneering a new technology ordinarily involves overcoming limits set by both scaling and Carnot's theory on the efficiency of machines. The curves relating the rate of progress to time tend to be S-shaped because the process of pioneering a new technology is much like that of mining gold. In the initial phase, when the degree of uncertainty is the largest, the potential for making impressive discoveries is also likely to be the greatest. But eventually engineers will become frustrated in their search for significant advances and will turn their attention toward more predictable and less ambitious advances. However, the cost of bringing about even incremental advances will eventually become so high that other engineers will go off in search of new gold mines. For example, although it brought about a smaller advance, the DC-7 commercial airliner cost about ten times as much as the DC-3.[7] Likewise, even though they represented relatively tiny advances, the radars developed after World War II cost several times as much to develop as those developed during World War II.[8]

Where do the discoveries come from to make new S-shaped curves? Assuming that the industry has already reached the stage of slow history, the advances will seldom come from major firms in the industry. In fact, of some fifty inventions—most of which were included in the Sawers, Jewkes, and Stillerman study—that resulted in new S-shaped curves in relatively static industries, I could find no case in which the advance in question came from a major firm in the industry.[9] In some cases (Bessemer steel, the electric steel process, jet engines, the Polaroid Land Camera) the inventions came from newly established firms. In others (the Diesel locomotive, synthetic fibers, computerized machine tools) the inventions came from firms in other industries or from universities. In other words, as long as organizations remain highly dynamic they can produce a series of important advances—for example, as have been produced by Bell Telephone Laboratories. But once firms in an industry become static the discoveries will come from newcomers. Evidently the process of going from a dynamic to a static organization is highly irreversible, for otherwise firms that had remained static for a period of years could have made major discoveries.

In Figure 4, three examples of dynamic processes are shown. In the first, computer technology, there is no evidence of a slackening in the rate of progress, because semiconductors played more or less the same role in providing a new S-shaped curve as did the jet engine in the case of aircraft. Likewise, turbine engine performance shows no slackening in the rate of progress, even after almost twenty-five years. On the other hand, propeller-driven airliners follow the more typical pattern of fast history followed by slow history. Measured in terms of operating costs, more progress was made from 1925 to 1935—from the trimotored Ford airplane to the DC-3—than was made during the following twenty years. Not shown on the chart are jet airliners, which provided the industry with a new S-shaped curve, in terms of both speed and flying times. However, it should not be assumed that simultaneous progress can forever be made in reduc-

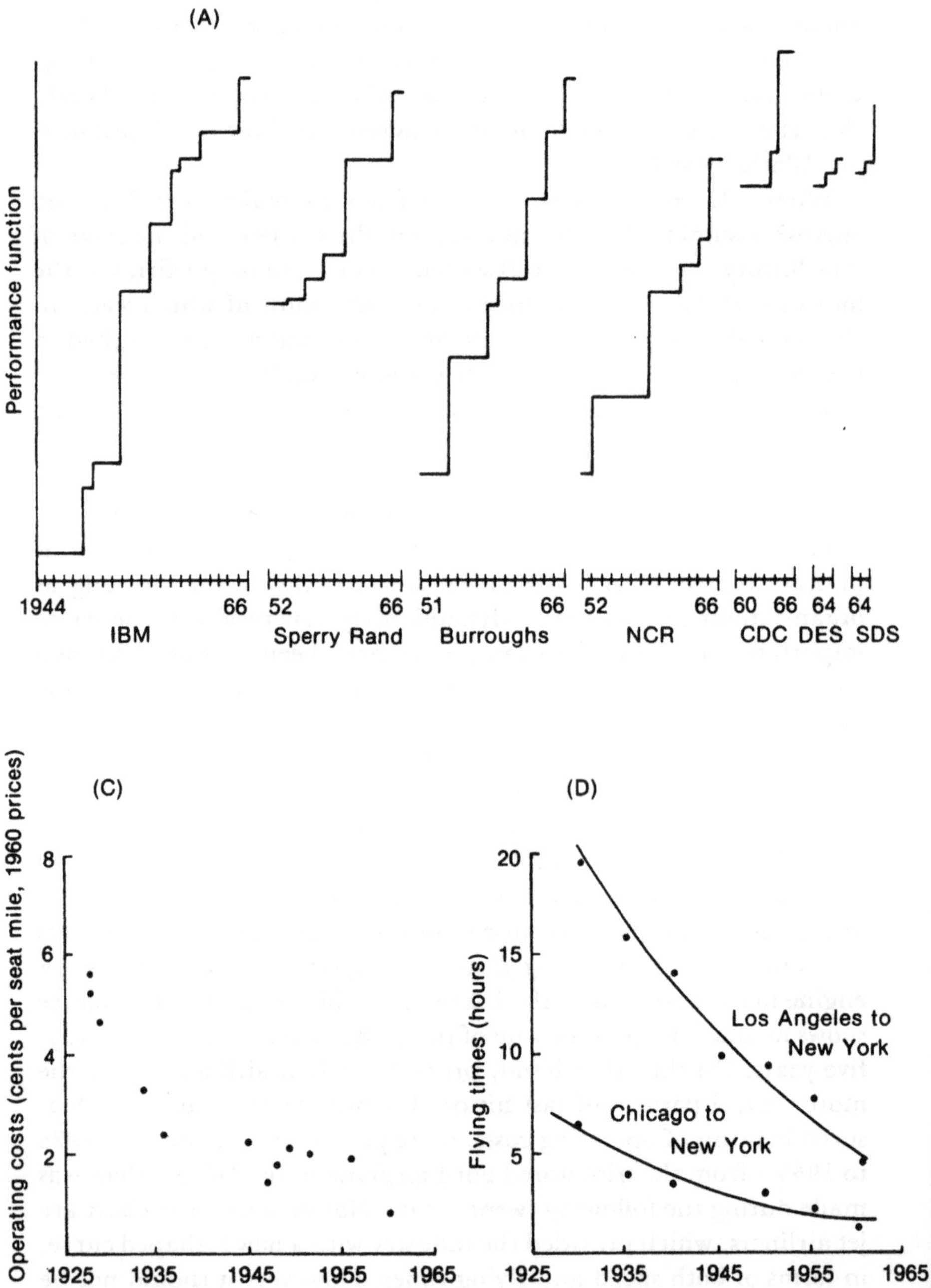
(A)
Performance function
1944
66
52
66
51
66
52
66
60
66
64
64
IBM
Sperry Rand
Burroughs
NCR
CDC
DES
SDS
(C)
Operating costs (cents per seat mile, 1960 prices)
8
6
4
2
1925
1935
1945
1955
1965
(D)
Flying times (hours)
20
15
10
5
Los Angeles to New York
Chicago to New York
1925
1935
1945
1955
1965

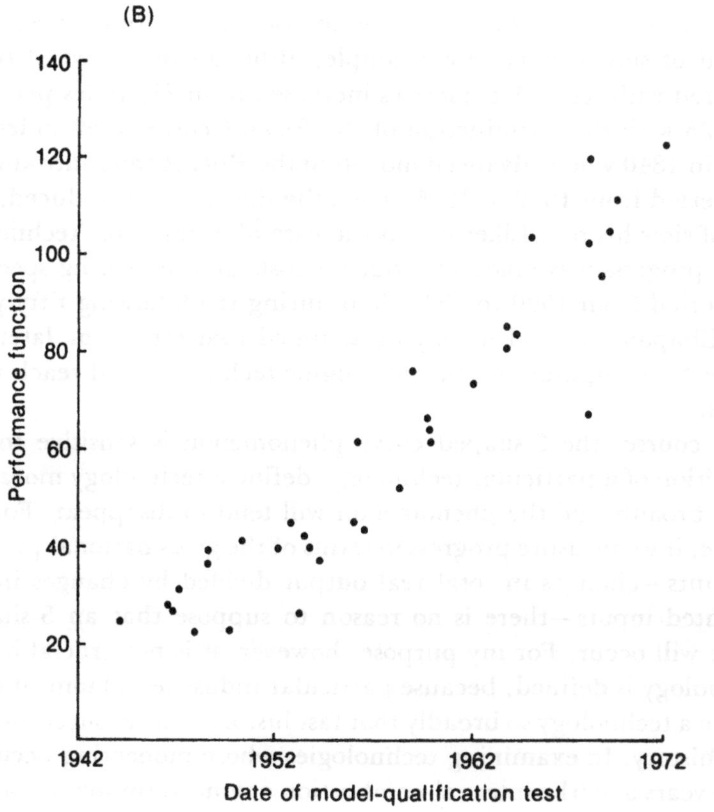

Figure 4. Dynamic processes. (*A*) Actual computer performance. Data from Alvin J. Harman, *The International Computer Industry* (Cambridge, Mass.: Harvard University Press, 1971). (*B*) Aircraft turbine-engine performance. Data from Robert Shishko, *Technological Change through Product Improvement in Aircraft Turbine Engines* (Santa Monica, Calif.: RAND Corp., 1973). (*C* and *D*) Indicators of efficiency, propeller-driven aircraft. From Ronald Miller and David Sawers, *The Technical Development of Modern Aviation* (New York: Praeger, 1970).

ing both costs and flying times. Indeed, with the advent of supersonic aircraft this era may be over.

The aircraft case is typical: a period of fast history followed by a period of slow history. For example, although the speed of trains powered with steam locomotives increased from 2½ miles per hour in 1826 with the introduction of the Royal George to 50 miles per hour in 1840 when advanced models of the Rocket were introduced, the period from 1840 to 1925, when the diesel was introduced, was one of slow history. Likewise, in the case of automobile technology more progress was made in reducing costs and increasing speed in the period from 1900 to 1925 than during the following fifty years (see Chapter 4). And it may be assumed that sooner or later the curves for computer and turbine engine technology will reach their limits.

Of course, the S-shaped curve phenomenon is sensitive to the definition of a particular technology: define a technology more and more broadly and the phenomenon will tend to disappear. For example, if we measure progress in terms of the gross national product accounts—changes in total real output divided by changes in the weighted inputs—there is no reason to suppose that an S-shaped curve will occur. For my purpose, however, it is not crucial how a technology is defined, because particular industries seldom, if ever, define a technology so broadly that fast history is never succeeded by slow history. In examining technologies whose pioneering occurred some years ago (the internal-combustion engine automobile, piston-engine aircraft) there is no problem in distinguishing fast history from slow history.

To be sure, not all progress can be regarded as fast or slow history. In fact, both trivial advances and fundamental discoveries occur as more or less isolated events rather than as parts of a recognizable dynamic process. However, the theory advanced in this book does not purport to predict such isolated discoveries.

The Fallacy-of-Composition Error

A theory is needed (1) to explain the regularity of a dynamic process; and (2) to predict the difference in microbehavior associated with slow and fast history. And not only that; we also want a theory that can provide a reasonable description of the driving mechanism involved. Was Schumpeter correct in his belief that progress is becoming automatic—automatic in the sense that the size of the advances sought by particular firms in an industry is independent of the size of the advances sought by their competitors?[10] Or was Adam Smith more nearly correct in believing that progress and competition go hand in hand?

The reason neither static classical theory nor Bayesian probability theory can be used to explain a smooth dynamic process is that either explanation would involve the fallacy-of-composition error: an error in what is true or seems to be true of the parts (microbehavior) is assumed to be true of the whole (macroperformance) or what is true or seems to be true of the whole is assumed to be true of the parts.

To construct predictive theory it is imperative to avoid this error. For example, when Keynes discovered that the savings habits favoring the stability of the individual did not necessarily favor the stability of the nation, he not only recognized an important illustration of the fallacy-of-composition error, but also found a way to make better predictions of the macroperformance of an economy. In a dynamic world the error applies not only to savings decisions; it applies to microbehavior in general. Smooth overall performance cannot be predicted on the basis of classical microtheory, because if entrepreneurs behave as profit maximizers—restrict themselves to a choice among known or assumed-to-be-known alternatives—they will not possess the freedom of choice to generate new alternatives. To provide himself with the necessary freedom of choice the entrepreneur must believe that all he knows is but partial truths. In other words, if he acts upon the assumption that the only type of rationality is choosing among known alternatives, he will not be able to generate new alternatives.

To be sure, even the general-equilibrium theorists have discovered that entrepreneurs do not have perfect information. However, they assume that buying better information is no different from buying any other commodity.[11] For example, an entrepreneur decides how much it is worth to him to have more accurate weather information and he continues to spend until the costs and benefits are equal. One problem with this point of view is the failure to recognize that unless prodded by necessity (for example, a competitor) entrepreneurs are unlikely to search for new alternatives. Another is the failure to recognize that even when prodded by necessity entrepreneurs do not buy new knowledge on the same basis they make best use of existing knowledge. While the former involves dealing with apparent dilemmas, in order to correct errors in previous theories and discover new ideological mutations, the latter consists of solving well-defined problems. In short, the willingness of general-equilibrium theorists to concede that information may be imperfect is less a concession to reality than a steadfast unwillingness to acknowledge that the economic universe is composed of human beings.

By buying information to reduce variances a Bayesian entrepreneur has a greater freedom of choice than a classical profit maximizer when dealing with uncertainty. Bayesian probability theory is designed to permit the entrepreneur to make choices when, by experimentation, he can improve his knowledge prior to taking action. Yet, an entrepreneur thinking in Bayesian statistical terms would not have the freedom of choice to correct errors in older theories. Nor would he have the freedom of choice required to dissociate hints from particular experiences in order to guess at new ideological mutations. The Bayesian entrepreneur would not possess the required freedom of choice, because Bayesian probability theory assumes that man's knowledge improves as a result of a more or less continuous and cumulative learning process and not as a result of discovering errors in theories when they are extrapolated to deal with new phenomena.[12] In other words, like classical microtheory, Bayesian probability theory assumes that entrepreneurs have no imagination. And as a substitute for imagination it provides a quite mechanical process for revising prior probability distributions.

Although Bayesian probability theory has not been generally accepted by economists, the semiclosed system upon which it is based is a paradigm that is generally accepted by social scientists. According to this generally accepted model, the environment does change, but so slowly that all change can be regarded as incremental change. For example, in terms of the semiclosed system paradigm, the electric light bulb would be looked upon as the result of many tiny steps made to improve the kerosine lantern.

On the other hand, the fallacy-of-composition error is also committed when smooth microbehavior is deduced from smooth macroperformance; that is, when all firms are regarded as microcosms of the GNP accounts, as is done by Denison. In fact, the cornerstone of the argument to be advanced is that smooth macroperformance can occur only when firms cannot predict each other's actions, which is to say, microdiversity is the hidden hand of macrostability. If firms could make perfect predictions of their competitors' behavior they would have no need to insure themselves against uncertainty by generating new ideas, and smooth progress could never occur!

To avoid making the fallacy-of-composition error it is necessary to recognize a wider variety of behavior than is accounted for in terms of classical theory. In particular, whereas classical microtheory assumes that in a world of perfect competition there is but one type of firm—a profit-maximizing entity whose rationality consists of choosing among known alternatives—in the real world one can postulate a spectrum of firms classified according to their ability to deal with uncertainty:

Type 1: "Happy-warrior rationality" is associated with ideological outbreeding and is commonly employed in making fast history.

Type 2: "Middle-class rationality" is associated with ideological inbreeding and is commonly employed in making slow history.

Type 3: "Accounting rationality" is associated with a zero rate of ideological change and is commonly employed by profit-maximizing firms in a temporary equilibrium with an unchanging outside environment.

Type 4: "Conservation-of-power rationality" is associated with organizations which have such a low ability to deal with unpredictability that they must manipulate the rules of the game if they are to survive.

If my argument is correct, a fundamental requirement for economic stability is an appropriate mix of firms and corresponding rationalities. Assume, for example, that the United States adopts as a meta-objective being self-sufficient in ideas, not because it is adverse to borrowing this or that idea from other countries, but because depending on other countries for its ideas could jeopardize its future stability. And also assume that because generating ideas requires dealing with a greater degree of uncertainty than borrowing ideas, and because firms cannot be simultaneously optimized for dealing with higher and lower degrees of uncertainty, they must be specialized in the functions of generating and borrowing ideas in more or less the same way they become specialized for producing different goods and services. Under such assumptions the dynamic stability of the United States (its ability to make more or less continuous progress) would require two sets of firms, generators of ideas (Type 1 firms) and borrowers of ideas (Type 2 firms). Quite clearly, Type 1 firms could not long survive without Type 2; and Type 2 could not long survive without Type 1. In such a world macrostability does not depend on any one kind of rationality; rather, it depends upon a diversity of behavior.

Of course all types of rationality do not necessarily contribute to the macrostability of a country. Consider, for example, business firms that have a very low capacity to deal with uncertainty, but possess the resources and political power to manipulate their environments to enhance their survivability (by lobbying for higher tariffs). Such behavior (Type 4 rationality) protects the stability of the firm in question by jeopardizing the dynamic stability of the nation, that is, its ability to make steady progress. In other words, it makes the lives of the members of the firm more predictable at the expense of making the lives of consumers more unpredictable. Or consider labor union leaders who protect the microstability of the members by imposing practices that have the effect of seriously jeopardizing productivity gains, for example in the construction industry. Again the lives of some people (labor union members) have been made more predictable at the expense of making the lives of others (prospective home buyers) more unpredictable.

So it can be seen that in a dynamic world economic stability is not merely a matter of pursuing the right mix of monetary and fiscal policies. Fundamentally speaking, it is a matter of enjoying the right mix of rationalities. Indeed it may be assumed that the fundamental reason the United States did enjoy a high degree of stability for many years is that whereas Types 1 and 2 behavior predominated, Types 3 and 4 behavior played relatively small roles.

The Concepts of Macrostability and Microstability

In one and only one kind of world can microstability and macrostability be equated, namely, a classical world in which no unpredictable progress occurs. Therefore, to avoid making the fallacy-of-composition error, it is necessary, in a world in which unpredictable and irreversible change occurs, to introduce concepts for describing reality that are not contained in classical theory. The term "macrostability" will be used to describe an overall dynamic process in which the advances come about quite regularly. It must be emphasized that this is a *dynamic* concept of stability and as such is opposed to the conventional definition. The conventional concept of stability implies an unchanging world; and a dynamic concept of stability depends on the ability to make smooth adjustments to new circumstances. It might seem that the higher the degree of macrostability the more smooth will be the process. However, since our fundamental interest is in progress, and since the very essence of progress is being able to deal with new circumstances, it is assumed that when an industry demonstrates the ability to bring about smooth progress at a more rapid rate (which implies a greater ability to deal with new circumstances) it also demonstrates a higher degree of macrostability. Thus, when the S-shaped curve shown in Figure 1 is rising rapidly (fast history) the degree of macrostability is said to be high. And when it is rising slowly (slow history) the degree of macrostability is said to be low.

Admittedly, a dynamic concept of stability is completely opposed to common wisdom. But it must be remembered that, whereas the conventional concept of stability applies to an unchanging environment, the dynamic concept of stability applies to an environment subject to quite unpredictable changes. Consider, for example, two marriages. In the first, every move the couple makes is completely predictable on the basis of initial conditions. In the second, the partners are constantly encountering new matrimonial dilemmas. But, while it cannot be predicted when a dilemma will arise, much less how it will be resolved, the couple can be counted upon to discover some way to resolve their dilemmas. Therefore, this marriage can be described as a predictably unpredictable system. In other words, whereas the first marriage is based upon a static concept of behavior and a static concept of stability, the second is based upon a dynamic concept of behavior and a dynamic concept of stability.

Now, which marriage is more stable? This question can be answered only with reference to the environment. In a completely stable environment (as in heaven) the first type of marriage would be more stable. But in an environment subject to unpredictable change (as on earth) the second would be more stable.

"Microstability" is conventionally defined as "the stability associated with an unchanging environment." For example, the British labor unions can be said to exhibit a high propensity for microstability. Whether this insistence on preserving a way of life is due to the psychological make-up of British workers or the quite rational desire of British union leaders to conserve their own power, there can be little question that British labor unions are obsessed with a desire for the security and predictability associated with an unchanging environment. On the other hand, the pioneers of the Industrial Revolution in Britain, and those who left Britain during the Victorian Age to pioneer the development of the United States, Canada, Australia, and New Zealand, evidently were not obsessed with a desire for microstability.

In a classical world in which no dilemmas arise, and no irreversible ideological change occurs, microstability and macrostability are equivalent concepts. But in the real world, the concepts of microstability and macrostability are diametrically opposed. A world that enjoyed 100 percent microstability would be absolutely predictable, and have no capability to respond to new circumstances, displaying, therefore, a zero degree of macrostability. Conversely, a world that enjoyed 100 percent macrostability would be inhabited by people who were constantly discovering that their ideas were but partial truths; and it would evince a zero degree of microstability.

In short, predictability and stability are associated concepts only in a Keynesian long run: the long run in which we all will be dead. In the short run, here on earth, stability consists of dealing successfully with a variety of matrimonial, economic, scientific, and personal dilemmas; and in the process men and women discover that the history of their world has changed.

The concept of macrostability can be applied to individual industries. And various industries can be expected to bring about progress at widely different rates. In the economy as a whole, the degree of macrostability depends upon the mix of firms: the greater the proportion of Types 1 and 2 firms, the higher the degree of macrostability; and the greater the proportion of Types 3 and 4 firms, the lower will be the degree of macrostability.

At first glance this dynamic concept of macrostability seems to bear no relationship whatsoever to the Keynesian concept of macrostability: prosperity without inflation. However, steady increases in productivity can permit increases in money wages without inflation. And it is easy to imagine that if the United States' economy had not been characterized by a high degree of macrostability it would have suffered much earlier from a chronic inflation problem.

It is surprising that Keynes adopted a static concept of macrostability. As is evidenced in his earlier writings, no one was more critical of classical equilibrium theory. For example, Keynes compared Marshall's concept of an equilibrium with "a whole Copernical System by which all the elements of the economic universe are kept in their places by mutual counterpose and interaction."[13] Moreover, not only did Keynes deeply understand the problems of classical microtheory, but his *General Theory* can be regarded as the first step in the introduction of dynamic considerations into economics. His theory anticipated some of the key ideas in modern cybernetics theory insofar as it does not depend on initial value predictions. For example, a captain of a ship does not rely upon initial value predictions. As far as he is concerned, rational behavior does not consist of presetting the rudder in New York before taking off for Le Havre. Rather, he continually observes the interaction between the ship and the waves, and then on the basis of short-term predictions makes his course corrections. Similarly, the members of the President's Council of Economic Advisors or the British Treasury observe the interaction between public and private spending decisions, and on the basis of short-term predictions they develop recommendations that hopefully will keep the nation's economic ship of state on a course of full employment without inflation.

To be sure, Keynesian dynamics is not dynamics in the sense used in this book. To qualify as a dynamic open system the captain of the ship and the Council of Economic Advisors would, when confronted with necessity, have to use their imaginations to make new discoveries. Nevertheless, Keynes' theory is a far cry from the degree of determinism associated with equilibrium theory.

It is somewhat surprising, therefore, that when describing the private economy in *The General Theory* Keynes took a point of view that was even more static than Marshall's: "We take as givens the existing skill and quantity of available labor, the existing quality and quantity of available equipment, the existing technique, the degree of competition, and habits of the consumer."[14] As a result the Keynesian model provides cures only for depressions when there is a shortage of effective demand for goods, and not for chronic inflation when there is a shortage of effective demand for progress.

True, Keynes' mission was to provide a rationale for deficit spending, and for that purpose it was not essential to ask economists to give up their sacred concept of a static equilibrium. It is also true that by ignoring the degree of competition, as defined by the risk competitors impose on each other, Keynes may have committed no serious error as far as Britain is concerned. Nevertheless, he left economic theory with two strange contradictions that are not easy to explain. By ensconcing economic theory in a Ricardian world he does not permit the entrepreneur to possess the same degree of imagination as an enterprising chimpanzee, who, when confronted with dilemmas, invents new tools for himself. And, by assuming complete predictability, Keynes postulated a world that is at variance with the facts of life as revealed by the laws of nature.

Unfortunately, however, instead of completing the revolution that Keynes started by removing the artificial assumptions and bringing macrotheory closer to reality, Keynes' followers have been mainly engaged in constructing their own special brand of heaven: stable growth. And while Galbraith seemingly does not favor growthmanship, he would have us live in a completely planned and predictable society. Indeed, in his insistence on order and predictability, Galbraith has become even more Victorian than the Victorians. Marshall, for example, would permit some uncertainty in the way firms adapt to a given environment; but according to Galbraith, the imperatives of technology require the elimination of uncertainty.[15]

Keynes' followers not withstanding, if Keynesian economics is to be saved from the fallacy-of-composition error, it is essential to adopt a dynamic concept of stability that regards steady increases in productivity to pay for increases in real wages without inflation as one important aspect of a stable economic system.

The Properties of a Dynamic Economic System

If we are unwilling to regard the generation of productivity gains as a factor exogenous to the economic system, then our definition of an economic system must include properties (or elements) that determine both the regularity and the rate of productivity gains. A dynamic economic system has three major elements. First, it has a dynamic concept of efficiency, which acknowledges that business firms can improve their knowledge, and which regards the concept of static efficiency as a special case in which firms have perfect knowledge. Second, dynamic economics has a dynamic concept of competition, which permits firms to discover better or cheaper alternatives. In other words, whereas classical theory imposes pompous preconditions on entrepreneurs by permitting them to engage only in the rational behavior involved in making choices among known alternatives, the dynamic theory of competition assumes a world of imperfect knowledge, from which perspective the classical theory of perfect competition is regarded as a special and limiting case. Third, whereas the classical theory of competition is based on the concept of a closed system (one in which outputs can be precisely accounted for in terms of inputs), dynamic theory is based on the assumption of an open system, a system in which entrepreneurs interacting with their technological environments can change both their ideas and their environments by generating new knowledge: a system in which outputs cannot be precisely accounted for by inputs. The interaction may be small or large. And the degree of uncertainty an organization will encounter, as measured by the number of hypotheses it will have to get married to and divorced from before discovering a satisfactory resolution of the dilemma, will depend on the size of the interaction.

The ability of organizations to deal with uncertainty is a function of their internal characteristics: the diversity of their members (as measured in terms of their backgrounds and their personality characteristics) and the diversity of their interactions (as measured in terms of the randomness of their communications).

A dynamic concept of efficiency is needed not to predict particular discoveries, but rather as a first step towards making the statistical predictions necessary to understand the differences in microbehavior associated with fast and slow history. More specifically, it is important to understand why the necessity to deal with higher and lower degrees of uncertainty can result in differences in behavior as marked as those between criminal and probate law firms. The concept of dynamic efficiency also helps us understand that the main function of entrepreneurship is essentially one of discovering new ideological mutations, that is, of acting as a marriage broker between what is desirable from an economic point of view and what is possible from a technological point of view.

Because firms cannot buy insurance against competitive risk—the risk of having a market stolen away by a competitor who makes a discovery—their only alternative for dealing with such risk is to insure themselves against uncertainty the best they can by being prepared to do to their competitors what their competitors can do to them. The degree of competitive interaction—the degree of competition as defined in dynamic terms—is measured by the advances firms seek. When firms aim for nonincremental advances (a 20 percent rather than 2 percent increase in the efficiency of a machine) they must engage in major-league behavior to survive, and the degree of competitive interaction is high. When firms aim for modest advances and engage in minor-league behavior the degree of competitive interaction is low. When the degree of competitive interaction is zero, firms display identical behavior with respect to products and prices. And this can either occur because of an unwillingness to engage in risk-taking or because knowledge is complete (that is, the case of perfect competition).

Competition, as defined in dynamic terms, plays a major role in explaining both the regularity and the rate of progress (the degree of macrostability). Because firms cannot predict each other's discoveries they undertake different approaches towards achieving the same goal. And because not all of the approaches will turn out to be equally successful, the pursuit of parallel paths provides the options required for smooth progress. On the other hand, the rate of advance in an industry will depend upon the degree of competitive interaction. The more unpredictable the discoveries in a particular industry (the greater the diversity of behavior in that industry), the greater will be the rate of advance firms demand from each other. Conversely, if firms could predict each other's advances they would not have to insure themselves against uncertainty by taking risks. And no smooth progress would occur.

This is not to say that progress depends only upon a willingness of business firms to engage in risk-taking. It also depends upon consumers who have a sufficient sense of discrimination that they can distinguish better from poorer products. For example, Swiss chocolate firms may not feel obligated to improve the quality of their products because even if successful the consumer may not be able to notice the difference. And high-fidelity equipment may be reaching a similar state of development.

It is impossible to say which comes first: the consumer with a sufficient sense of discrimination or the new product. Typically new products and new tastes are developed more or less simultaneously, with positive and negative feedback playing major roles in the evolution of tastes and technology. And risk-taking is required not only on the part of business firms engaged in making experiments, but also on the part of consumers who are being experimented upon.

The third major property needed to describe an economic system is the concept of openness which explains how individuals and organizations can effectively deal with higher and lower degrees of uncertainty. In organizational terms, what is the operational significance of a high degree of openness, that is, one that permits a large change in the technological environment? Let us suppose that stealing markets away from competitors is the name of the game for a firm with a happy-warrior rationality, and its leadership decides that if this objective is to be achieved the firm must somehow bring about a 25 percent reduction in the cost of its product. If the firm wants to maximize the probability of achieving this objective, what is the required state of organization? The efficient state of organization for making fast history, it will be shown, is that of "organized disorganization": a state in which the organization includes people with a wide diversity of professional and social backgrounds, and, to make good use of this diversity, it imposes minimal constraints on their interactions. For example, in such an organization it is almost impossible to predict with whom the leader will be speaking next. And due to an unwillingness to precisely define responsibilities there is a good deal of internal competition. The state of organized disorganization, I will argue, will maximize the probability of achieving a nonincremental reduction in costs, because the ability to obtain hints from people with a wide diversity of backgrounds is necessary for dealing with a high degree of uncertainty.

Next let us consider a lower degree of openness. In particular, think of a semiclosed system as a special case of an open system in which the technological environment is taken more or less as a given. The classical example of a semiclosed system is Darwinian biology, as it was formalized by Darwin's successors, which assumes that only highly predictable types of evolution occur. (And as indicated in the Appendix, Bayesian probability theory is implicitly based on the concept of a semiclosed system.) However, when biologists discovered that a biological environment cannot be defined independently of the species from which it is composed and the interactions in which they engage, they discovered, in effect, that biological systems are open.[16] In the field of economics, Marshall based his theory on a semiclosed system.[17] And as it happens, his description of Victorian England in terms of this paradigm does no serious injustice to the facts. The Victorians did assume that what they knew constituted a set of everlasting truths—and apparently even a cat creeping through the Conservative Club could have been the cause of a dilemma.

The essential difference between an open and a semiclosed system is that inasmuch as the latter takes the environment as a given a smaller degree of uncertainty is assumed. This in turn means that a semiclosed system paradigm is useful for explaining slow, and not fast, history. However, even though a semiclosed system paradigm is associated with entrepreneurs who borrow ideas rather than those who generate ideas, it is practically impossible to borrow ideas from one environment to use in another without encountering dilemmas, however minor, and without changing the environment, if only a little. In other words, the difference between fast and slow history is a difference of degree rather than of kind—and a semiclosed system is to be thought of as a special and limiting case of an open system.

Because bringing about a lower rate of progress presupposes less randomness in hints, a semiclosed system should be associated with a more constrained organization: one in which presidents talk only to vice-presidents and to members of the board; and one in which the members of the stationary-parts department of an engine division of an automobile company seldom interact with those working in the moving-parts department—and these departments almost never interact with people in the research division.

Finally, a closed system is a special case of an open system in which there is no environment outside of the system itself with which to interact. In science the solar system is generally regarded as a system in which the interactions can be safely ignored. And Newtonian celestial mechanics provides the classic example of a closed system.

Walrasian general-equilibrium economics is Newtonian celestial mechanics extended to the economic universe. One set of "planets" consists of households that maximize their utility, the other, of firms that maximize their profits. And when maximization rules are employed to bring both sets of planets into an equilibrium we are back to celestial mechanics. However, this is not too surprising, because Walras' objective, as set forth in the introduction to *Elements of Pure Economics,* was "to make economics into a science which would rank with the mathematical sciences of astronomy and mechanics."[18]

The attempt to transform economics into a science by making it resemble Newtonian physics was not undertaken by Walras alone. For any discipline to be known as a "science" during the nineteenth century it had to appear quite as deterministic as Newtonian celestial mechanics. However, since the Middle Ages the basic mission of science, as generally understood by scientists, has been to better understand reality. And almost invariably scientists have based their theories not on assumptions but on the observation of reality. Newton, for example, based his theory on observations made by the sixteenth-century Danish astronomer Tycho Brahe, whose observations were in turn brilliantly analyzed by Johannes Kepler, a renowned German astronomer and mathematician of the seventeenth century.

And assuming that economists must follow the same path if economics is to evolve into a mature science, then Walrasian economics must be regarded as beautifully logical, but possessing almost no scientific content. To be more specific, it can be shown that the concept of an equilibrium implicitly assumes either (1) an organization whose members think exactly alike; or (2) an organization whose interactions are so tightly constrained that human diversity goes completely to waste.[19] In other words, if my argument is correct, from a twentieth-century point of view general equilibrium economics is unscientific because it does not include human beings in the definition of an economic system!

To bring our theories in closer harmony with reality, therefore, we must base them upon the concept of an open system. The concept of openness plays the same crucial role in dynamic theory as does the concept of specialization in static theory. First, it permits us to visualize how dynamic processes occur. Second, it provides us with a deep understanding from a statistical point of view of the relationship between (1) the degree of openness required of the firm as a function of the degree of uncertainty in its environment; and (2) the internal characteristics of organizations as a function of the requirement for openness.

Of course progress could come about in other ways. Logically speaking, progress could be brought about by Schumpeter's hero entrepreneur who, in Schumpeter's earlier writings, went from dilemma to dilemma much as Mozart's Don Giovanni went from adventure to adventure.[20] Or it could be brought about by a technostructure that institutionalizes this concept of entrepreneurship and makes it quite automatic. This, of course, was the concept of entrepreneurship stressed by Schumpeter in his later writings—a concept borrowed and simplified by Galbraith in his version of Schumpeter for the kiddies.[21] And as a logical possibility it certainly cannot be dismissed.

The principal difference between the arguments of Schumpeter and Galbraith, on the one hand, and that to be presented in the next three chapters, on the other, is that mine is essentially a statistical argument. The essence of my argument is:

1. Firms are likely to generate impressive advances only as long as they employ a wide diversity of people who engage in a good deal of conflict on how to achieve certain generally accepted goals.
2. Firms are likely to remain internally interactive and able to deal with a high degree of uncertainty only as long as they are prodded by their competitors.

3. Static Efficiency versus Dynamic Efficiency

Economists have long assumed that the only kind of efficiency is static efficiency. But Schumpeter not only recognized that an economic system can be characterized by a higher or a lower degree of dynamic efficiency, but acknowledged that it cannot achieve a high degree of static and dynamic efficiency simultaneously: "A system — any system, economic or other — that at every given point in time fully utilizes its possibilities to the best advantage may yet in the longer run be inferior to a system that does so at no given point of time, because the latter's failure to do so may be a condition for the level of speed of long-run performance."[1] In this chapter we shall see why Schumpeter's observation was correct.

From the viewpoint of a typical firm in an industry, the achievement of high degree of macrostability indicates it has attained a high degree of dynamic efficiency. The essential difference between static and dynamic efficiency is that whereas the former is the result of making choices along a production-possibilities frontier, the latter is the result of extending the frontier by exploiting as fully as possible a technological potential. Thus an engineer engaged in selecting from the best available technology those inputs that enable a firm to produce a particular output at minimal cost is dealing with a static-efficiency problem. By contrast, an engineer trying to determine why a particular hypothesis for increasing the efficiency of a machine does not work out as predicted is dealing with a dynamic-efficiency dilemma. And if he is to escape from this dilemma a hypothesis must be discovered that will provide him with an acceptable improvement in efficiency.

In real life, of course, the difference between static and dynamic efficiency is a matter of degree rather than of kind. Even with respect to older technologies, such as railroad technology, the potential for making new discoveries never becomes completely exhausted. Conversely, even when the entrepreneur's main objective is to extend the frontier he never can ignore the problem of how to combine inputs: the airplane may embody quite new technological features—but it must fly.

The principal difference between the achievement of static and dynamic efficiency is that the greater the emphasis placed upon extending a technological frontier the more uncertainty there is. In the pure case of static efficiency, which assumes knowledge as given, rational behavior consists of planning on the basis of initial conditions. But if an entrepreneur is to profit from an unexploited potential he must almost inevitably deal with a greater degree of uncertainty. To be sure, an entrepreneur may pretend that he knows ex ante the optimal combination of inputs. However, if he is dealing with a relatively unexploited potential he will find that the optimal trade-offs cannot be defined beforehand. Indeed, the essence of achieving a high degree of dynamic efficiency is to conduct the program so that in making tomorrow's decisions one does not become a prisoner of today's knowledge. If knowledge can be improved, the person who acts on the basis of perfect knowledge is proceeding irrationally. Or, as experienced engineers are fond of exclaiming: "It's not what you don't know that kills you; it's what you think you know."

Risk and Uncertainty

To show how entrepreneurs deal with uncertainty and risk it will be necessary first to define these concepts in operational terms. According to Frank Knight's definitions, there are two quite distinctive types of uncertainty: true, or unmeasurable, uncertainty and statistical, or measurable, uncertainty (which he defined as risk).[2] In the real world, however, the distinction between statistical uncertainty and true uncertainty is not nearly as sharp as Knight's definition implies. Indeed, in his informal discussion Knight indicated an awareness of this point. Even with respect to health, accident, and life insurance he acknowledged, "At best there is a large field for the exercise of judgement."[3] And he also observed: "It is hard to imagine an intelligent individual considering any single case as absolutely isolated except a decision in which one's whole fortune (or his life) were at stake."[4]

According to Knight, the difference between a measurable and unmeasurable uncertainty is a matter of degree. On the one hand, it may be assumed that insurance companies are seldom, if ever, able to base their calculations entirely upon actuarial considerations. On the other hand, it also may be assumed that new scientific and technological theories are seldom, if ever, devised without some hints from previous experiments or experiences.

It is necessary, therefore, to consider a spectrum of uncertainty in which there are no black and white distinctions between less uncertain and more uncertain states of the world:

1. A world of zero uncertainties is a completely deterministic world in which behavior is entirely predictable on the basis of initial conditions (for example, the world of general equilibrium economics).

2. A world of weak uncertainties can be accurately and completely described in probabilistic terms; it is a world wherein it should be possible, therefore, to obtain insurance against all unforeseen events. As long as insurance companies provide 100 percent insurance against fires, the action of a competitor, the loss of affection of a husband or wife, or any other event, the world is described as one of weak uncertainties. It is difficult, of course, to imagine a world in which all risks can be completely insured. In fact, a world of weak uncertainties is no less artificial than a completely deterministic world.

3. A second world of weak uncertainty is one of Bayesian uncertainties: a world in which an entrepreneur does not completely know a probability distribution, but his knowledge of the distribution can be gradually improved by experimentation. So, unlike classical economic man, Bayesian economic man has a limited ability to insure himself against uncertainty; his ability is limited because he is not required to use his imagination.

4. A world of strong uncertainties is one in which dilemmas occur; therefore, man must continually correct errors in previous theories to ensure smooth progress. In other words, this is the world in which

Schumpeter's famous process of creative destruction is more or less continually at work: newer theories supplant older theories to generate better or cheaper products. It is defined as a world of strong uncertainties because probabilistic predictions cannot be made as to when particular dilemmas will arise nor how they will be resolved.

Of these four states of uncertainty the following discussion will concern the first, second, and fourth, with the third to be elaborated upon in the following section.

There is no sharp boundary between a weak and a strong uncertainty. An entrepreneur who knows his costs within ten percent is dealing with a weak uncertainty. But if costs increase ten times over the initial estimate the uncertainties can be described as strong. Moreover, one can visualize an entire range of strong uncertainties measured in terms of whether the discontinuities that have to be overcome are relatively minor (the discovery of a new type of spark plug) or major (the elimination of the need for spark plugs).

Unlike Knight, I define "risk" as a hazard that is not fully insurable. To be sure, from the point of view of an insurance company, risk can be regarded as a measurable uncertainty. But from the point of view of an individual or a business firm, risk represents a hazard that cannot be fully insured. And rational behavior does not consist of ignoring such a risk. Business firms must deal with two main risks. One is the technological risk, which is measured in terms of the costs involved in experimenting with new products. The other is the competitive risk, which is measured in terms of the market loss for one firm if another is more successful in introducing a new product.

In terms of these definitions, a world of weak uncertainties would contain no risk. The formation of insurance companies converts a strong uncertainty for an individual into a weak uncertainty for society. And if we assume a world in which all risk could be completely insured—a world in which no regrets could occur—then why should not a rational person be completely indifferent as to whether or not his house burned down? Or if business firms could fully insure themselves against the actions of their competitors, why should they not be completely indifferent to the action of a competitor stealing away a market? To be sure, in the real world people are not indifferent to such risks. But this is only another way of observing that the real world is a world of strong uncertainties.

On the assumption that insurance can be completely effective in converting strong uncertainties into weak uncertainties, it is to be expected that in a world of weak uncertainties and total insurance behavior would be the same as that in a world of zero uncertainties. With 100 percent fire insurance, individuals would behave as if the loss of a house were no longer a risk to them; and with 100 percent insurance against competitive risk, business firms would assume that they could safely ignore such risk. In other words, from a theoretical point of view there is no difference between a world of zero uncertainties and a world of weak uncertainties: behavior in the two worlds is the same. In particular, in a world of weak uncertainties in which people could obtain 100 percent insurance against risks, they would need no capability for dealing with dilemmas, because, from their point of view, the world would be riskless. And like a completely deterministic world, a world of weak uncertainties and total insurance would enjoy 100 percent microstability.

Risk, therefore, arises *only* in a world of strong uncertainties. And when risk is present, rational individuals and business firms will behave differently than they would in a world of weak uncertainties. A rational individual will not take the probability of his house burning down as a given, for if he does the opportunity of comparing alternatives will be denied him: the alternative of buying more insurance versus the alternative of using his imagination to find ways to reduce the probability of a fire: the smaller his insurance coverage, the greater the incentive to use his imagination. Even though its leadership may not be keen about taking technological risks, a rational business firm will constantly weigh competitive and technological risks. Furthermore, it can be assumed that the larger the markets that are likely to be lost as a result of competitive risks, the more it will pay to become involved in technological risks.

That insurance can change incentives and behavior was pointed out by Kenneth Arrow in an article published in 1963.[5] It is interesting to note that the description of the phenomenon in question as a "moral hazard" was not invented by Arrow; rather, the term has long been used by insurance companies. According to insurance experts, when the very act of buying insurance has the effect of increasing the probability of the event insured against (for example, fires) the insured are acting immorally! This deviation from "true" moral behavior is described by actuarial experts as a "moral hazard." And, indeed, from the point of view of the insurance company the behavior in question is to be regarded, if not immoral, as irrational, because they obviously do not want to find that the effect of selling fire insurance is to increase the probability of fires. Indeed, it is for this reason that fire insurance companies will not provide 100 percent coverage. On the other hand, as was previously indicated, a person who insists upon taking the probability of his house burning down as a given is engaging in irrational behavior (he is prevented from comparing alternatives). So we see that rational behavior from the point of view of an insurance company is not necessarily rational behavior from the point of view of the insured (and vice versa). It also can be seen that their incentives are quite different. From the point of view of the insurance company, the more insurance coverage it provides, the greater is the incentive to minimize the probability of the event insured against. On the other hand, from the point of view of the insured, the more insurance coverage, the smaller is the incentive to take risks to minimize the probability of the event insured against.

Or to take another insurance example: malpractice insurance is said to provide an incentive for physicians to substitute computer diagnoses for more personal diagnoses, not because the former can make better predictions (quite the contrary), but because it is believed that computer diagnoses provide better evidence for defense against malpractice suits. So that which is rational behavior from the point of view of a physician is not necessarily rational behavior from the point of view of a patient (and vice versa). Now, to be sure, in the longer run the price of malpractice insurance might rise to such an extent that physicians would be driven to undertake more imaginative research on ways to make better diagnoses. However, if this occurred, the incentives facing the medical profession would also change. And physicians who did not compare increased insurance costs with the costs of doing more research would be engaged in irrational behavior inasmuch as they would not have considered alternatives.

The main point to keep in mind, however, is that the change in incentives as more and more insurance is provided not only applies to the relationship between insurance companies and the insured. Generally speaking, the more certain an environment, the poorer will be the incentives for risk-taking, and the higher will be the degree of microstability. Conversely, the less certain an environment, the higher will be the propensity for risk-taking and the degree of macrostability. For example, it is generally known that cost-plus contracts decrease the incentives for discovering ways to reduce costs, because with such contracts the risk of cost escalation is entirely transferred to the buyer.

The takeover of a company by a conglomerate may or may not result in a decline in risk-taking. The purpose of taking over the independent company might be to reenergize the entire organization by fostering more internal competition (and a more uncertain environment). On the other hand, when the basic purpose of forming a conglomerate is to provide a static form of insurance by manufacturing a wider range of products, the almost inevitable result will be a decline in risk-taking. This can occur either because of a decline in risk-taking in the company that has been taken over or by the imposition of constraints upon its behavior by the parent organization. Typically, however, there is a change in both the internal incentives and the imposition of direct controls. Therefore, greater insurance against uncertainty is purchased at the expense of a lesser ability to deal with uncertainty.

It is also reasonable to assume that cartels provide a static type of insurance at the expense of dulling the incentives for progress. The basic purpose of forming a cartel is to eliminate competitive risks. And with the elimination of competitive risks firms have little or no incentive to bring about progress. To be sure, as economists are fond of pointing out, cartels can sow the seeds of their own destruction by encouraging cheating in the form of price cuts. And it cannot be denied that such a short-run incentive does exist. However, it also seems likely that in the longer run the more important effect of cartels will be a decline in risk-taking, as such risk-taking affects the generation of lower-cost alternatives. Indeed, this may be one of the main reasons productivity increased no more rapidly in Germany than in Britain between 1900 and the end of World War II.[6] Evidently cartels had the same stifling effect on productivity in Germany as did a small degree of competitive interaction, coupled with a high degree of constraint imposed on productivity gains by the labor unions, in Britain.

Or, as another example, suppose that the government were to undertake the function of providing new technological knowledge, say, on the argument that because the benefits cannot be fully internalized such risk-taking ought to be a public activity. If knowledge is regarded as a public good, how might private firms be affected? Quite obviously they would no longer have an incentive to generate knowledge. And with socialization of the risk-taking function new knowledge would be generated at a slower rate.

In fact, the main advantage of a capitalist society based on decentralized risk-taking over a socialistic society based upon centralized planning is the ability of the former to "internalize risk." Risks are said to be internalized when the incentives favor dealing with an uncertainty in order to reduce it rather than ignoring the uncertainty. For example, when a firm deals with a technological uncertainty in order to escape from a competitive risk, "risk internalization" occurs. Without a mechanism to internalize risk a society based upon centralized planning cannot hope to achieve the same degree of *dynamic* efficiency as a society that provides genuine incentives for the internalization of risk. To be sure, a country like Russia can borrow its technology from the United States and other capitalistic societies. But, because technology must be adapted to the environment in which it is to be used and to the tastes of the consumers who are to use it, in order to be good borrowers firms must be highly flexible. For example, Japanese firms are highly flexible borrowers, which is to say, they are very good at reacting to negative feedback. Negative feedback, however, presupposes that some risk-internalization mechanism is at work, because those firms making unfortunate guesses in the risks they take can either suffer serious losses or fail entirely. And a country that relies upon centralized planning rather than on decentralized risk-taking will be at a serious disadvantage when adapting itself to new circumstances, because negative feedback will always be in short supply.

To summarize the preceding discussion: The achievement of a high degree of dynamic efficiency requires dealing with a high degree of uncertainty. And the willingness to deal with uncertainty will depend upon the extent to which the incentives favor internalization of risk.

Risk, Uncertainty, and Diversity

How should the entrepreneur go about dealing with a greater degree of uncertainty in order to achieve a higher degree of dynamic efficiency? There are numerous ways to describe the dynamic-efficiency games of real life, but the best analogy I have come across is the game of Scrabble. A capsulized description of Scrabble is that it challenges the ability of a player to work out a crossword puzzle against one or more opponents. It is played on a board marked with squares on which to place letters, seven of which initially are chosen at random from a limited supply; there are more of some letters and fewer of others. Extra high points are earned for using scarce letters such as Z's and J's and for putting letters on special squares, and an additional 50 points are earned if all seven letters are used on one play. The dictionary is the final judge of permissible words; and the penalty for having used an unacceptable word is a loss of that turn to score. The players, of course, only know a small fraction of the words contained in the dictionary, so during the game words can be discovered that are not previously known to any of them (that is, if they play as entrepreneurs). If one plays to make longer-run profits as large as possible (higher and higher scores over a series of games), and if one plays with an entrepreneur who cooperates to make his opponent's environment highly uncertain, then it will pay to take large risks when guessing at new words. Only in the final moves of the game, when the opportunities for making Scrabble history are used up, does each player tend to take the configuration of the board as a given. This does not imply that no risks are taken, but, rather, that players are forced to act as specialists in finding ways to make best use of their remaining letters when the opportunities for making brilliant new words become more and more constrained.

In one respect, Scrabble is a simpler game than the dynamic-efficiency games of real life. A player may have to guess about the "whole" (the new words to be constructed), but he knows the "parts" (the letters he has picked); whereas in the dynamic-efficiency games of real life a player must often guess about both the parts and the whole. For example, if a new compressor design is described as a "part" and a new aircraft engine as a "whole" the player must guess about both.

Nevertheless, Scrabble does incorporate some of the principal features of the dynamic-efficiency games of real life. In the first place, if one player is skillful enough to present the other with real dilemmas, improvements in productivity—dynamic efficiency—can be measured in terms of the growth of the individual and total scores when the game is played a number of times. In the second place, like the dynamic-efficiency games of real life, Scrabble is a nonzero-sum game. Now it is true a player would like to win as often as he can, and that each game is a zero-sum game inasmuch as it is either won or lost. But what makes it a positive-sum game is that one player's gain is not another's loss: new words are learned. In the third place, it is a game that highlights the relationship between risk and learning new tricks. Suppose that a boy named Dennis and his rival Bruce play Scrabble as two entrepreneurs just entering a field in which there are serious dilemmas. In this case each is subject to two risks: the risk of guessing wrong versus the risk of having an opportunity stolen from him. Obviously the growth in their scores will depend on how skillful each becomes in taking such risks.

What, then, determines how well Dennis and Bruce might be able to do? One factor is the amount of randomness (or diversity) in the letters each draws. With a wider assortment of letters each will count himself more lucky than if he drew, say, all E's. Therefore, on the "supply" side of the equation there is the randomness of the letters the player picks. And on the "demand" side is the freedom of choice he exercises when making use of his randomness.

Freedom of choice is determined by the willingness and ability of a player to make good use of his diversity. Leaving for the moment the task of pinning down the meaning of freedom of choice under conditions of weak uncertainties, Bayesian uncertainties, and strong uncertainties, it can be noted here that the growth in the scores (S) made by Dennis and Bruce will be determined, in part, by the diversity of the letters they pick (D), in part, by their freedom of choice in making use of this diversity ($F.C.$), and by luck (L).

$$S = f(D, F.C., L)$$

In Figure 5 the functional relationships for a fairly typical situation are illustrated by a pair of diagrams. I have assumed that, in a "typical" situation, diversity can be measured in terms of the variety of letters picked. This, of course, is an oversimplification. But our present purpose is simply to understand the general relationship between diversity and freedom of choice. As Figure 5 shows (and common sense suggests), freedom of choice does not mean a lot when diversity is low, but it does when diversity is high. When there is a possibility for making a four-, five-, six-, or seven-letter word, a player whose freedom of choice was, say, 75 percent would have a substantial advantage over one whose freedom of choice was only 50 percent. Such an advantaged player would lose only when luck was decidedly against him. Though there are definite limits on the amount of uncertainty or diversity an entrepreneur can tolerate, the more diversity he can utilize the greater will be his freedom of choice.

Specifically, how does freedom of choice affect outcomes? The ef-

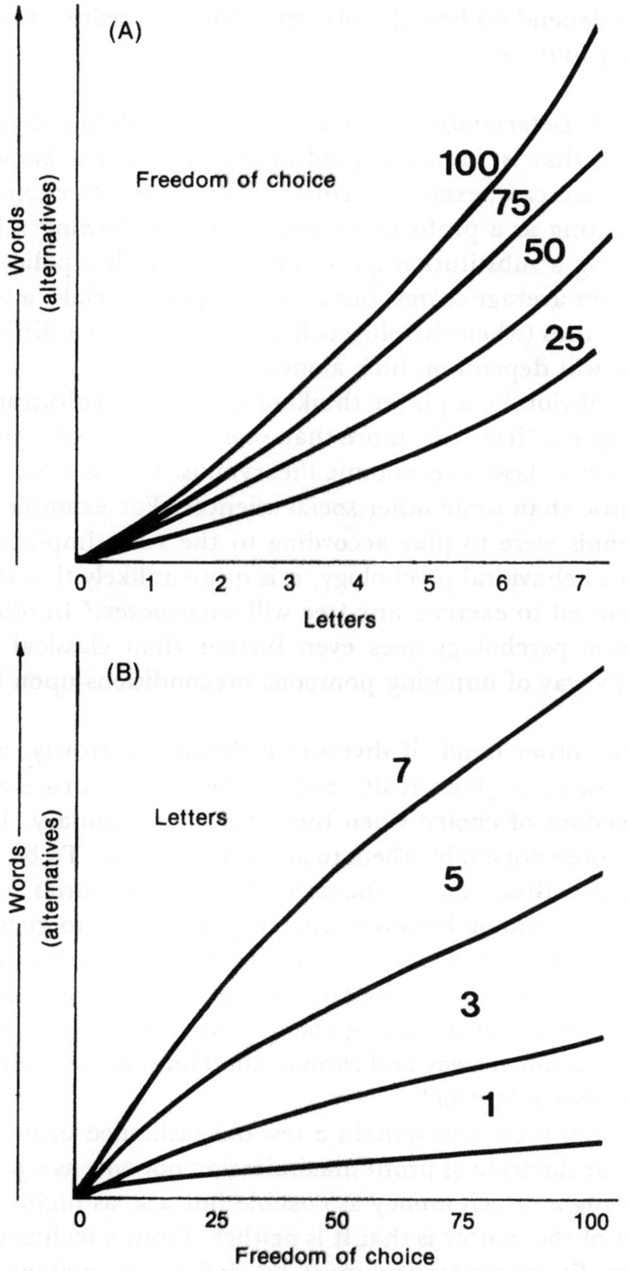

Figure 5. Making words. (*A*) Alternatives versus letters (freedom of choice constant). (*B*) Alternatives versus freedom of choice (number of letters constant).

fect will depend on how the players define "diversity." Consider the following four cases:

Case 1: A Deterministic World. The players define diversity very narrowly, that is, as making substitutions within a known vocabulary. In this case, exercising close to 100 percent freedom of choice means acting as a profit maximizer by never allowing a possibility for making a substitution go to waste. And such a policy buys not only higher average scores, but also, in repeated trials, a lower variance of scores (when the players find themselves in a difficult situation less will depend on luck alone).

Quite obviously, a player thinking in terms of substitutes will be exercising his "free will" more than one who does not. And for this reason, even classical economic theory must be regarded as less deterministic than some other social sciences. For example, if Bruce and Dennis were to play according to the rules implicit in B. F. Skinner's behavioral psychology, it is quite unlikely that they would be permitted to exercise any free will whatsoever.[7] In other words, behavioral psychology goes even further than classical economic theory by way of imposing pompous preconditions upon its subject matter.

On the other hand, if diversity is defined narrowly, as making substitutes among known alternatives, Dennis and Bruce will have a zero freedom of choice when their known vocabulary, large as it may be, does not enable them to act in a tight spot. To be sure, after Dennis and Bruce have exhausted their opportunities for making substitutions among known words, they might like to guess at possible words. But by acting as strict profit maximizers—restricting themselves to choices among known alternatives—they cannot compare the alternatives of taking chances on uncertain words and having a bonus stolen away and cannot, therefore, make their profits as large as they might be!

Although there still remain a few old-fashioned economists who regard the doctrine of profit maximization not only as a prescription for making as much money as possible but also as highly scientific, the fact of the matter is that it is neither. From a technical point of view, profit maximization must be defined as making as much money as possible subject to a given menu of alternatives. And if it is so defined, profit maximization can result in its intended objective in one and only one kind of world: a world whose knowledge is perfect. By contrast, if firms in the real world maximize profits subject to a given menu of alternatives they will ultimately go out of business. The railroads offer a good example of an industry in which firms defined their alternatives so narrowly that they ultimately failed. But not only railroad executives live in the past. For example, several years ago I asked George Dantzig (the inventor of linear programming) what he had learned in the course of advising petroleum companies about linear programming techniques. His answer: "A common problem in the petroleum industry is maximization of profits subject to an obsolete set of constraints; thereby activities are kept alive which do not pay their own way." To be sure, the doctrine of profit maximization might be salvaged by making it subject to the best available alternatives. A more basic problem with the doctrine, however, is that by acting upon the assumption that there is some definite limit on total profits, firms preclude themselves from making as much money as they otherwise might make.

Nor can the doctrine of profit maximization be regarded as a great contribution to economic science. To make a scientific statement it is not necessary to put it in mathematical terms. It is essential, however, to make a sufficiently unambiguous statement that it can be proven either right or wrong. And it is unscientific to proclaim that firms are maximizing their profits, because in the real world the alternatives are constantly changing; and furthermore, in a changing real world it is humanly impossible to know all the alternatives. Therefore, proclaiming that such firms maximize their profits is tantamount to proclaiming that the alternatives chosen are those which God meant to be chosen!

Case 2: A World of Weak Uncertainties. This is a world in which the players are willing to act on the basis of uncertain information because they can insure themselves against uncertainty. For example, to encourage him to act on the basis of uncertain information, Dennis's mother might offer to compensate him for any losses he incurs as a result of guessing wrong when playing Scrabble with Bruce. With 100 percent insurance against guessing wrong, Dennis obviously will be provided with an incentive to act on the basis that uncertain knowledge is equivalent to certain knowledge. But while such insurance will encourage entrepreneurs to take chances they would not otherwise attempt, it will provide them with no incentive whatsoever to learn from their mistakes. If entrepreneurs are to learn from their mistakes there must not only be positive incentives to encourage mistakes, but negative incentives to insure that something will be learned from them.

Case 3: A World of Bayesian Uncertainties. In this world Bruce and Dennis have the same incentive as in Case 1 to make good use of substitutes. But if the definition of diversity is broadened to include words they think they know, then the strength of their beliefs will be determined by the amount they are willing to bet on a given possibility. Now, if Bruce and Dennis define diversity to include alternative likelihood functions characterized by two parameters—the mean and variance of a distribution—they obviously will have a greater freedom of choice for dealing with uncertainty. They will be able to compare the risk of guessing wrong with the risk of having an opportunity stolen away by a competitor. Therefore, if Bruce adopts a Bayesian strategy by introducing more uncertainty into Dennis's environment, Dennis must act in a like manner if he hopes to succeed.

Actually, in such a Bayesian world, entrepreneurs have two incentives: to take chances when threatened by a competitor and to regard the taking of such chances as experiments with which to buy information—thereby gradually reducing the uncertainty in their world. And with these incentives Bruce and Dennis are encouraged to be men about town, because the more words they know on some kind of probabilistic basis the better they will be able to deal with uncertainty.

But, while Bayesian players will have a clear advantage over those who refuse to think in terms of buying information, it is nevertheless true that thinking in Bayesian terms will make the entrepreneur's freedom of choice and his profits smaller than they might otherwise be. In particular, because Bayesian probability theory is based upon a semiclosed system, thinking in terms of such a paradigm does not enable the entrepreneur to deal with genuine discontinuities. To deal with a genuine discontinuity requires generating a hypothesis previously assigned a zero probability. To indicate the flavor of the argument, suppose that an entrepreneur believes he can discover genuine Rembrandts at bargain prices. And also suppose that the process of proving whether a guess is right or wrong is not costless; for example, it might involve a rather expensive x-ray analysis of the would-be Rembrandt paintings. If the entrepreneur desires to make the probability of a discovery as large as possible how should he go about his task? An entrepreneur who took a Bayesian point of view would bet with himself as to whether or not a particular discovery was interesting enough to warrant the x-ray outlay on the basis of previously viewed Rembrandts. Assuming for the moment that Rembrandt's style changed more or less continuously, the probability of spotting a true treasure obviously would depend on the number of Rembrandts he had seen before.

But would an entrepreneur brought up on happy-warrior rationality bet on a particular picture being a Rembrandt on the basis of its resemblance to paintings he had seen before? Never! By following such a strategy an entrepreneur would be destined to become a prisoner of his own experiences: if Rembrandt had made a significant change in his style of painting, it is unlikely the entrepreneur would be able to recognize a "new" Rembrandt painting. Assuming that Rembrandt's technique did not completely change, the entrepreneur could not afford to ignore the dozens of previous hints that might be relevant to the discovery of a "new" Rembrandt painting.

Or consider the parable of the ducks. Suppose that an expert in the general field of birds observed specimens of a newly discovered bird in North Dakota, in Texas, in Norway as well as in other places —birds that, in addition to a distinctive walk and distinctive quack, are white. When announcing this new species, which he names "duck," to the world, the ornithologist predicts that wherever this bird is encountered a distinguishing characteristic will be its white color. Now suppose that after this has become the generally accepted paradigm millions of black duck-like birds appear. Would a Bayesian recognize this newly discovered bird for a duck? To be sure, it might quack like a duck. And it might walk like a duck. But in terms of the logic of a semiclosed system, upon which Bayesian probability theory is based, changes in knowledge come about only in a cumulative and incremental manner. And on the basis of such a model a zero probability would be assigned to hypotheses that resulted from genuine breaks in the data. Only if the appearance of a black duck had been preceded by off-white ducks, light-gray ducks, and dark-gray ducks might a black duck be taken for a real duck. And again the entrepreneur who insists upon thinking all uncertainty can be expressed in terms of likelihood functions is not engaged in rational behavior if in fact he is dealing with strong uncertainties. To compare the alternatives of guessing, either on a Bayesian basis or by using his intuition, the entrepreneur must be willing to entertain the hypothesis that ducks might be black without attaching a prior probability estimate to the guess. Indeed, by acting on the basis of a prior probability distribution that freezes the likelihood function, many of his hints will go to waste! Therefore, Bayesians impose pompous preconditions on their subject matter by constraining man from dealing with discontinuities. In other words, what the Bayesians overlook is that when dealing with real world uncertainties (strong uncertainties) the really important matter is not arriving at the right answer, but asking the right questions (for example, Could it be a duck?).

Case 4: A World of Strong Uncertainties. Let us think of diversity not only as known and probabilistically defined substitutes, but also as hints that can be detached from particular experiences to guess at new substitutes (that is, new probability distributions). If Bruce and Dennis want to rapidly expand their vocabularies (and their profits), hints received on the structure of the English language will be treasured and they will think of themselves as conducting experiments to revise their theory so better predictions can be made. And a player with only a miniscule imagination should be able to do better than a Bayesian. To take an obvious example, if Bruce and Dennis thought about possible uses of the prefix "pre" they would obviously be in a better position to compare alternatives in a difficult situation than an entrepreneur who thought that life was more or less like flipping coins.

Now, thinking about words that might be formed with the prefix "pre" is only a beginning in understanding the structure of the English language. And obviously Dennis would like hints that apply to a wide variety of words, because the more randomness in his hints the better he will do when necessity prods him. If it is assumed that the more randomness in the hints the greater will be the capability of an entrepreneur to deal with uncertainty, then it should be apparent that Bruce and Dennis are provided with an incentive to diversify their experiences, by playing Scrabble with other imaginative players. The greater the diversity of their experiences and the more randomness in their hints the larger is likely to be their bag of tricks.

In a zero-sum game, in which the gains must precisely offset the losses, competition and cooperation can be thought of as opposites. However, in a positive-sum game, in which the meta-objective is to develop new knowledge, competition can be regarded as a form of cooperation. For example, when scientists compete to win Nobel prizes they cooperate to expand knowledge in the world. And the same is true of Dennis and Bruce: if Dennis is to expand his knowledge of the English language as rapidly as possible Bruce must cooperate by creating strong uncertainties!

To conclude this discussion: The more uncertainty individuals or organizations must deal with, the broader must be their concept of diversity. In a certain world diversity is defined most narrowly and consists of known alternatives. In a world of weak uncertainties it consists of alternative probability distributions. In a Bayesian world diversity consists of alternative likelihood functions. In a world of strong uncertainties it consists of more or less randomness in hints.

Once these elementary distinctions have been made, the concept of openness will not seem as elusive as when it was introduced in the last chapter. Openness—the ability to interact with an external environment to change it and the entrepreneur's ideas—depends on the ability of the entrepreneur to define diversity more and more broadly, as he encounters more and more risk. When Dennis and Bruce make substitutions only within a known vocabulary they are behaving as "closed systems." When they make choices among alternative likelihood functions they are behaving as "semiclosed systems": systems whose degree of openness is only slightly above zero. And the more random the hints that can be efficiently utilized, the greater will be the degree of openness.

This is not to say, however, that Dennis and Bruce can hope to acquire a high degree of dynamic efficiency without giving up something in static efficiency. Because the job of using one's imagination to construct new hypotheses is a very difficult one, if Dennis constantly used his imagination to guess at new words he might find himself completely unable to spell a simple word like "goose." Conversely, if Dennis were to concentrate on being a highly methodical player who rarely makes a mistake in spelling he might find it almost impossible to use his imagination. Indeed, if money were no object, Dennis would really like to have two teams of specialists working for him: one composed of highly methodical players (people with a relatively low degree of openness) and the other composed of highly imaginative players (people with a relatively high degree of openness).

In the real world, however, resources are limited. Therefore, it is impossible to demand more dynamic efficiency without giving up something by the way of static efficiency (and vice versa). Furthermore, the entrepreneur desiring to achieve a high degree of dynamic efficiency will want to undertake programs to limit his financial risk should he guess wrong. He should regard all research and development activities as experiments with which to buy knowledge—experiments that should be conducted as inexpensively as possible. For example, an aircraft company developing a new airplane will give up something in the way of static efficiency by using one wing-assembly feature instead of three. Why? If there are technical problems with the leading edge of the wing (and there usually are) it is much cheaper and quicker to incorporate new knowledge.

In summary, achievement of dynamic efficiency will require: (1) defining "diversity" to include the ability to use hints from previous experiences and experiments, and (2) highly flexible programs to minimize the cost of incorporating new knowledge.

Specialization in Risk-Taking

Because an entire economic system (as distinct from an individual firm) must be oriented toward achieving both a high degree of dynamic efficiency (as in fast history) and a high degree of static efficiency (as in slow history), it is fortunate that people are not the same in their capacity to deal with uncertainty. And no doubt such basic differences in personality are in part, at least, determined by genetic factors. Some years ago biologists were of the opinion that individual personality traits were associated with different races. But today there is general agreement that within any reasonably large population there is a wide diversity of personality differences; indeed, the differences are much larger within than between the races.[8]

Nevertheless, it is easy to exaggerate the importance of genetic factors in determining basic personality drives. To be sure, there are those born with such an enormous appetite for adventure that they are constantly seeking new adventures—almost to their dying day. Conversely, there are those with such an enormous appetite for security that they behave like old men—almost from the day they were born. And genetic factors may play an important role in explaining such large differences. However, most people seem to fall in the middle of the distribution; that is, they are dominated neither by a desire for adventure nor a desire for security. It seems safe to assume that the environment in which these people live plays a decisive role in molding their personalities. For example, children of overly protective parents have been observed to develop a genuine distaste for dealing with dilemmas. Religious training can give people a tremendous fear of unpredictability. And while personality plays an important role in determining which occupation a person enters—for example, whether a lawyer goes into criminal or probate law—conversely, a vocation can have a significant effect on one's personality. In German computer companies today you will find people who are the direct antithesis of the so-called authoritarian personality; on the other hand, it is easy to imagine that when German firms were highly cartelized the business environment did not favor the development of personalities with a high degree of openness.

There are, of course, a few economists who still live in the nineteenth century inasmuch as they believe, like Marshall and Freud, that man's dominant drive is for security. However, it is no less of an exaggeration to assert that people live only for adventure than it is to insist that they live only for security. In fact it is quite as wrong to assert people are all alike in their personality characteristics as it is to insist that they are all alike in their tastes. Indeed, it is fortunate that people are not all alike in their personality characteristics. In a world where the only permanent truth is that all truths are but partial truths, risk lovers are needed to develop new truths, and risk averters are needed to insure that older truths are not easily discarded. In other words, for dynamic processes to occur both Franklin Roosevelts and Herbert Hoovers must play vital roles.

If it is granted that the pursuit of dynamic efficiency requires dealing with more uncertainty than does the pursuit of static efficiency, and that people differ in their capacity to deal with uncertainty, then we should expect to observe a division of labor between firms engaged in dealing with more and less uncertainty. To be sure, within a single firm a wide diversity of behavior can be observed. For example, it can be assumed that the research and development department of a highly dynamic firm would not have the same degree of constraint imposed upon it as, say, the bookkeeping department. However, highly dynamic firms differ from highly static firms not only in their research and development activities. If the research and development activities are successful, more often than not new production tools will become necessary—and a good deal of learning will have to be undertaken by the tooling department. Moreover, if the feedback process is to work, the sales people must become involved in transmitting information from the customers to the people in research and development. And the newer the technology in question, the more important will be the feedback.

Not only is the argument for specialization, in terms of the degree of uncertainty, appealing, such specialization actually does occur. For example, although some joint ownership of aircraft and airline firms occurred during the 1920s, the development of commercial aircraft and the operation of commercial airlines were later undertaken by entirely different firms. Vertically integrated companies did not endure, because substantial diseconomies would have been incurred if either airline companies had owned aircraft firms or aircraft firms had owned airline companies. In the former case, static efficiency would have been imposed at the expense of dynamic efficiency; and in the latter case dynamic efficiency would have been imposed at the expense of static efficiency. In other words, with joint ownership the chance of having both reasonably dependable airline companies and highly progressive aircraft firms was quite unlikely. For the same reason it may be assumed that public utilities buy substantially all of their progress from firms such as Westinghouse and General Electric. And, as was pointed out by Lawrence White in his book on the automobile industry, in recent years practically all the progress in this industry has been brought about by subcontractors.[9] Considering the fact that the automobile industry has not featured much progress in recent years, how is this to be explained? Apparently the automobile industry is so specialized to the static-efficiency function it has an almost zero ability to deal with uncertainty.

Finally, as a different kind of example, consider Bell Telephone Laboratories and Western Electric, both of which are owned by American Telephone and Telegraph. Here we find within a single firm quite different types of organizations. And it certainly can be argued that AT&T's success has rested upon having within it one organization specialized for dynamic efficiency and the other for static efficiency. If there had been only a Bell Telephone Laboratories much progress might have been made—but at the expense of static efficiency. On the other hand, if there were only a Western Electric we would have dependability and static efficiency—but at the expense of dynamic efficiency.

Why is it, then, that AT&T has been able to combine both types of efficiency? The reason, it would appear, is that AT&T is not under real pressure to quickly introduce new equipment into the telephone system. For example, although the invention of the transistor occurred in Bell Labs, AT&T was not one of the first, but rather one of the last, firms to introduce transistorized equipment into operational use. On the other hand, industries in which competitive pressures force the early introduction of new products cannot enjoy the best of both worlds. For example, in order to introduce new pharmaceuticals early, pharmaceutical firms find themselves unable to produce them at the lowest possible costs. Or, to take another example, although during World War II the tooling practices of the aircraft firms resembled those of the automobile industry, after World War II they returned to the so-called "inefficient" practices they had engaged in during the 1930s. Why? As has already been suggested, it can be assumed that if tooling had been designed so as to minimize production costs it would have been impossible to quickly introduce new commercial aircraft into operational use without inflating the cost of changing the tooling in order to incorporate new knowledge.

To be sure, the trade-off between static and dynamic efficiency will not always take the same form. In the preceding examples, production at minimal cost was given up. Dynamic efficiency can also be bought by failing to optimize the design of a new system in the highly detailed manner it would be optimized if static efficiency were the goal. Or dynamic efficiency can be bought at the expense of static efficiency by sacrificing the reliability of the product.

What is the implication for the theory of the firm of the trade-off between static and dynamic efficiency? What is the principal difference between a theory of the firm based upon a fully exploited technology and a theory in which it is assumed progress has not come to an end? The principal difference is that whereas in the former case a completely deterministic model is implied, in the latter it is not.

Consider, first, the chief clerk of a pin mill. As Figure 6 shows, he obtains demand bids from consumers and supply bids from factor markets, and from these price information is generated that is turned over to an auctioneer (the market). In other words, the classical theory of the firm is based upon a closed-system paradigm (a zero degree of interaction between competitors). In fact, if an economy consisted entirely of fully exploited technologies there is no log-

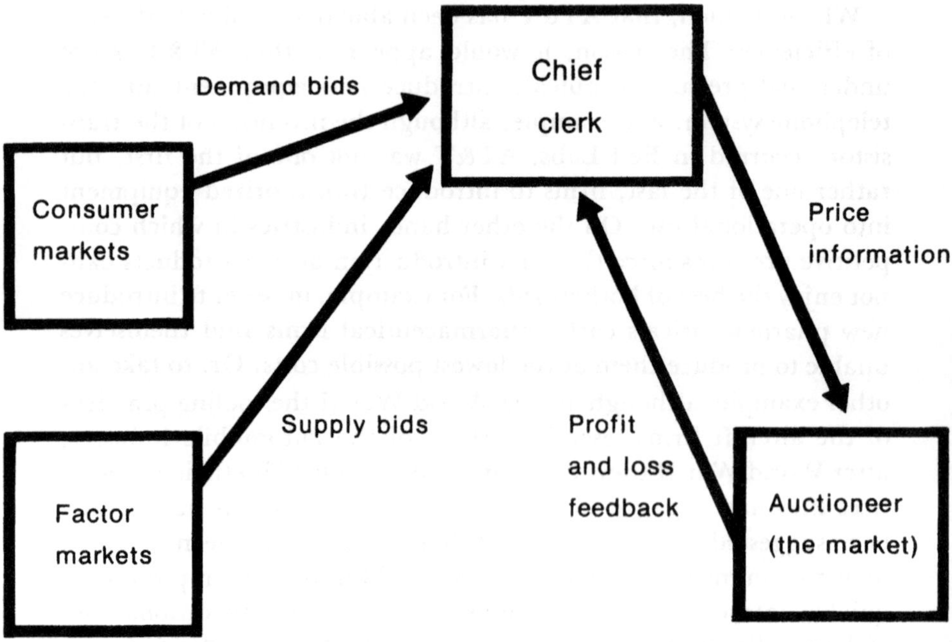

Figure 6. A fully exploited technology.

ical reason why computers could not be substituted for chief clerks and the entire job taken over by a centralized planning bureau.

On the other hand, in a world in which progress is to occur there must be both Type 1 firms (generators of ideas) and Type 2 firms (borrowers of ideas)—each practicing a quite different rationality (Figure 7). The chief requirement for Type 2 firms is that they must have highly flexible and adaptive organizations. Flexibility is necessary because borrowed ideas do not typically turn out to be good or bad; rather, they can be both good and bad. To be successful the firm must be good at improvising in the face of numerous minor dilemmas (and some major dilemmas). This, in turn, requires a highly flexible research-and-development organization and getting ideas into test at the earliest possible moment.

Highly adaptive organizations are required if the best use is to be made of a technology. Indeed, even before the United States became a technological leader, flexible firms were responsible for its increasing rate of productivity. However, the more structured and predictable firms become, the less adaptive they are likely to be.

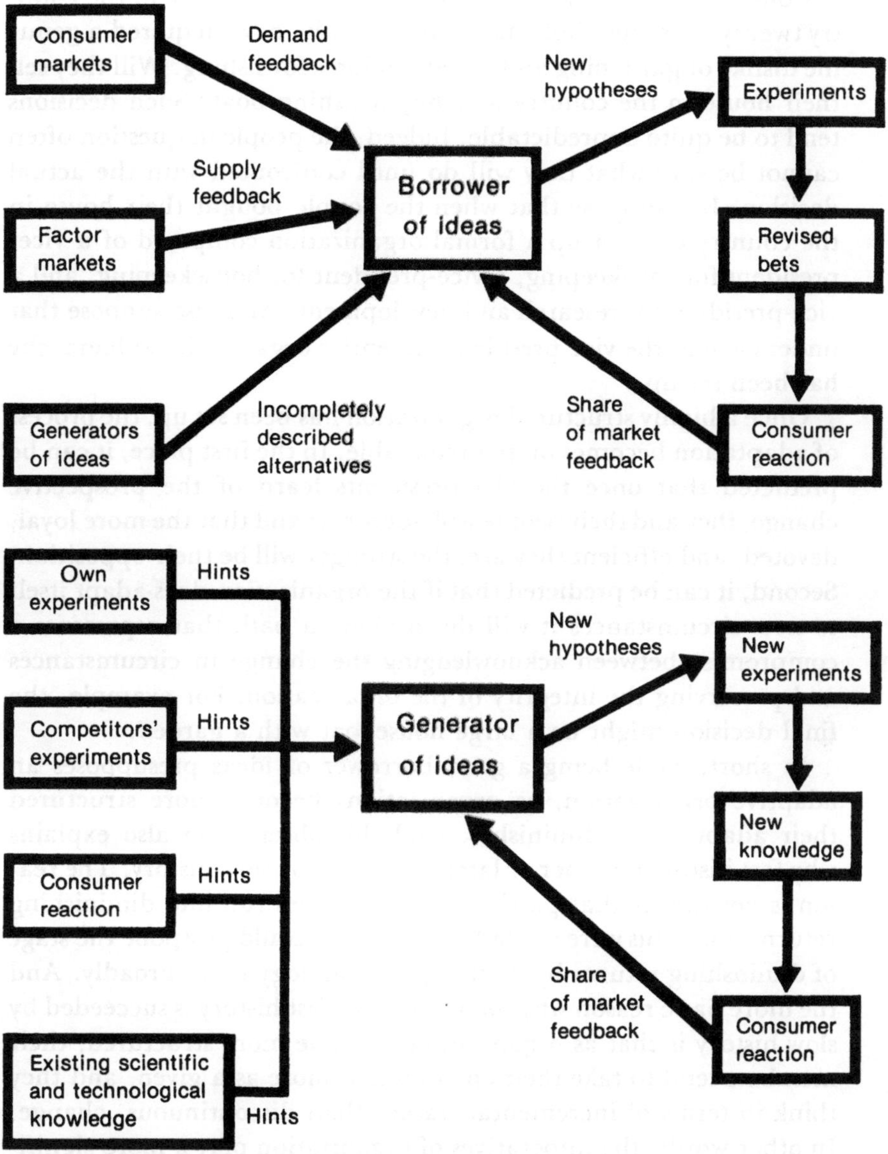

Figure 7. An exploitable technology.

Generally speaking, highly structured organizations are inefficient when dealing with changes in their environments.

Consider, for example, a couple who bought a house in the country twenty years ago, but who, more recently, have acquired a genuine dislike of gardening and a real fondness for fishing. Will they sell their house in the country and buy a fishing boat? Such decisions tend to be quite unpredictable. Indeed, the people in question often cannot be sure what they will do until confronted with the actual decision. But suppose that when the couple bought their house in the country they set up a formal organization composed of a vice-president for yardkeeping, a vice-president for housekeeping, and a vice-president for research and development. And also suppose that under each of the vice presidents an entire organizational hierarchy has been set up.

Once a highly structured organization has been set up, the process of adaptation becomes more predictable. In the first place, it can be predicted that once the vice-presidents learn of the prospective change, they and their people will oppose it; and that the more loyal, devoted, and efficient they are, the stronger will be their opposition. Second, it can be predicted that if the organization does adapt itself to new circumstances it will do so along a path that represents a compromise between acknowledging the change in circumstances and preserving the integrity of the organization. For example, the final decision might be a large houseboat with a garden.

In short, while being a good borrower of ideas presupposes an adaptive organization, as organizations become more structured their adaptiveness diminishes. And this observation also explains why fast history is sooner or later succeeded by slow history. The reason is not simply that particular technologies run into diminishing returns, for if this were the only factor firms could postpone the stage of diminshing returns by defining a technology more broadly. And the more basic reason why sooner or later fast history is succeeded by slow history is that as organizations become more structured, their members tend to take their environment more as a given, and they think in terms of incremental, rather than discontinuous, change. In other words, the imperatives of organization play a more significant role in slow history than they do in fast history.

The principal distinction between Type 2 and Type 1 firms is that if the latter are to be dynamically efficient they must not only be flexible, but highly capable of regarding their activities and their competitors' activities as hints to be used for constructing new experiments. And as we already have seen, to be favored by luck in the hints they receive entrepreneurs must have the ability to ask the right questions. For example, when people at the Douglas Corporation asked themselves what particular changes in aerodynamic configuration and aircraft engine design might permit significant advances in operating costs, as well as speed, over the Boeing 247 airplane, they were posing relevant questions. Or to take another example: When Ford Motor Company people asked why an automobile could not be built which would be both more inexpensive and more rugged than the Oldsmobile, they were raising questions that helped to put luck on their side.

In short, if Type 1 and Type 2 firms are to remain dynamically efficient there must be a reciprocal relationship between them. Type 2 firms need to be good at adapting their organizations to new knowledge. And Type 1 firms need to be good at asking the right questions. As Simon Kuznets made the point in his Nobel Prize lecture: "If technology is to be employed efficiently and widely, and indeed, if its own progress is to be stimulated by such use, institutional and ideological adjustments must be made to effect the proper use of innovations generated by the advancing stock of human knowledge."[10]

Illustrations of the Trade-off Between Static and Dynamic Efficiency

The following examples are intended to show (1) that although the trade-off between static and dynamic efficiency can take many different forms it is nevertheless very real; and (2) that internal incentives play a very important role in determining the degree of dynamic behavior.

The Trade-off Between Progress and Specialization. The problem here is to explain why, until about 1960, Pratt and Whitney in the United States and Rolls Royce in Britain were responsible for more than three-quarters of the aircraft engine sales in their respective countries.[11] There can be little doubt that whereas they appreciated the fact that success in jet engine development would require a high degree of dynamic efficiency, their competitors operated within the confines of the rules of static efficiency. Thus, both Pratt and Whitney and Rolls Royce placed a good deal of emphasis on conducting programs so that they could quickly adapt themselves to new circumstances. For example, both companies developed inexpensive demonstrator engines to test novel components. Because both had a sufficient menu of technology under development, each could quickly reorient programs to exploit current opportunities (for example, the turbofan engine). And during the period prior to 1960, it was an unwritten law in both companies that an engine could not be developed for a specific application until the technology was well in hand. As members of both companies have described their strategy of research and development: "You develop an aircraft engine by testing it."

By contrast, the competitors of these companies were more devoted to planning on the basis of initial conditions. Westinghouse and General Electric initially set up their jet engine divisions with engineers taken from their steam-turbine divisions, on the premise that the technologies were sufficiently alike to furnish an important carry-over of experience. And these engineers went about their business as if they were engaged in the careful optimization process associated with a mature technology; that is, they put considerable emphasis on specializing aircraft engines for particular applications. In Britain there was a similar emphasis by Rolls Royce's competitors, but for a different reason. All of the other British aircraft-engine companies were parts of vertically integrated firms, and they gave careful attention to mating one of their own engines with one of their own aircraft.

The results? A good deal can be said for specializing aircraft engines in terms of particular applications. For example, in developing an engine for fighter planes it is important to obtain a high engine-thrust relative to engine weight. On the other hand, in commercial aircraft and bomber applications minimizing fuel consumption is more important than minimizing engine weight. But good as these arguments might seem, they did not win the day. Although Westinghouse could and did develop an engine for use in fighter planes, and General Electric an engine for use in a bomber, more often than not in each generation of engines a Pratt and Whitney engine stole the market in all applications: bombers, fighters, and transports. And as Eli Devons showed in an unpublished study undertaken for the British Ministry of Aircraft, the number of times a vertically integrated firm succeeded in mating one of its engines with one of its aircraft was less than the number determined by chance![12]

How are these results to be explained? In the case of aircraft engines, the trade-off was between improving engine technology applicable to several applications and optimizing engines for particular applications. To take best advantage of this trade-off it was not necessary to completely ignore the opportunities for specialization, because after a basic new engine was developed it could be optimized for different applications. Nevertheless, as Figure 8 shows, in terms of improved performance the curve for product-improvement engines (engines specialized for particular applications) is flatter than for new engines. And the basic reason Pratt and Whitney and Rolls Royce were so successful is that they were more aware of this trade-off—they recognized better than their competitors that to cook rabbit stew the first requirement is to find the rabbit.

What was the response of the competitors of Rolls Royce and Pratt and Whitney to their success? As of the late 1950s, when his study was completed, Eli Devons found no evidence of a general willingness to adopt the Rolls Royce strategy. On the contrary, the integrated firms regarded the Rolls Royce approach to planning as highly unscientific, and their spokesmen insisted that Rolls Royce succeeded despite Lord Hive's rules. Following Lord Hive's departure, Rolls Royce became a more typical British company by the way constraints were imposed on dynamic behavior.

As far as the United States is concerned the story is quite different. Westinghouse finally went out of the aircraft-engine business, and in the middle 1950s General Electric changed both its strategy and its team, after which it was able to increase its share of the market. Evidently negative incentives do play a role in changing behavior.

The Trade-off Between Dynamic Efficiency and Durability. Although we economists are only now discovering dynamic efficiency, H. J. Habakkuk has shown that the progress ethic was very deeply rooted in American society. And by quoting an American friend of de Tocqueville he provides an interesting example of another type of trade-off between static and dynamic efficiency:

> I asked our steamboat builders on the North Bank a few years ago why they made their vessels so weak. They answered that perhaps they might even last too long, because the art of steam navigation was making daily progress. In fact, these boats which made 8 or 9 knots could not, a little time afterwards, compete with others

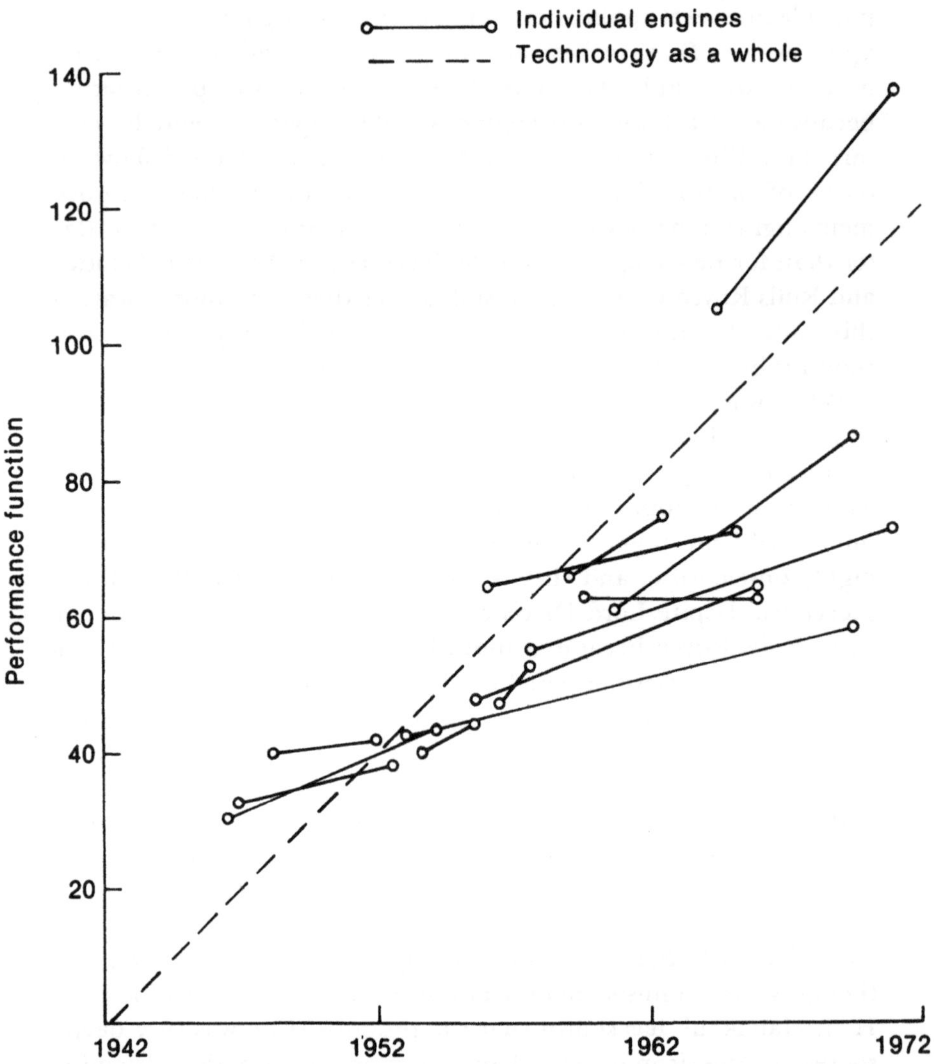

Figure 8. Performance improvements in individual aircraft turbine engines compared to the performance improvement in the technology as a whole. Data from Robert Shishko, *Technological Change through Product Improvement in Aircraft Turbine Engines* (Santa Monica, Calif.: RAND Corp., 1973).

whose construction allowed them to make 12 or 15 knots. . . . There is a feeling among us about everything which prevents us aiming at permanence; there reigns in America a popular and universal belief in the progress of the human spirit. We are always expecting an improvement to be found in everything.[13]

Evidently there was dynamic competition in America as early as the 1830s when de Tocqueville wrote. Without such competition there probably would not have been the pressure on steamboat builders to press for greater and greater speed.

The Trade-off Between Dynamic Efficiency and Excess Capacity. Theoretical economists who cannot tolerate the uncertainty associated with competition define competition so as to eliminate rivalry. And practical policymakers who are intolerant of uncertainty sometimes go even further by arguing that because competition is a wasteful activity it must be eliminated. For example, prior to the nationalization of airlines by European governments in the early 1930s, politicians likened competition to a state of confusion and blamed the underutilization of capacity upon such chaos. In the United States a similar reaction helped lead to the establishment of airline regulation in 1938. During the period between its establishment and the end of World War II, the Civil Aeronautics Board (CAB) certainly cannot be blamed for a lack of effort to eliminate chaos from the United States' airline industry. On practically all major routes no competition whatsoever was permitted. Moreover, even to this date the CAB has not allowed a single new firm to enter the major trunkline business.

Only after World War II, when there was a good deal of pressure from aircraft companies, did the CAB allow competition on trunklines. However, because no price competition was allowed, first priority was given to building faster and more luxurious planes rather than more economical planes. To be sure, quality competition costs something. And there is a greater degree of constraint on keeping airliner costs down with such competition than without it. Moreover, the jets turned out to have a cost advantage over propeller-driven airplanes that was not foreseen in their early development. Nevertheless quality competition is not the type of competition the United States featured during the 1930s when it became the leader of the world in commercial aviation.

Let us suppose that in 1930 airline regulation of the type employed between 1938 and the end of World War II was promulgated. To obtain a higher degree of static efficiency in the form of less excess-capacity, what sacrifices might have been required in dynamic efficiency? To put the question more specifically, according to Miller and Sawers, between the Fokker and the Ford trimotors and later versions of the DC-3 airplanes there was a reduction of about 50 percent in per mile seat costs (including depreciation).[14] What is the probability such a reduction would have occurred if regulation had been adopted in 1930?

It is not necessary to argue at length that competition between the airlines played a significant role in stimulating aircraft engineers to develop more efficient planes. Consider, for example, the role played by the Boeing 247, a sleek ten-passenger airplane developed to provide a significant advantage in speed over the Ford and Fokker trimotor airplanes. Because of its performance United Air Lines ordered sixty of these airplanes. Then, to meet this new competitive threat, TWA requested from several aircraft companies designs that would provide advantages in terms of cost as well as in speed. The companies included Curtiss-Wright, Ford, Martin, Consolidated, and Douglas. And it was this challenge that provided Douglas engineers with the incentive to develop the DC-1, the forerunner of the DC-3. In fact, as Miller and Sawers have pointed out, Douglas himself later said: "It was the challenge of the 247 that put us into the transport business."[15]

By developing the 247, Boeing was cooperating with Douglas in the same manner Bruce would have had to cooperate with Dennis if the total scores they earned playing Scrabble were to increase as rapidly as possible. And it also should be apparent that without competition between the airlines incentives for such cooperation would have been lacking.

Evidence like this convinces me that with a highly regulated and less uncertain environment in civil aviation during the early years, it is quite unlikely anything like a 50 percent reduction in costs could have been achieved. Moreover, a less competitive environment would certainly seem to be one of the main reasons why, after leading the United States in civil and military aviation during the 1920s, Europe made very disappointing progress during the 1930s. If it is assumed that European designers were quite as capable as American designers, how else to explain why no European airliners were sold in the United States until after World War II?

This is not to say, however, that with no regulation the prospects for bringing about substantial cost reductions were quite as favorable in Europe as they were in the United States. For progress to come about rapidly, two conditions have to be fulfilled: there needs to be a high degree of rivalry between both airline companies and between aircraft companies. And while both of these conditions were fulfilled in the United States, in Europe there was less rivalry among airline companies. Indeed, the very fact that government ownership and regulation were undertaken suggests that incentives were weak. Therefore, while it can be said that regulation certainly worsened incentives and had a negative impact on cost performance, it cannot be said just how much better performance might have been in its absence.

On the other hand, there also seems to be little doubt that by introducing regulation in 1938 the United States took a step that was bound, sooner or later, to lessen its competitive advantage. And as the following table shows, while the best American jets cost about 40 percent less per seat mile than the best European jets, it may be assumed that the American cost advantage has been narrowing from the 1930s, at which time American airlines purchased no European-developed airliners.

Moreover, while Boeing's recent performance has been quite impressive, there is good reason to suppose that without a really first-rate competitor its performance will sooner or later become as sluggish as Douglas's in the early postwar years. Past experience suggests that when a firm no longer faces genuine challenges it has a very small chance of remaining dynamic.

What, then, might be done to remedy the prospective shortage of risk-taking? In the case of commercial aviation the answer seems to be crystal clear: the government should stop regulating airline fares and restricting the entry of new firms. If government policies place major stress upon preventing excess capacity from developing, twenty-five years from now the airlines may find themselves in exactly the same predicament as the railroads.

To some people this may seem like a very radical proposal when in fact it is conservative. The longer such measures are postponed, the more firms will become accustomed to dealing with a relatively low degree of uncertainty, and the more irreversible will be the process. In other words, the longer the United States waits, the more radical will be the required measures. And the purpose of deregulating now is to minimize the need for more radical measures later.

To conclude this chapter: Dynamic theory gives us a better way to

Table 1. Airliner costs (cents per seat mile).

Plane	Passenger capacity	Year put into operational use	Costs: Operations	Direct maintenance	Subtotal	Depre-ciation	Total
Turboprops							
Fokker F-27	—	—	1.183	.763	1.946	.332	2.278
Viscount 700	52	1958	1.203	.524	1.727	.377	2.104
Lockheed Electra	132	1959	.935	.597	1.532	.498	2.030
Jets							
Sud Caravelle	64	1961	1.205	.482	1.687	.707	2.394
BAC-111	79	1965	.888	.415	1.303	.408	1.711
Douglas DC-9	90	1965	1.172	.260	1.432	.630	2.062
Boeing 720	110	1960	.839	.281	1.120	.228	1.348
Boeing 729	110	1964	.829	.275	1.104	.338	1.442

Source: Ronald Miller and David Sawers, *The Technical Development of Modern Aviation* (New York: Praeger, 1968), appendixes 1 and 2.

understand economic reality because it provides a new trade-off—the trade-off between static and dynamic efficiency. The former type of efficiency is mainly concerned with making good use of existing inputs, and the latter with either improving the inputs or using existing inputs in such a manner that new economic opportunities are realized. Which type of efficiency will be favored depends on the extent to which incentives favor internalization of risk.

4. Dynamic Competition

Perfect Competition: A Science or a Religion?

The concept of competition upon which this book is based is hardly new. As George Stigler pointed out in an article written in 1957, economists from the time of Adam Smith to the time of Alfred Marshall regarded competition as rivalry either among buyers or sellers.[1] Adam Smith observed rivalry among buyers to bid up the price when the item in question was scarce.[2] And he also observed rivalry among adventurous entrepreneurs to pioneer a new industry.[3] But on the eve of the Industrial Revolution, when Adam Smith wrote, competition was apparently not the normal state of affairs in the British economy. According to him, the norm was behavior aimed at manipulating the environment to enhance the survivability of the firm (Type 4 rationality): "People of the same trade seldom meet together, even for merriment and diversion, but the conversation ends in a conspiracy against the public, or in some contrivance to raise prices."[4]

Why, then, did economists reject Adam Smith's concept of competition in favor of Cournot's, which, inasmuch as it assumes perfect knowledge and so large a number of sellers in a market that each can have but a negligible impact on price, represents a more deterministic theory? According to Stigler, "Cournot's definition was enormously more precise and elegant than Smith's so far as the treatment of numbers was concerned."[5] And given the conception of science that rules the minds of many economists even today, there is little doubt that the virtue of a more deterministic theory of competition was to make economics more like a science by making it rival Newtonian celestial mechanics. To be sure, none of the deterministic thinkers argue for deterministic theories per se. Rather, the argument is usually couched in such terms as "more precise definitions," "a more analytic treatment," "a more scientific point of view," and so forth.

What about the often-made criticism that perfect competition is unrealisitc? Stigler's answer: "all concepts sufficiently general and sufficiently precise to be useful in scientific analysis must be abstract: that, if a science is to deal with a large class of phenomena, clearly it cannot work with concepts that are faithfully descriptive of even one phenomenon, for then they will be grotesquely undescriptive of others."[6]

Now, physical scientists certainly do not argue that the test of a good theory is its ability to deal with "a large class of phenomena." Indeed, if physical scientists had always been as enamored of static theory as Stigler, and as unperturbed by experimental evidence as he is by economic experience, it can be safely assumed that to this day physics would be dominated by the kind of thinking contained in the first law of thermodynamics (wherein the accounts are always in perfect balance) and completely oblivious to the thinking contained in the second law (which acknowledges physical change). However, physical scientists are well aware that a single theory need not be used to explain everything. They know that when theories are extrapolated to deal with new phenomena, sooner or later they will break down. And for this reason they have long held: "The principle of science, the definition, almost, is the following: *The test of all knowledge is experiment*."[7]

To be sure, economists do not have the ability to make experiments or fine-grained predictions that physical scientists have. Nevertheless, economic experience can be regarded as experiments conducted for the benefit of economists. And economists can content themselves with the kind of predictions they can make, namely, coarse-grained predictions. Indeed, if economics is to evolve into a mature science it must take as its operational principle that the test of all knowledge is economic experience. In other words, economists should be less concerned with borrowing the appearance of a successful science and more concerned with borrowing the substance.

Granted, the theory of perfect competition could make good predictions if the world it was premised upon bore a reasonably close relationship to the real world. The real world, however, is no more related to the world of perfect competition than heaven is related to earth. Let us suppose we live in the world alleged by the theory of perfect competition: a world so deterministic that entrepreneurs can have but a negligible influence on their environments. Clearly in such a world the seventeenth and eighteenth century scientific and technological revolutions could not have occurred. And neither could the technological revolutions that have taken place in Stigler's lifetime. It is evident, therefore, that if the assumptions underlying the theory of perfect competition were reasonable, as far as economic evolution is concerned we would still be living in the sixteenth century! But since we are not, it must be concluded that when it comes to making reasonably good coarse-grained predictions the theory of perfect competition is somewhat lacking.

The theory of perfect competition is an unscientific doctrine from the viewpoint of a mature science because it essentially precludes the development of a predictive theory. There is no close relationship between the effectiveness of competition and the number of firms in an industry, at least when the actual number is closer to a dozen than it is to infinity. If the degree of competitive rivalry is high, industries such as the aircraft industry can bring about an impressive rate of progress with fewer than six firms. On the other hand, if the degree of competitive interaction is low, industries such as the steel industry can display behavior strikingly similar to that of nineteenth-century trusts—and find themselves unable to compete with more flexible foreign firms.

Therefore, if progress is to be made towards the development of a predictive theory it is imperative not to eliminate the rivalry to generate cheaper or better alternatives. As the many unsuccessful attempts to develop a satisfactory theory of duopoly strongly suggest, if competition is restricted to price competition among firms producing standardized commodities it is impossible to formulate a predictive theory. When all firms in an industry are free to copy a price cut, who can predict whether that industry will act in a highly disciplined manner to avoid price cuts, or in a highly nervous manner in anticipation of each other's actions?

It is only by acknowledging that firms do take risks to develop better or cheaper alternatives that we can hope to develop a predictive theory. True, we may not be able to predict why some industries feature more risk-taking than others, but we can predict the relationship between risk-taking and the rate of progress, which certainly would be a start in making economics a more scientific discipline than it is today.

Conversely, the theory of perfect competition is unscientific because, by assuming a world of perfect knowledge in which firms cannot interact to change their economic environments, such a theory imposes pompous preconditions on our subject matter: competitors are so constrained in the behavior in which they can engage (making choices among more or less known alternatives) we are precluded from understanding economic reality or developing a testable theory. As it happens, I did not invent the expression "pompous preconditions." I borrowed it from Richard Feynman, who used it to describe the philosophical lessons physicists learned from the introduction of the uncertainty principle in physics: "What is necessary 'for the very existence of science', and what the characteristics of nature are, are not to be determined by pompous preconditions, they are determined always by the material with which we work, by nature herself. We look, and we see what we find, and we cannot say ahead of time successfully what it is going to look like."[8]

To be sure, the introduction of the uncertainty principle does not represent the only time physicists freed themselves from one set of pompous preconditions to adopt another. The same lesson has to be learned almost every time new scientific paradigms are established. However, freshmen and sophomores learn this fact of life on the first page of the *Feynman Lectures on Physics:* "Each piece, or part, of the whole of nature is always merely an approximation to the complete truth, or the complete truth so far as we know it. In fact, everything we know is only some kind of approximation, *because we know that we do not know all the laws as yet*. Therefore, things must be learned only to be unlearned again or, more likely, to be corrected."[9]

It is evident that Feynman is well aware of the mental attitudes required to generate advances in knowledge. And it may be assumed that the same is true of practically all the famous discoverers in physics. Consider, for example, Maxwell's parody on "Coming Through the Rye," which physicists often quote to illustrate what they mean by the "scientific method."[10]

Gin a body meet a body
Flyin' through the air,
Gin a body hit a body,
Will it fly? and where?
Ilka impact has its measure,
Ne'er a ane hae I,
Yet a' the lads they measure me,
Or, at least, they try.
Gin a body meet a body
Altogether free
How they travel afterwards
We do not always see.
Ilka problem has its method
By analytics high;
For me, I ken na ane o' them,
But what the waur am I?

This parody reveals an attitude towards science almost the precise opposite of laying down pompous preconditions.

To be fair to Stigler, he does not say that reality should be completely ignored in the development of economic theory, but rather that rigor should be given first priority and reality, second. This is indicated by a quotation from another of Stigler's articles: "The dominant influence upon the working range of economic theorists is the set of internal values and presures of the discipline. The subjects for study are posed by the unfolding course of scientific developments. . . . This is not to say that the environment is without influence, for every great economist injects some portion of it into the developing theoretical corpus."[11]

The main difference between a mature and an immature science is that in the former the priorities are reversed: first, attention is given to describing reality, and second, to rigor. A number of noted physicists, Maxwell included, have played important roles in developing the mathematics and statistics needed to describe the physical reality in question. In contrast, by relying almost entirely upon second-hand mathematics economists have attached second priority to dealing with economic reality.

Of course not all economists have been so reverent towards existing theory as Stigler. Obviously Keynes had very different ideas on the role of theory. And so does Kuznets. Nevertheless, I suggest that the fundamental reason economics has not matured nearly as rapidly as physics is that whereas in physics theoreticians quite commonly take the attitude of Maxwell, in economics they do not.

As it happens, Adam Smith believed in formulating theories on the basis of observation and used them in making predictions. For example, he predicted that if Britain did not begin competing economically on the continent of Europe it would one day find itself in serious trouble![12] And we can honor Adam Smith and bring economics closer to a mature science by adopting a behavioral concept of competition rather than a numerical one.

Competition and Nineteenth-Century Values

The desire to make economics resemble a successful science was not the only reason for abandoning Adam Smith's concept of competition. A more basic reason was the change of values that took place between the eighteenth and nineteenth centuries. Indicative of this change is the manner in which the eighteenth and nineteenth-century historians described the Italian Renaissance.[13] To the eighteenth-century historians the Renaissance represented a revival of learning, and the Middle Ages was a period of monkish ignorance and superstition. On the other hand, to the nineteenth-century historians the Renaissance represented a cast of Machiavellian characters engaged in various assassinations, while the Middle Ages was a period of angelic purity.

In many ways Marshall's works reflect the values of British Victorian society. Although adhering to Adam Smith's concept of competition, Marshall was far more defensive than Adam Smith about the evils associated with rivalry. For example, Marshall felt obliged to argue: "Man is not more dishonest than he was."[14] But perhaps there was an unwillingness to face up to reality in British Victorian society, just as there is today in the New American Victorian State. And perhaps rivalry became distasteful because it could no longer be described as Adam Smith described it, namely, as a competition in deeds. Consider, for example, the rivalry for political favors when American firms make large political-campaign contributions. Or consider American aircraft manufacturers' rivalry to bribe foreign officials for the purpose of obtaining contracts. It would be easy to blame all ills on rivalry. However, I suggest that rivalry in manipulating the political and economic environment is symptomatic of a decline in competition in deeds. When entrepreneurs no longer have the self-confidence to compete in terms of deeds, competition does not die out—it merely assumes different manifestations. Political candidates, for example, may compete in terms of dirty politics or in terms of projecting a pious image.

Although it is too early to tell whether the New American Victorian State will evolve towards a renunciation of all forms of rivalry, there can be little doubt that in Victorian England the system of values did change. For example, according to Marshall there was a tendency in Britain to blame all problems—from the loss of colonies to the great French War to a series of bad harvests—on "unrestrained competition."[15]

A specific type of competition greatly criticized by Lenin and others was international competition for markets. As Keynes later made the argument: "War has several causes. Dictators and others such . . . But, over and above this, facilitating their task of fanning the popular flame, are the economic causes of war, namely, the pressure of population and the competitive struggle for markets."[16] At the present time British economic historians are engaged in a bitter dispute as to the role played by the competitive struggle for markets during the new period of British imperialism, that is, the period after 1880. According to John Gallager and Ronald Robinson, competition for foreign markets at the time was the driving force in British foreign policy.[17] But according to D. C. M. Plott, British foreign policy was merely responding to pressures from both increased foreign competition and increased tariff barriers.[18]

But to show the main flaw in Keynes's argument, it is not necessary to determine either the true motives of British foreign policy or the relationship between wars and the competitive struggle for markets. According to Keynes's argument, the pressure for economic imperialism resulted from the inability to maintain full employment at home, and economic stagnation resulted from oversavings. Keynes's difficulty, and that of all British economists since the time of Ricardo, is that he took the marginal efficiency of capital as a given and failed to recognize that, in varying degrees, new capital can embody new knowledge—that is, profitability will depend on the degree of advance over existing capital. In turn, the degree of competitive interaction determines how rapidly knowledge advances. If this argument is correct, then the way to alleviate the pressure for foreign markets is to prevent the marginal efficiency of capital from declining by promoting competition.

Prior to the great depression of the 1870s and 1880s there was no need for British foreign policy to be concerned with finding outlets for British products, because Britain was highly competitive in world markets. However, in its 1886 report, the Royal Commission on the Depression of Trade and Industry concluded that Britain had lost her competitive advantage in part because the superior adaptability of the Germans had put them ahead.[19] And in the sense that British firms never regained a propensity for risk-taking, even today Britain's main economic problem is that it never recovered from the great depression of the 1870s.

While Keynes was wrong in failing to appreciate that competitive risk-taking does have a very noticeable impact on the marginal efficiency of capital, the much broader subject of the relationship between economic competition and wars is complicated and will require a great deal of further research. Does competition lead to nationalism and nationalism to wars? Or might the truth be precisely the opposite? My hypothesis is that competition is not a cause of wars, but rather a substitute for wars. Assume that while environment may play an important role in determining people's personalities, there are limits on how monotonous their work can become before they seek other outlets, such as drugs, extramarital activities, or wars. Given this assumption, the way to minimize the probability of wars is to keep countries so busy civilizing themselves they will not have enough energy left to civilize others. In other words, the probability of war can be minimized if societies have a good deal of openness, and competition certainly helps to achieve this goal. Conversely, when countries begin civilizing others they are driven to a lower degree of openness, their ideological development becomes impeded, and the probability of war is likely to be higher. Indeed, it was for this basic reason that Thomas Jefferson, among others, preached the cause of isolationism.

A good deal of research will be needed before we can tell whether Thomas Jefferson's hypothesis is a reasonable one or not. But a superficial examination of history suggests that the hypothesis deserves further examination. Is it not possible that Europe was so peaceful during the nineteenth century not so much because of the policies of Metternich and Castlereagh, but rather because countries were so busy with their own development? Conversely, when Germany and Britain began to compete in civilizing other countries, did not this constrain their degree of openness? Or to take another example, can we not see from our own experience in the United States that achieving the status of a "great leader" leads to an effort to "civilize" other countries in terms of our system of values, and as a consequence there occurs a decline in openness? Or, to consider still another example, is it not possible that the incentive for Russia's foreign policy might come from an effort to cover up or excuse the lack of accomplishments at home? And if this is the case, might not more competition with the rest of the world help change the incentive? And will not a society that is more democratic by virtue of being able to create a wider diversity of ideas be a society less likely to go to war? In other words, was not competition rejected by Keynes and many of his followers because it coincided with nineteenth-century values (which disdained all forms of conflict) rather than because of any serious analysis of the relationship between competition and wars?

To be fair to Keynes, he did appreciate the relationship between business firms engaged in generating a diversity of ideas, on the one hand, and political democracy, on the other. This is indicated in the following passage from the *General Theory:* "But, above all, individualism, if it can be purged of its defects and abuses, is the best safeguard of personal liberty in the sense that, compared with any other system, it greatly widens the field for the exercise of personal choice. It is also the best safeguard of the variety of life, which emerges precisely from this extended field of personal choice, and the loss of which is the greatest of all the losses of the homogeneous or totalitarian state."[20]

Keynes, unfortunately, did not appreciate how a competitive society that creates a diversity of ideas not only can widen the realm of personal choice, but can also prevent the marginal efficiency of capital from declining. If he had been willing to recognize this point, Keynes may have appreciated that to promote both progress and political democracy it is essential to embrace Adam Smith's concept of competition.

Behavioral Assumptions

Dynamic theory is based on the assumption that firms in a particular industry are likely to undertake advances of a similar size. Obviously, firms cannot survive while bringing about modest advances if their competitors are making major advances; for not only will their share of the market decline, they will eventually have to go out of business. But in the hope of capturing a larger share of the market why do not some firms undertake more ambitious advances? In other words, why in a particular industry are there not steady increases in the degree of competitive interaction? For example, there are Ford and Chrysler engineers who complain bitterly that while they are permitted to undertake some research-and-development projects to prevent General Motors from obtaining a lead, they are seldom permitted to undertake projects that would enable their companies to obtain a significant lead. Why are engineers from these companies so highly constrained? The reason is that what is rational behavior from a creative engineer's point of view is not necessarily rational behavior from the point of view of the Ford and Chrysler top management. Because the firms in question are optimized to deal with a low degree of uncertainty, they dare not impose risks upon their competitors to which they cannot respond.

To be sure, the same would not be true of a new firm entering the automobile industry. Nevertheless, one of the fundamental reasons newcomers to the automobile industry have done so poorly is that they have not been sufficiently imaginative in the introduction of new designs. In other industries, such as the semiconductor industry, it is the newcomer who typically brings about the most ambitious advance. It should be noted, however, that because newly established firms are usually better able to cope with uncertainty than well-established firms their incentives are different.

That established firms display a high degree of similarity in behavior would seem to be true in most industries. A major exception, however, is the petroleum industry, where some firms evidence a much greater willingness to take risks than others. Moreover, those firms more inclined to take risks are better organized to deal with uncertainty. For example, they employ professional "skunks" in corporate headquarters to constantly remind the vice-presidents about unexpected events that may occur. And these professional skunks have funds to explore promising ideas not acted upon by the regular research and development divisions. How is this difference in behavior to be explained? As it happens, the progressive oil companies are more poorly situated with respect to assured supplies of crude oil, which provides them with a greater incentive to engage in risk-taking.

The oil industry is not, of course, the only industry in which some firms display higher degrees of openness than others. In almost any industry, those firms that have been recently successful in introducing new products will be less open than those in a less fortunate position. It is not necessary to assume that each firm in a given industry seeks the same degree of advance; but to develop a predictive theory, it is necessary to assume that differences within given industries are smaller than those between industries. And, while further research will be required to pin down the validity of this assumption, it seems to be a reasonable first approximation.

What is the relationship between the number of firms in an industry and its ability to engage in dynamic behavior? When there are only a few firms, with the market dominated by one particular firm (as General Motors tends to dominate the automobile industry), and when such dominance is the result of scale economies, we can expect that sooner or later the degree of macrostability in the industry will decline. Moreover, even in the absence of dominance there is probably some minimum number of firms required for the undertaking of a sufficient diversity of experiments to permit smooth progress. To be sure, firms in the chemical industry have sponsored a good deal of internal competition. And so has IBM. But generally speaking, individual firms are intolerant of a wide diversity of ideas. It is reasonable to assume, therefore, that for smooth progress to occur there must be some minimum number of firms in an industry—as a rough guess, about four to eight firms must account for 50 percent of the market.

The assumption that dynamic workable competition can occur with a relatively small number of firms in an industry, providing one firm does not succeed in dominating the industry, is consonant with the empirical findings of Frederic Scherer[21] and Frederick Knickerbocker.[22] Scherer was concerned with the relationship between inventive activity (measured in terms of the number of scientists and engineers employed in an industry) and the degree of concentration. He found that inventive activity tended to be greatest when four firms accounted for about 50 percent of the market.

Knickerbocker was concerned with the relationship between American firms establishing subsidiaries abroad and the degree of concentration. He found that when eight firms accounted for 70 percent of the market a substantial bandwagon effect occurred in the establishment of subsidiaries abroad. Quite clearly, a relatively small number of firms can engage in dynamic competition. And the real question is not whether firms in different industries behave differently in their propensity to engage in risk-taking, but how such risk-taking contributes to the performance of an economic system.

A Dynamic Insurance Policy

In the last chapter we saw how diversity and uncertainty are related. To deal with more and more uncertainty in their environment, Scrabble players, for example, must define diversity more and more broadly. We also saw how competition has the effect of internalizing risk. A competitive risk may be likened to an unwelcome tax collector who might assess the entrepreneur an amount he can only very roughly calculate. If after comparing the market risk with the technological risk the entrepreneur decides the latter is the lesser of the two evils, then the risk is said to be "internalized": to escape from a competitive risk the entrepreneur has to engage in a technological risk, and if successful he will make the future rate of progress more predictable. Roughly speaking, this is what is meant by thinking of competition as a "dynamic insurance policy."

Before pursuing the argument, however, I will briefly contrast the type of stability associated with competition under static and dynamic conditions, respectively. When Marshall discovered the concept of the "elasticity of demand," he in effect found that redundancy provides an economy with a policy that ensures low-variance outcomes: the greater the degree of redundancy in the form of substitutes, the more constrained price increases are likely to be. When ecologists speak of "diversity" and "stability" they also have in mind "substitutes" and "redundancy."[23] This is apparent in their argument, because they use the Claude Shannon and Warren Weaver information-theory formula, which in effect measures redundancy.[24] And the more substitutes in an ecosystem, the greater its stability. On the other hand, there is the diversity created by imaginative people who, when confronted with risk, can provide an economic system with more dynamic stability by generating new ideological mutations. This type of diversity provides an economy with the ability to buy a dynamic insurance policy: a policy to permit smooth progress in overcoming discontinuities.

What determines (1) the rate of advance (whether history will be fast or slow) and (2) the smoothness of progress (whether or not the advances will come about quite regularly)?

If we look upon the degree of risk internalization as the premium paid for a dynamic insurance policy, then larger and larger premiums will buy a greater and greater ability to overcome discontinuities. The more risk in an environment, the more widely firms must search for hints if they are to survive. In other words, the more risk in an environment, the more openness is required; the less risk, the less openness. And the greater the degree of openness when searching for hints, the more rapid will be the rate of progress.

For example, it seems to be no accident that in recent years firms in the computer and pharmaceutical industries have depended more on outside sources for their research than have firms in other industries. Is this because firms in these industries do not possess effective in-house research capabilities? Or is it that firms in the computer and pharmaceutical industries have had to face a high degree of competitive risk? Conversely, firms in the steel industry contract for relatively little of their research. Is this because they possess such excellent research capabilities? Or is it because they feel less competitive risk than firms in the computer and pharmaceutical industries?

Those who would like to see the government play a larger role in research and development often cite the experience of the agricultural experimental stations. Even before their establishment, however, the advent of county fairs and county newspapers led to a good deal of rivalry in agriculture as of the time of the Civil War. And might not the willingness to take risks have been an important reason why there was a keen demand for new ideas? Conversely, unless public research and development can be undertaken in ways that increase the degree of competitive interaction, what reason is there to believe that supplying more ideas will automatically increase the demand?

Or, to consider a quite different example: It has been said that the Newtonian revolution in physics was first exported to the Continent and then reimported into England via Scotch universities.[25] Why did the Newtonian revolution have an impact on Scotch universities before British universities? As it happens, a number of well-known Scotch scholars did attend the University of Leyden in Holland. And my guess is that, because professors at Scotch universities felt themselves in competition for good students more keenly than did professors at Cambridge and Oxford, the Scotch universities were more outward looking. Conversely, consider present-day

American scholars who write in such specialized languages they can be understood only by a small inner circle and who, academically speaking, become millionaires simply by selling diamonds to each other. How is such behavior to be explained other than that the people involved feel a very small degree of risk?

In short, more risk drives people and organizations to higher degrees of openness, less risk, to lower degrees of openness. Therefore, from a statistical point of view we should expect to observe higher degrees of competitive interaction associated with higher degrees of macrostability (that is, higher rates of smooth progress).

However, because when quality improvements are involved it is not easy to devise ways to measure the size of advances sought by firms, it is necessary to recast dynamic theory in terms of a less equivocal measure of the degree of competitive interaction. To qualify as "scientific," the theory does not have to be formulated in terms of mathematics. But it does have to be stated in sufficiently unambiguous terms that economists can, on the basis of empirical research, say whether the theory makes good or bad predictions.

Let us assume that the relationship between the size of the advance embodied in a product (whether measured in terms of a reduction in cost or an improvement in quality) and the total quantity of the product sold is nonlinear. In other words, let us assume that as the price is progressively lowered (or the quality progressively increased) the elasticity of demand will become greater and greater. The reason for this assumption is that both individuals and business firms tend to be somewhat sluggish in their buying habits. Moreover, changing affiliations is not always costless. For example, when airline companies buy a new type of airliner, mechanics must be retrained and a significant investment in spare parts is required. However, as costs are reduced more and more, at some point we should expect to observe a marked change in affiliations. According to people engaged in the development and production of new airliners, it is hardly worthwhile to develop a new airliner which will only result in a 5 percent cost savings. But a 20 percent cost savings is a quite different matter.

If it is reasonable to assume that the relationship between the size of the advance embodied in the product and the quantity demanded is nonlinear, then we should expect to observe larger differences in market shares with a high degree of competitive interaction than with a low degree (that is, we should expect to observe more dramatic changes in market shares with fast history than with slow history). It is conceivable that each firm in an industry might bring about equally impressive advances. However such an occurrence is very unlikely.

What determines the regularity of dynamic processes? In the first place, in order to explain why firms conduct experiments, strong uncertainties must be assumed. Quite obviously, if they could predict each other's experiments there would be no incentive to obtain a competitive lead. Second, it is safe to assume that the smoothness of progress will be a function of the number of experiments undertaken and the degree of risk involved. When the S-shaped curve is rising steeply only about one out of five projects will provide the degree of advance required to make steady progress. On the other hand, when it is rising slowly only one out of five projects will turn out to be disappointing. This is not to say, however, that slow history is less expensive than fast history. For what it cost to develop the Edsel (measured in 1910 dollars) the Ford Motor Company probably could have developed two dozen versions of the Model T.

Third, it can be assumed that the number of experiments conducted is related to the number of firms in an industry. To be sure, by engaging in internal competition individual firms can pursue parallel paths towards the achievement of the same objective. But, with the major exceptions of the chemical industry and IBM, such behavior is relatively rare. In most industries, firms are too small during their fast history phase to simultaneously carry on several competing research-and-development programs. And in most industries, when firms become large they no longer feature internal competition. Therefore, while a larger number of firms is required for fast history than for slow history, some minimum number of firms is needed if history is to be smooth. For example, if only three or four firms had been involved in pioneering automobiles, the progress made during the period 1900 to 1925 might have easily taken another fifty years. Conversely, large costs of entry make it very difficult to introduce new ideas into a relatively static industry. If history teaches us anything, it is that even during the fast-history phase progress is highly dependent on the establishment of new firms. In fact, low barriers to entry not only permit progress to be smooth; but they are very important in maintaining a high propensity to engage in risk-taking.

In short, the rate of progress is determined by the degree of risk-taking: the higher the degree of competitive interaction, the more rapid will be the rate of progress. And the easier entry is into an industry, the higher is likely to be the degree of risk-taking. The smoothness of progress is mainly determined by the number of firms in an industry.

To sum up this discussion: Because it constrains opportunities for wage and price increases and thereby provides insurance against specific events, static competition that consists of a greater rather than a lesser number of firms can be likened to a static insurance principle. On the other hand, dynamic competition that permits smooth progress in reducing uncertainties because it internalizes risk can be equated to a dynamic insurance principle. Are these independent insurance principles? Certainly one can imagine an economy consisting of many small firms that provides the first, but not the second type of insurance. In particular, the concept of perfect competition implies an infinite capability to deter price increases—but a zero capability to produce the same output with fewer inputs. When there is perfect competition firms are so small they simply cannot interact with an environment to change it. In fact, from a classical point of view, firms imposing substantial risk upon each other to bring about progress would have to be described not as competitors but rather as monopolists!

However, dynamic competition not only provides a dynamic insurance policy—in the sense that it acts as a stimulus to productivity increases—it also provides the same benefits as a static insurance policy inasmuch as it acts as a deterrent upon wage and price increases. Productivity advances come about because firms actively search for ways to cut costs. And because the name of the game is to enlarge your market at the expense of your competitors (or to prevent your competitors from doing the same to you), dynamic competition acts as a deterrent on wage and price increases. Indeed, the time to worry is when the happy warriors disappear from the scene and firms insure themselves against uncertainty by engaging in highly consonant behavior. Under such circumstances not only will productivity gains be less rapid, but there will not be the same stringent degree of constraint on wage and price increases.

Let us grant that a high degree of competitive interaction can play a major role in stimulating progress. Can we be sure that the reverse is true—that without competition there can be no progress? When explaining the behavior of particular firms we cannot dismiss the possibility advanced by Schumpeter and Galbraith that progress is automatic inasmuch as it does not depend on the degree of competitive interaction. Certainly we can find some firms in which there is a drive to bring about progress for its own sake. The theory presented here, however, does not allege to explain the behavior of every firm in the economy at every moment of time. My proposition, rather, is a statistical one: examine a period in which there has been a significant increase in the degree of macrostability and you are likely to find a significant increase in the degree of competitive interaction. For example, very rapid progress has been made in reducing the fatalities associated with certain heart operations. How is this progress to be explained? Surgical teams compete to make discoveries and cooperate by having regular meetings to exchange information. However, a good deal of the expertise cannot be easily communicated; for example, it may reside in nurses trained to make very quick decisions in postoperative care. And because there cannot be a complete exchange of information the more successful surgeons are able to build up their practices more rapidly. Now there obviously are some physicians who would make discoveries without such an incentive, just as there are scientists who would have discovered the structure of DNA without the incentive of competing with Linus Pauling. My proposition is that the incentive provided by competition makes discoveries more likely. Hence, when significant changes in the rate of progress are observed, we should expect to find significant changes in the degree of competitive interaction.

For example, how is Germany's spectacular post-World War II increase in the rate of productivity-advance to be explained? How was it possible for Germany to surpass Britain in per capita GNP? I am confident that if the degree of competition were measured in terms of changes in market shares it would be found that in post-World War II Germany there was more competition than in the period 1900 to 1938. And I am also confident that it would be found that Germany's products were more competitive in foreign trade in the latter period than in the former period.

Or to take another case: Suppose we were trying to explain why, in the British economy, productivity was slowing down in the third quarter of the nineteenth century, and why the British standard of living has been declining relative to other industrialized countries. I am confident that the explanation is related to the decline in rivalry among British firms. And it is my prediction that when British economic historians get around to undertaking the necessary research they will find that in the period 1850 to 1870 changes in business fortunes were more pronounced than in the period after the great depression of the 1870s. In other words, I predict they will find that macrostability is not to be confused with microstability.

Dynamic Competition: A Positive-Sum Game

Why was not research aimed at an understanding of dynamic competition undertaken years ago? My guess is that, while to understand dynamic competition it is necessary to think in terms of a positive-sum game, the theory of competition, which even today rules the minds of economists, assumes a zero-sum game. Indeed I suspect that Adam Smith did not get across his message as well as he might because he too thought in terms of a zero-sum game. Consider, for example, his discussion of the probable effect of shortening apprenticeships:

> The master, indeed, would be a loser. He would lose all the wages of the apprentice, which he now saves, for seven years together. In the end, perhaps, the apprentice himself would be a loser. In a trade so easily learnt he would have more competitors, and his wages, when he came to be a complete workman, would be much less than at present. The same increase of competition would reduce the profits of the masters as well as the wages of workmen. The trades, the crafts, the mysteries, would all be losers. But the public would be a gainer, the work of all artificers coming in this way much cheaper to the market.[26]

Adam Smith seems to have had in mind a fixed pie, in which what is gained by the public is lost by the masters and the apprentices. To be sure, he was aware how change in such a tidy feudalistic relationship leads to significant inventions. For example, in discussing the impact of the division of labor on discoveries he said: "A great part of the machines made use of in those manufacturers in which labour is most subdivided, were originally the inventions of common workmen, who, being each of them employed in some very simple operation, naturally turned their thoughts towards finding out easier and readier methods of performing it."[27]

However, Adam Smith seemed to assume that once the initial discoveries were made the dynamic process would stop. To be more specific, let us suppose that a master and two apprentices are engaged in pin making, with each of the apprentices trained as a craftsman fully responsible for the product, from drawing the wire to pointing it, to cutting and attaching the head. In such an operation output per person is unlikely to exceed, say, 500 pins per day. But as a result of shortening apprenticeships, twenty young apprentices may go to work for an enterprising master who organizes a pin mill into fifteen quite distinct operations. According to Adam Smith, the output of such an operation is about 5,000 pins per worker per day.[28] And it is reasonable to assume that he had in mind an order-of-magnitude improvement in productivity as a result of the direct and indirect gains from specialization.

What Adam Smith's model did not contemplate was the possibility of competition between pin mills leading to further improvements in machinery and in the degree of specialization—improvements that might easily result in another order-of-magnitude improvement in productivity within a period of ten years. Nor did Adam Smith's model contemplate competition between firms engaged in developing and producing pin mill machinery, the later export of pin mill machinery to other countries, and the impact of such trade on increasing the wealth of other nations.

Adam Smith, however, hardly can be blamed for his incomplete model. As it happens, he wrote the *Wealth of Nations* in 1776, only ten years after the invention of the steam engine, and long before anyone could have foreseen the impact of the Industrial Revolution. In fact, it can be assumed that realist as he was, if Adam Smith could have written the *Wealth of Nations* in 1850 he would have been less impressed with the writers of the Age of the Enlightenment (who tended to believe the character of the races was fully determined and man was so enlightened no further enlightening was possible) and more impressed with British entrepreneurs. And as a result, Adam Smith's economics might have been different in two respects. In the first place, he might have observed that the cities in which the Industrial Revolution was born—Nottingham, Birmingham, and Manchester—were, on the eve of the Industrial Revolution, inhabited almost entirely by people from Scotland and dissenters from the Church of England—people who were risk-takers.[29] Some of these risk-takers were inventors. Others were entrepreneurs who undertook the role, as American firms did after World War II, of transferring the Industrial Revolution to the Continent.[30] And still other risk-takers established firms that became involved in dynamic competition in Britain. It is likely that on the basis of such observations Adam Smith would have become aware that the pursuit of self-interest is not enough to explain increases in the wealth of nations: people must cooperate by imposing risks upon each other.

Secondly, it would also have become evident to Adam Smith that when people do so cooperate they can change the history of the world. And this observation would have forced Adam Smith to adopt a quite different theory of international trade. With a static theory of international trade aimed at making best use of existing resources, it can be appreciated that to obtain the best performance from an international symphony orchestra countries must send those types of musicians in which they have a comparative advantage. But when they feature a good deal of dynamic competition, countries can change both the repertoires and the instruments.

Actually the Industrial Revolution seems to have had a greater impact on the rest of the world (and most notably on the United States) than it did on the older and more established cities in Britain, which were more structured in terms of feudalistic relationships. No doubt, it was the inability of such cities to cope with change that led many historians to take a dim view of the Industrial Revolution. And no doubt, when the more traditional type of entrepreneur introduced steam power into his factory, the end result was to substitute a newer for an older type of feudalism. One would like to believe that technological discoveries have the effect of improving the lot of the worker, as, for example, they did when Henry Ford paid the almost unheard-of salary of five dollars a day. But if we can believe John Stuart Mill, inventions did not play this role in Britain:

> Hitherto it is questionable if all the mechanical inventions yet made have lightened the day's toil of any human being. They have enabled a greater population to live the same life of drudgery and imprisonment, and an increased number of manufacturers and others to make fortunes. They have increased the comforts of the middle classes. But they have not yet begun to effect those great changes in human destiny, which it is in their nature and in their futurity to accomplish.[31]

As was noted, during the Victorian Age there was a common tendency to blame all of the problems of British society on competition. But perhaps the real problem was a lack of competition. If technology is to play a constructive role in human destiny, a relatively unstratified society is required which will promote a natural instead of an artificial aristocracy. However, this is possible only in a society in which competition performs the role of a dynamic insurance policy more or less continuously.

5. Case Studies of Dynamic Competition

The Automobile

In a number of industrial innovations, including the jet engine, computers, piston-driven and jet aircraft, and the automobile, European countries surpassed the United States in the initial pioneering work. At the time of the famous Paris to Bordeaux auto race of 1894 the French had already acquired a reputation for building the best racers in the world. And it was not until 1896 that an American, Frank Duryea, developed a car that could defeat a racer built by Panhard of France. Moreover, French, German, and British firms had begun producing automobiles more than five years earlier than American firms.

By 1926, however, American firms accounted for almost 85 percent of the world output of automobiles.[1] Moreover, despite import duties and other taxes on American cars, which typically added about 100 percent to their price, American firms, including foreign subsidiaries, sold nearly as many automobiles abroad as were produced by all non-American firms.

How did the United States become a technological leader in the production of automobiles? What special advantages did it have? No doubt because of higher per capita income the potential market for automobiles was greater in America than in Europe. But because there is no automatic mechanism for exploiting a potential, becoming a technological leader was hardly preordained.

In order to overtake European firms, American firms had to possess a relative advantage in generating two types of knowledge: knowledge that would make it possible to decide which type of propulsion system—steam, electric, or gasoline—would provide the most economical automobile; and knowledge that would make it possible to minimize the cost of the system finally chosen—the gasoline engine.

As of 1895 there was no question about the technical feasibility of steam, electric, or gasoline automobiles. But the gasoline engine was by no means a sure bet from an *economic* point of view. Understandably, there was a good deal of skepticism among engineers and scientists as to whether or not it would ultimately prove to be a safe and reliable engine. In fact it seems likely that if engineers at the more respectable Eastern universities had been polled, the steam and electric engines would have been chosen over the gasoline engine. *Scientific American,* which provides a fairly good indicator of the generally accepted points of view in science and technology, did not declare itself in favor of the internal-combustion engine until 1895.

A second uncertainty concerned the design and production of low-cost gasoline automobiles. On the basis of Schumpeter's theory of the "hero" entrepreneur, it might be concluded that the revolution in lowering costs was based largely on Henry Ford's boldness in adopting mass-production techniques. The problem with this "great man in history" theory is that it is not in accord with the facts. Reductions in the cost of automobiles were not the product of a single stroke of genius, but rather of a long series of discoveries and innovations, which neither began nor ended with the Model T. At the beginning of this dynamic process the 1904 Ford two-cylinder Model F, which for its day was a moderately priced car, sold for $1200. However, due to a series of discoveries that nobody could have foreseen, by 1924 a four-cylinder Model T cost only about $180, measured in 1904 dollars—an 85 percent reduction in real terms![2] Moreover, the Model T was not the only car with an impressive cost history. For example, measured in constant dollars, the 1924 Packard cost only about 25 percent as much as its 1904 model.[3] Such histories reflect more or less continuous pressures to reduce costs. But it seems unlikely that progress in cost reduction can be explained independently of the degree of competitive interaction.

What, then, was the role of competition in (1) the choice of the internal-combustion engine and (2) in subsequent reductions in the price of gasoline automobiles?

The classic example of the pursuit of parallel paths to weed out less promising alternatives is the Manhattan Project; as is generally known, the problem of producing a self-sustaining reactor was tackled by four independent groups of physicists, and at least five different approaches were followed. The essential difference between the Manhattan Project and the early development of automobile technology is that whereas in the former case J. Robert Oppenheimer was mainly responsible for weeding out less promising alternatives, in the latter case customers' responses were the deciding factor as to which approach would survive. And as of 1900 the purchaser was confronted with a wide variety of choices: the choice between electric, steam, and gasoline engines, between air-cooled and water-cooled internal-combustion engines, and between several types of transmissions.

As of 1900 there was also a good deal of uncertainty as to where automobile production would be centered in the future. Steam and electric vehicles accounted for about three-fourths of the four thousand automobiles estimated to have been produced by fifty-seven American firms.[4] Interestingly, in the United States there was a geographical division of labor in the development of steam, electric, and gasoline vehicles, with the older sections of the country specializing in the older and more predictable technologies, and the younger and less developed sections specializing in the newer gasoline technology. Thus, New England accounted for about 75 percent of steam-vehicle production, 50 percent of electric-vehicle production, and 15 percent of gasoline-vehicle production. Firms in Pennsylvania and Western New York produced both electric and gasoline automobiles. And firms in the Midwest concentrated mainly on the production of gasoline automobiles.[5]

The leading American automobile producer in 1900 was the Pope Company of Hartford, Connecticut. Before entering the automobile business the Pope Company was the largest bicycle manufacturer in the world. It entered the automobile business when Hiram Percy Maxim, an inventor who had built a gasoline-powered tricycle, was hired as its chief engineer. However, Colonel Albert A. Pope, the head of the company, predicted that gasoline carriages were unlikely to have a future because "You can't get people to sit over an explosion!" So in the first two years of operation, the Pope Company manufactured five-hundred electric and only forty gasoline carriages.[6]

It is not surprising that steam and electric engines were the early favorites. British inventors had developed steam carriages even before the development of steam locomotives. And as of 1885, there were dozens of custom-made steam and electric vehicles in operation—purchased mainly by the rich as a hobby. Some American inventors, including Ransom Olds, experimented with steam and gasoline vehicles before deciding the latter were more promising. As of 1895, the electric car could not be ruled out because no one could be sure that provision of a reasonably light battery for traveling distances up to, say, a hundred miles would prove a stumbling block. Nor was it foreseeable that gasoline automobiles would be easier to maintain than those powered by steam—anymore than it was predictable that jet airplanes would be easier to maintain than piston-engine airplanes.

We see, then, that while initially a great deal of uncertainty prevailed as to which particular automobile—steam, electric or gasoline—would provide the best choice, competition, in the form of pursuing parallel approaches, played a major role in reducing the degree of uncertainty. Indeed, it may be assumed that without such competition it simply would have been impossible to narrow the range of alternatives. Without genuine incentives to engage in imaginative behavior, how else could it have been determined that the steam-and electric-powered automobiles would turn out to be high-cost alternatives, and the gasoline-powered a low-cost alternative?

This is not to say, of course, that competition determined that the gasoline engine would be the best choice for all time to come. Given the technologies and constraints that existed as of 1900, it provided the best choice for that time. And one cannot be sure that under different conditions the internal-combustion engine represents the best choice. For example, today the Stirling engine is being discussed as an alternative to the internal-combustion engine, because of its apparent advantages in both low gasoline-consumption and low emissions.[7] As it happens, the Stirling engine was seriously considered as a successor to the steam engine in 1850, even before consideration of the internal-combustion engine. But it was subsequently dismissed because the technological difficulties seemed to be too formidable.

Next, let us turn to the role of competition in reducing the cost of gasoline automobiles. Rivalry to produce an inexpensive car existed almost from the beginning of the American automobile industry. In 1903, Ransom Olds introduced a two-horsepower lightweight car (about 750 pounds) for $650, and the following year, when four thousand were sold, his firm became the top producer in the United States. In retaliation, Colonel Pope, who had been the number-one producer, introduced a six-horsepower runabout for a price of $660. Moreover, between 1905 and 1910 Hupmobile entered the low-cost market with a four-cylinder, twenty-horsepower car selling for about $750, Sears & Roebuck with a $495 car, and Maxwell and Overland with relatively inexpensive runabouts. Moreover, the Century Motor Vehicle Company of Syracuse, New York, brought out a $750 steam vehicle.

At the time of the development of the Model T, however, Ford's main competitor was not one of the low-cost producers. In 1908, the Buick Company, which in that year became a division of the newly established General Motors Company, was the top producer; and its sales accounted for about 25 percent of the market, as compared with about 10 percent for Ford. Unlike most other pioneers of the American automobile industry, William C. Durant, the founder of General Motors, was not an inventor, but rather a partner in one of the largest carriage-manufacturing firms in the country. In fact, when Durant entered the automobile industry by buying the bankrupt Buick Company in 1904, he was already an expert on the application of mass-production techniques in industry. The Durant-Dort Carriage Company set up specialized plants for manufacturing bodies, wheels, upholstery, paint, varnish, springs—and even whip sockets. Moreover, as a carriage manufacturer Durant had the experience of setting up a nationwide system of dealers and distributors.

To the more cautious men who took over the direction of General Motors in the 1920s, Durant no doubt seemed like a reckless promoter. Within two years after establishing General Motors he had acquired a controlling interest in Olds, Cadillac, Oakland, and six other automobile companies, three truck firms, and ten parts and accessory companies. In 1910, however, the market and technical uncertainties were stronger than in 1920. And as the following statement indicates, Durant was a man who believed in hedging his bets: " 'They say I shouldn't have bought Cartercar,' he said. 'Well, how was anyone to know that Cartercar wasn't to be the thing? How could I tell what these engineers would say next? Maybe friction drive would be the thing . . . I was for getting every kind of thing in sight, playing safe all along the line.' "[8]

Another key principle of Durant's theory of entrepreneurship was to find capable people to run the companies purchased by General Motors—and leave them alone. For example, Durant hired Charles W. Nash and Walter P. Chrysler to take over the management of the Buick Company while he concentrated his own energies on building a sales organization. And that "noninterference" remained his policy is indicated by the fact that until 1918 Durant ran the General Motors Corporation with a total staff of three personal assistants.

If Henry Ford wanted to increase his share of the market well above 10 percent he was in a real dilemma: in the low-price field he faced stiff competition from several companies; in the medium-price field he faced Buick, which in four years had become the top producer in the nation. Moreover, Buick's performance in increasing its share of the market is not difficult to understand, because Buick built a more rugged car than did its competitors. It is not altogether surprising, therefore, that Henry Ford chose to escape from his dilemma not by sacrificing durability, but by making automobiles quickly and exactly alike. Even as early as 1903, he is said to have told one of his partners: "The way to make automobiles is to make one automobile like another automobile, to make them all alike, to make them come from the factory just alike—just like one pin is like another pin when it comes from a pin factory."[9]

However, Ford's dream of a low-cost car was not realized in one giant step. The first step consisted of producing a rugged, mechanically simple, lightweight car, whose development involved resolving a number of difficult scaling problems. Ford had noticed that European models had smaller and stronger parts than American cars. And because the American steel industry could not make the vanadium steel needed for a stronger structure, Ford sent to England for a metallurgist to help introduce the process into a small steel company in Canton, Ohio. Of equal importance in resolving the scaling problems was the development of an amazingly simple engine and transmission embodying a number of ingenious inventions.

How was this progress brought about? According to common wisdom, the Ford Company was a one-man operation from the beginning. But according to the Ford biography written by Allan Nevins and Frank E. Hill, the Ford organization that pioneered the Model T was entirely different from that which emerged during the 1920s.[10] In fact, the principal conclusion I draw from their work is that just as there was a great change in Franklin Roosevelt's administration between the time it dealt with the depression and the time Roosevelt became a great wartime leader, so was there a great change in Henry Ford's administration from the time it brought about its "new deal" to the time it became a great leader in the automobile industry. Henry Ford's new-deal administration was like Franklin Roosevelt's New Deal administration in several respects. First, within both administrations there was a good deal of internal competition brought about by a steadfast refusal to precisely define responsibilities.[11] Second, and related, both organizations contained a good deal of internal conflict. And like Roosevelt, Henry Ford was a highly accessible person, "a man that nobody need to be afraid to approach at all."[12] And because of this, like the Roosevelt New Deal administration, the Ford new-deal administration was highly interactive: Visitors wishing to see Ford usually had a search on their hands, for he might be in the shop, the experimental department, the drafting room, or the power plant; he came and went as he liked.[13] Third, both the Roosevelt and Ford administrations contained a wide diversity of people. Ford himself is pictured as a highly intuitive engineer who detested working in a tightly structured environment. C. Harold Wills, who became Ford's chief engineer, was in this respect much like Ford. But he was tougher than Ford when it came to getting things done. Neither Ford nor Wills were college graduates. But the same was not true of all the engineers who played important roles in the development of the Model T and its forerunners. For example, Joseph Galamb was a well-trained engineer who had worked in automobile firms in Germany. James Couzens, who became the chief lieutenant in charge of business affairs, was almost the complete opposite of Henry Ford in every respect. Couzens insisted upon precise rules and regulations, and was more convinced than Ford of the role of a good cost-accounting system. Unlike Ford, he detested experimentation and change. In a battle that continued for some years, Couzens constantly accused Ford of being a perfectionist in searching for ways to improve the automobile. And if he had had his way Couzens would have frozen the design long before the advent of the Model T.

As for the engineering work on new models, the Ford Company utilized an organization (to be described in some detail in Chapter 6) commonly known today as a "skunkworks." This is an organization in which engineers work directly with machinists, and its purpose is to quickly generate new knowledge by getting new hardware into test very rapidly. Robert Grant, who was involved in this activity, described it as follows: "Our job was to get the advanced designs, the ideas that Mr. Ford and others would bring in to us, and actually put them together and test them. We would machine them all up, even get the castings and everything, and take them and build them in a car, and take the car out and test it."[14] Charles E. Sorensen, who got his start in this activity, is said to have been a genius in translating Ford's ideas into hardware. But it should not be assumed that all the ideas came from Ford. There is to this day a good deal of uncertainty as to who supplied this or that invention.[15] And this is exactly what we should expect in a highly interactive organization that makes good use of human diversity.

What role did competition play in cutting production costs on the Model T? In the first place, it should be noted that the movement towards mass-production techniques began long before the Model T. The first step in the introduction of mass production techniques was to make interchangeable parts. And Henry Leland, who had worked in a gun factory during the Civil War, transferred the concept of interchangeable parts to the Cadillac Company when he became its head in 1905. However, Leland was interested in the concept of interchangeable parts primarily to obtain high quality rather than low cost. The second step was to reorganize the process of producing automobiles. Previously, departments were organized around processes using particular types of machines (for example, milling machines). But it was found that automobile production could be speeded up by organizing in terms of a more or less continuous production process rather than by type of machine. About a dozen firms, including Ford, adopted this step more or less simultaneously, and almost invariably in connection with the building of a new plant. Apparently there was so much resistance from machinery operators that building a new plant was the only way to bring about the change. The newer form of organization was, of course, an important step in the evolution towards moving production lines. But not only that: once the organizational change was made, the automobile firms found many opportunities for developing more efficient machines by making them more automatic. For example, replacement of the vertical turret lathe by a more automatic horizontal lathe doubled output per worker. Or to take a more spectacular example, an automatic machine for making camshafts increased output per worker by a factor of ten. And literally dozens of cases can be found in which better machines permitted output per worker to increase by a factor of between two and ten.[16] To be sure, this does not mean that output per unit of input (including capital) increased by as much. But nonetheless, the reductions in costs tended to be highly discontinuous. In some cases the new machines were developed by machinery companies, and in others by the automobile firms themselves. But in either case the incentive was furnished by rivalry between automobile firms to capture a larger share of the market.

When it was first introduced, the Model T was stronger and faster than other low-priced cars, but not cheaper: it sold for $850, compared with $650 for the Oldsmobile. Moreover, in 1909 its price rose to $950 and Ford's share of the market declined. However, at that point Couzens, the tough-minded business manager of the Ford Company, insisted that if the Model T was to dominate the market for low-priced cars the price would have to be brought down to $600.[17] And acceptance of this target figure as a company objective apparently supplied the same element of necessity in the further evolution of mass-production techniques as flying to the moon did in the development of spacecraft. More particularly, attainment of the objective included obtaining interchangeable parts, moving production lines (to which moving component lines are geared), and speed in production.

To be sure, the concept of moving production lines was not new: disassembly lines, including moving overhead trolleys, had been used for some time in the meat-packing industry. Was it then a matter of luck that the Ford Company rather than some other company recognized the potential of this idea for the automobile industry? No doubt it was in part a matter of luck. But no doubt at that time the Ford production organization was well prepared to be lucky: it had a firm objective and, as in the skunkworks, it featured a good deal of internal competition. In particular, the person who is given most credit for introducing the concept of moving production lines into Ford and the automobile industry is Clarence W. Avery, a college graduate who supervised manual training in a Detroit high school where Edsel Ford was a student. However, others also were involved. And Nevins and Hill have this to say about the introduction of moving production lines:

> It is clear that the impression given in Ford's *My Life and Work* that the key ideas of mass production percolated from the top of the factory downward is erroneous; rather, seminal ideas moved from the bottom upwards. To be sure, Ford took a special interest in the magneto assembly. But elsewhere able employees like Gregory, Klann, and Purdy made important suggestions; Sorensen and others helped work them out, while Ford gave encouragement and counsel. The largest single role in developing the new system, however, was played by this university-trained thinker (Avery) so recently brought in from his schoolroom.[18]

Progress in reducing costs at Ford did not stop with the attainment of the $600 target figure. And as Table 2 suggests, demand turned out to be more elastic than anyone might have predicted. From 1909 to 1916, the price of the Model T fell about 60 percent, and sales increased by nearly a factor of 50. In 1909, when the cost reduction program began, Ford's share of the market was about 10 percent, compared with 23 percent for General Motors. By 1916, Ford's share of the market had risen to about 40 percent, while General Motors' had declined to about 8 percent. Moreover, by 1921 Ford's share was 60 percent, and every other car in the United States was a Model T![19]

From 1908 to 1920, the Ford Company's profits on net worth are

Table 2. Marketing of Model T Fords, 1908-1916.

Year	Price	Total sales (number)
1908	$850	5,986
1909	950	12,292
1910	780	19,293
1911	690	40,402
1912	600	78,611
1913	550	182,809
1914	490	260,720
1915	440	355,276
1916	360	577,036

Source: John B. Rae, *The American Automobile* (Chicago: University of Chicago Press, 1965), p. 61.

estimated to never have been less than 20 percent per year and sometimes as high as 300 percent per year—by far the highest in the industry.[20] Yet, until the 1920s there was but one serious attempt to challenge Ford's supremacy in low-priced automobiles. General Motors tried to develop a low-priced car based on an air-cooled engine developed by Charles Kettering. However, although a few Chevrolets with air-cooled engines were produced, the idea was finally given up, with Kettering claiming that the Chevrolet engineers were dragging their heels, and Chevrolet engineers claiming that the idea was impractical.[21]

In any event, the agent of creative destruction, as far as the Model T was concerned, was the second-hand car market. As of the early 1920s, many people who might have purchased a Model T were buying instead an "enclosed" second-hand car. Moreover, competition also came from Chevrolet, Essex, and Star, closed cars that cost only $150 to $200 more than a Model T. And as a result, from about 1921 to 1926 Ford's share of the market declined from 60 percent to about 35 percent.[22]

To return to the initial question, what enabled America to develop such a substantial lead in automobile technology? After a slow start, the United States quickly became not only the dominant exporter of automobiles in the world but, partly as a result, the dominant exporter of machinery. Granting that the size of the market was greater in America than in Europe, what can be said about the relative ability of American and European firms to exploit the potential?

Although it is not possible with the data available to make direct comparisons, I feel confident that in America there was more risk-taking, which in turn attracted a wider diversity of people into the industry—thereby making it better able to deal with uncertainty. For the 181 companies that produced automobiles between 1903 and 1926, the mortality data are as follows:[23]

28 percent lasted 3 years or less.
49 percent lasted 6 years or less.
36 percent lasted 10 years or more.
19 percent lasted 16 years or more.

It would be wrong to conclude from these data that the entire story of the early history of the automobile industry is one of Ford's rise and the downfall of many small companies. Unfortunately for the period under consideration, published data for production of cars, other than those produced by Ford and General Motors, is not available. However, in his pioneering study of the automobile industry, Ralph C. Epstein did collect data for the twenty-eight most successful cars (in terms of the quantity sold) produced during the period 1903 to 1924, on the promise that he would not disclose the names of the automobiles in question.[24] The left side of Figure 9 shows the rank of the ten largest producers as of 1903. If there had been no competition, as measured by changes in market shares, the chart would be composed of horizontal straight lines. But as the chart indicates, on the basis of 1903 sales it would have been impossible to pick the top ten in 1924. After 1910, automobile *A* never regained first rank. *B,* which was second in 1903, declined below tenth place; the same is true of *G*. Moreover, *C, E, F, I,* and *J,* which were also in the top ten in 1903, were made by firms that went out of business within a relatively few years. And of the leaders in the industry in 1924, only three were produced by firms that were in

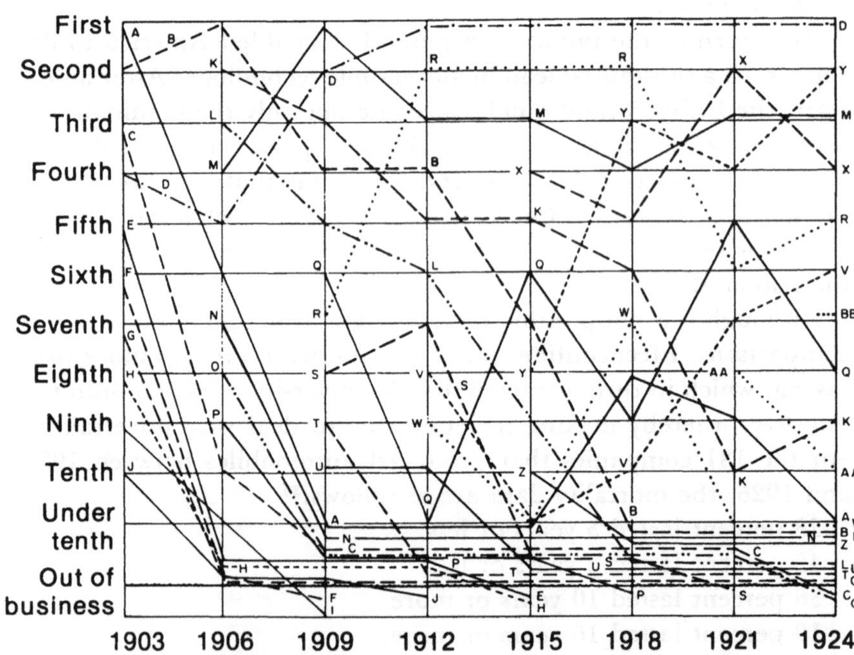

Figure 9. Twenty-eight leading automobile producers, ranked according to size of production, 1903-1924. From R. C. Epstein, *The Auto Industry* (A. W. Shaw Co., 1928), p. 206.

business prior to 1908. The positions of several of the leading makes oscillated greatly during this period. Generally speaking, the firms that did worse were those engaged in making expensive cars. Apparently, as early as 1910, it was difficult for automobile producers to change their products in response to changes in demand.

It is also likely that compared with the European automobile industry, a wider diversity of people, in terms of their education and the wealth of their parents, were associated with the American automobile industry. To be more specific, while a person like Henry Ford, who was the son of poor parents and had no college education, probably would have been the exception in Europe, he was by no means the exception in America. And as Table 3 shows, it would be hard to argue, a la Denison, that the success of the American automobile industry rested upon the superior education of its pioneers.

The advantage of an industry with a wider diversity of people is that it is better equipped to deal with uncertainty. For example, it may be assumed that, given the cookbook methods typically employed in teaching, engineering college graduates are taught to be more skillful at the expense of being made less imaginative. And granting that a mix of skillful and imaginative people is desired to deal with strong uncertainties, then a country that did not rely mainly upon college graduates for its top posts would be at an advantage.

Moreover, it also may be assumed that with entrepreneurs coming from poor families the probability of developing an inexpensive car for the masses would be greater. This is not to suggest, of course, that the poor necessarily have any aversion to making money by selling to the rich or that the rich are loath to make money by selling to the poor. The point, rather, is that being poor it is easier to imagine the difference a $1000 car and a $600 car might make to another poor person. By contrast, one who has been thinking in terms of $2000 or $3000 cars will almost certainly underestimate the elasticity of demand. Therefore, I do not think it any accident that the automotive entrepreneurs who came from poor families—Olds and Ford in the United States, and William Rich Morris (Lord Nuffield) in Britain—played major roles in pioneering low-cost automobiles.

Just as important in the more rapid evolution of the automobile industry in the United States was the attitude of American consumers. Unlike the highly skeptical consumer of today, in 1900 there

Table 3. Pioneers of American Automobile Industry.

Name	Education	Father's occupation	Principal activities
Apperson, Elmer (1861-1920)	Public school	—	Cofounder of Apperson Bros; first side-door touring car; first eight-cylinder car.
Buick, David D. (1854-1929)	Public school	Farmer	Founded Buick Mfg. Co.; valve-in-head engine.
Chalmers, Hugh (1873-1932)	Public school	Stone-cutter	A founder of Chalmer's Motor Co.; helped pioneer mass production techniques.
Chapin, Roy D. (1880-1936)	Univ. of Michigan	—	Sales Manager, Olds Motor Works; helped organize Hudson Co.
Chevrolet, Louis (1878-1941)	Public school	Farmer	Designed and built first Chevrolet with William Durant.
Chrysler, Walter P. (1875-1940)	Public school	Locomotive engineer	Pres. of Buick Co.; Exec. Vice-Pres. of Willys Overland; Pres. of Maxwell, which later became Chrysler Corp.
Coffin, Howard E. (1873-1937)	Univ. of Michigan	—	Built automobile while a student; Head of Engineering, Olds Motor Works; known as "Father of Standardization."
Dodge, John F. (1864-1920)	Public school	Machine shop worker	A founder of Dodge Bros., 1914; manufactured auto parts.

Dodge, Horace E. (1868-1920)	Public school	Machine shop worker	Made engines and other components mainly for Ford Co.; a founder of Dodge Bros. Motor Co., 1914.
Durant, William C. (1861-1947)	Public school	Banker	Backed David Buick and later founded General Motors.
Duryea, Charles E. (1861-1938)	Gittings Seminary	Farmer	Designed and built one of first American autos, 1893, with brother, J. Frank Duryea.
Ford, Henry (1863-1947)	Public school	Farmer	Chief Engineer, Edison Co., Detroit; founder of Ford Motor Co.; played major role in revolutionary mass-production techniques.
Haynes, Elwood (1857-1925)	Worcester Polytechnic Institute	Judge	Built one of first autos, 1894; helped found Edgar & Apperson Automobile Co.; discovered a number of alloys; first to use aluminum in auto engine.
LeLand, Henry M. (1843-1932)	Public school	Farmer	Founder of Cadillac and Lincoln companies; helped pioneer interchangeable parts, V-8 engine, and, with Charles Kettering, the self-starter.
Maxim, Hiram P. (1869-1936)	MIT	Inventor, farmer	Designed and built gasoline-powered tricycle, electric automobile.
Maxwell, Johnathan D. (1864-1928)	Public school	Merchant	Helped build first Haynes automobile and first Oldsmobile; a founder of the Maxwell-Briscoe Co., 1904.

Table 3. (Continued)

Name	Education	Father's occupation	Principal activities	Name	Education	Father's occupation	Principal activities
May, Henry (1861-1944)	Public school	—	A founder of the Pierce-Arrow Motor Corp., 1901.	Packard, James W. (1863-1928)	Lehigh Univ.	Lumberman and hardware merchant	Founder of Packard Auto Co., 1899; also inventor of incandescent lamps, etc., with brother, William.
Olds, Ransom E. (1864-1950)	Business school	Machine repair	Built steam and internal-combustion engines; built first American self-propelled vehicle for export, 1893.	Roos, Delmar G. (1887-1960)	Cornell Univ.	Architect	Chief Engineer for Pierce-Arrow and later for Studebaker Co.; designed Jeep for Willys.
Packard, William D. (1861-1923)	Lehigh Univ.	Lumberman and hardware merchant	Founder of Packard Auto Co.; invented and manufactured electric lamps, transformers, and dynamos, with brother, James.	Sloan, Alfred (1875-1966)	MIT	Tea and coffee importer	President of General Motors, 1923-1937; perfected the roller bearing, shaft for hanger, and hanger boxes.

Studebaker, Clement (1831-1901)	Public school	Farmer	Blacksmith; world's largest wagon manufacturer; built electric and gasoline cars with brothers John, Peter, Henry, and Jacob.
White, Rollin H. (1872-1962)	Cornell Univ.	Sewing machine inventor	Designed White steam automobile, 1899; built White truck.
Willys, John N. (1873-1935)	Public school	Manufacturer of brick, tile, and wood boxes	Bicycle repair and sales; organized the American Motor Car Sales Co., 1906; Willys-Overland Co., 1908.

seemed to be no lack of consumers with a genuine sense of adventure. And such risk-taking by consumers may have played quite as important a role in America becoming an automobile leader as did risk-taking by business firms.

Early in the 1920s fast history was succeeded by slow history in the automobile industry. And, while automobile manufacturers continued to regard their industry as fiercely competitive, there was a decline in risk-taking. Even as early as the 1920s, the emphasis in competition had shifted from quality and price to style. For example, when in 1922 General Motors began to produce both Chevrolets and Pontiacs on the same production line, it was essentially engaged in a form of price discrimination based upon making the latter appeal to more prestigious owners than the former. However, in the main, competition took the form of improvements in quality, but at a less impressive rate than during the 1900s. For example, during the period 1920 to 1950 the most important advances made by the General Motors research laboratories included the refrigerant "Freon," tetraethyl lead as a cure for engine knock, more durable paint, elimination of vibration from engines via an improved crankshaft, high-compression V-8 engines, and the diesel locomotive. Of these advances only the diesel locomotive was significant from the perspective of fast history. And it resulted in creative destruction in the locomotive rather than the automobile industry. Conversely, none of the advances for the automobile industry were as significant as, say, the self-starter—an invention made by Charles Kettering in 1911 before he became head of the General Motors research laboratories.

During the 1930s, General Motors and Chrysler rose to first and second places in automobile sales. What is surprising about the Ford Company, given an organization that became more and more intolerant of diversity and uncertainty, is that it remained in business. By 1921 Ford had become an organization that tolerated only "yes-men." The point is made by Nevins and Hill describing the change in Henry Ford as he neared the age of sixty: "He was working towards the concentration of power, to be exercised by his own intuitive judgment. He wanted a responsive organization, a smooth-running company unimpeded by brilliant individualists."[25] As a result, some of the most creative engineers left the Ford Company in the early 1920s—C. Harold Wills to form his own company, and Charles Knudsen to become head of Chevrolet. In the 1930s, Henry

Ford's control became even more rigid when he set up his own internal-security organization to engage in various Machiavellian schemes to weed out dissidents and to assure the continuance of his monarchial organization.

However, while much that happened in the Ford Company was no doubt influenced by the changing personality of Henry Ford, there was throughout the industry a movement of management practices towards static efficiency. For example, when Pierre du Pont took over the presidency of General Motors during the crisis of 1921, he replaced Durant with an entirely different type of person. Whereas Durant was an outgoing person whom his employees called by his first name, Alfred Sloan, Durant's replacement, was aloof, and few, if any, employees ever called him by his first name. Sloan's reorganization plan called for a more logical regrouping and consolidation of General Motors' operating divisions. And while the new system continued to give division managers a good deal of discretion, it also imposed more controls upon them. In particular, accounting practices were tightened and each division was required to pay its own way.

No doubt such practices were necessary if the industry was to move towards a higher degree of static efficiency. However, although it is rarely pointed out, it seems quite unlikely that the United States would have been the leader of the world in pioneering automobiles if the management practices instituted in the 1920s had been followed from the beginning.

Closely associated with the higher degree of constraint imposed on entrepreneurship was a decline in the degree of competitive interaction. As Figure 10 shows, on the basis of past performance it was easier in 1927 than in 1903 to predict the ten top producers of a decade later (see Figure 9). To be sure, in terms of present-day standards the degree of competition was still high. That there were some quite significant shifts in market shares is indicated by Figure 11, which shows that from 1926 to 1940 General Motors' share of the market increased from one-quarter to nearly one-half, while Ford's declined from about two-fifths to about one-fifth. And the rise of Chrysler to overtake Ford certainly was impressive. Nevertheless, company fortunes during the period 1925 to 1940 were far more predictable than they were during the period 1900 to 1925.

It is, of course, impossible to say which was cause and which was effect, the lower degree of competition or the higher degree of in-

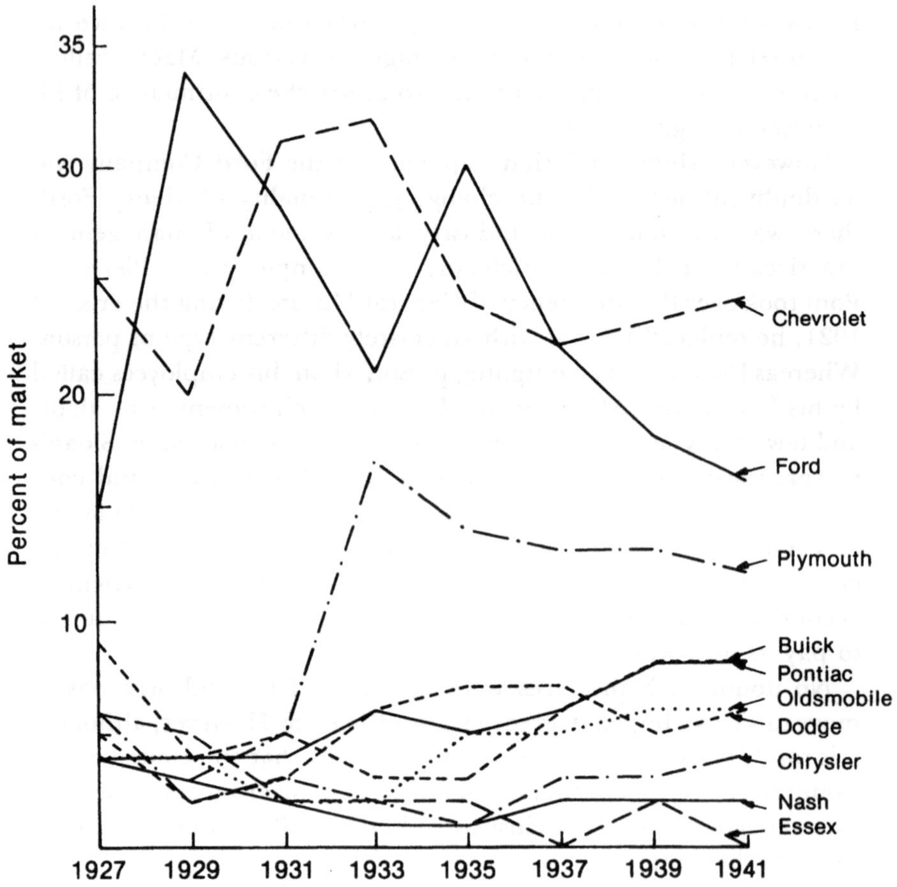

Figure 10. Share of market, ten leading United States automobiles, selected years, 1927-1941. From *Automotive Industries Annual Statistical Issues* (Detroit: R. L. Polk and Co., 1927-1941), reprinted with permission.

ternal structure. In terms of dynamic theory, one cannot make the neat separation of causes and effects that might seem possible in terms of static theory. Nevertheless, it can be said that when firms begin to act on the assumption of a lower rate of progress there is likely to be both an increase in the degree of organization and a decline in the degree of competitive interaction. And when such changes occur, firms will find themselves less able to deal with uncertainty. For example, according to Alfred Sloan, who was president of General Motors during the Great Depression, General

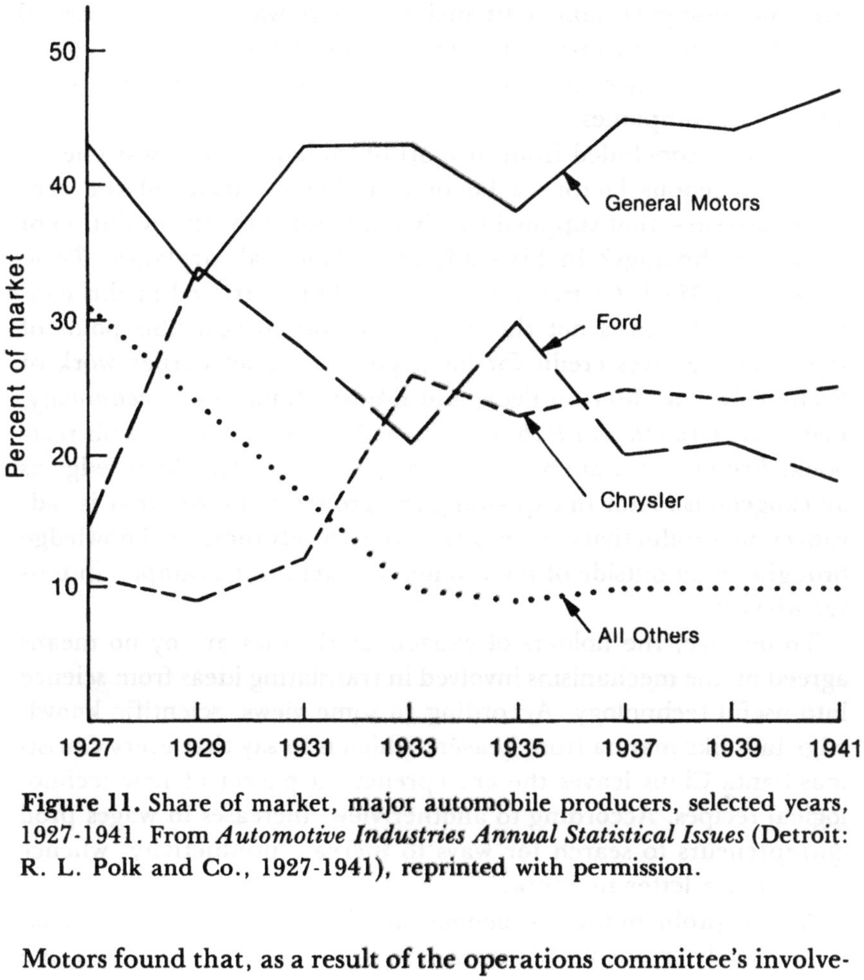

Figure 11. Share of market, major automobile producers, selected years, 1927-1941. From *Automotive Industries Annual Statistical Issues* (Detroit: R. L. Polk and Co., 1927-1941), reprinted with permission.

Motors found that, as a result of the operations committee's involvement in day-to-day decisions, the firm was overcentralized.[26]

Commercial Aircraft and Aircraft Engines

In one important respect the development of commercial aircraft and aircraft engines was different from the development of automotive technology. In the case of the automobile the government played no significant role. But government support for the development of military aircraft and aircraft engines generated technology applicable to commercial aircraft. Research sponsored by the National Advisory Committee on Aeronautics (NACA), made available to all aircraft companies, also played a very significant role. Moreover, because government financial support was available, several universities became involved to a great extent in the development of aeronautical science, and, like the NACA, made their research available to all companies.

Can it be concluded from this sort of evidence that it was science as an exogenous factor—a factor completely outside of the economic system—that supplied the dynamic force for the evolution of aircraft technology? In his study of commercial airplanes, *Technology and Market Structure,* Almarin Phillips arrived at this conclusion.[27] Phillips is not the only economist to take this point of view, and he gives credit for his hypothesis to an earlier work of Richard Nelson, Merton Peck, and Edward Kalachek: *Technology, Economic Growth and Public Policy.*[28] And even earlier, in his textbook, *Economics,* Paul Samuelson regarded scientific knowledge as an exogenous factor in explaining the growth paradox, that is, advances in productivity were attributed to advances in knowledge brought about outside of the economic system (for example, in universities).[29]

To be sure, the holders of exogenous theories are by no means agreed on the mechanisms involved in translating ideas from science into useful technology. According to some views, scientific knowledge falls like manna from heaven, which is to say that every Christmas Santa Claus leaves the entrepreneur a packet of new technological recipes. According to another view, increases in wages prod entrepreneurs to search for ways to increase productivity, whence they write a letter to Santa.

A basic problem with exogenous theories is that they are based on a completely erroneous notion of how advances in technology come about: scientists working in isolation are seen to be engaged in adding to the stock of scientific knowledge more or less continuously; and via some mysterious process ideas from science are translated into useful technology. But the fact remains that whether one is considering airplanes or other machines, the gist of Sadi Carnot's argument about the efficiency of machines remains exactly the same. Engineers may know quite well the changes (for example, engines with higher thrust relative to their weight and fuel consumption, aerodynamic configurations that will result in a reduction in drag) required to produce an improvement in physical efficiency. But, especially if the improvements are significant, they cannot predict which particular technical measures are most likely to succeed.

Typically, the technical measures that provide the largest advances are those engineers are initially most skeptical about.

Indeed, until engineers find themselves in a real dilemma, which results from the need to bring about an improvement they do not know how to accomplish, they have no way of assessing the relevance of ideas arising out of scientific research. For example, after World War II the Air Force had four bombers under development—the B-45, the B-46, the B-47, and the B-48—with four firms engaged in a prototype competition for the bomber to be awarded a production contract. As it happens, the aerodynamicists at one of these companies—Boeing—felt that with an improved design it would be possible to obtain much better performance. But their ideas on how to proceed were very hazy. However, about the same time under United States government sponsorship, a team of aerodynamicists was sent to Germany to unearth useful ideas from German World War II research. And although the information was made available to all aircraft companies, only the people from Boeing immediately appreciated the significance of an idea for using swept-back wings to reduce drag at high subsonic speeds. As it also happens, an earlier article in the open German aircraft literature proposed the same idea, but not until the significance of the advance was generally appreciated did several aerodynamicists remember having read it.

The reader may or may not regard a theory to use swept-back wings to reduce drag as "science." But in many cases, the knowledge which makes an advance possible cannot by any stretch of the imagination be regarded as "scientific" knowledge. For example, in developing the Sidewinder air-to-ground missile, a problem arose in the development of the guidance system, because, while there was not enough money to develop a system with linear responses, the people involved did not know how to develop one with nonlinear responses; in this case a German toy provided the needed clue.

In the case of the swept-back wings cited above, the relevant aerodynamic knowledge happened to be available before it was used for the development of an American plane. But in most cases, when fundamental problems arise, the relevant scientific information is simply not available. And more often than not the difficulties encountered in development provide the driving force for expanding the stock of scientific knowledge. For example, Theodore von Karman is pictured by associates as a man who, on the one hand, had a very deep understanding of science, but who, on the other, derived much of his stimulation from working on practical problems. Engineers from aviation companies credit him with having played a significant role in pioneering the practical side of aviation. To my knowledge, most significant advances in aerodynamics, whether brought about by NACA Laboratories or by universities, not only affect technology by supplying useful knowledge, but also are affected by the many problems that arise when attempts are made to improve the physical and economic performance of aircraft.

It is no accident, therefore, that when progress is rapid in an industry, firms in the industry are highly interactive with universities. And it is competition that generates pressure on both business firms and university departments.

The most that can be said for exogenous theories of economic change is that by permitting classical economic theory (or near variants of it) and scientific and technological change to exist side by side, they supply a peaceful coexistence theory of economics. However, our understanding of economic reality is substantially obscured, because we are prevented from understanding the role played by real-world competition. For example, according to Phillips, the history of aviation depicts an order-of-magnitude reduction in costs. Moreover he even goes so far as to acknowledge that "sharp increases in the share of the market held by particular manufacturers, that is, have been associated with the development of planes which, as compared with former models, are better in a number of significant ways."[30] Yet, nothing is said in Phillips's account about the role played by competition in bringing costs down. Indeed, according to his exogenous theory of technological change, almost everything that has happened in aviation seems to have been preordained by forces outside of the economic system. Apparently, for an economist trained to think in terms of the model supplied by perfect competition, in which firms have no power whatsoever to affect prices, stealing markets from other firms is not to be regarded as competition but as evidence of monopoly power. To be sure, Phillips grants that, because knowledge is constantly changing, firms had to live with a good deal of uncertainty; but their role is seen to have been a quite passive one. On the other hand, if we are to believe Arthur Raymond, who was in charge of Engineering at Douglas from the time of the DC-3 to the time of the DC-8, one of the most important factors to be taken into account in aircraft design, if an aircraft manufacturer hopes to be successful, is his competitor:

> What is my competitor doing? Is he so entrenched that it will be extremely difficult, if not impossible, to make headway against him? On the other hand, has he been established in the field so long that he is perhaps growing complacent? Should he have brought out a new model some time ago and failed to do so, thus giving me an opening?[31]

It can be seen, therefore, that while science did play a larger role in the development of the airplane than it did in the development of the automobile, the role science played did not preclude competition.

Another difference of note between the automobile and aircraft industries is the degree of vertical integration. Although early pioneers in the automobile industry were almost exclusively engaged in the assembly of automobiles (as airframe developers are almost exclusively engaged in the assembly of airframes), at a relatively early date vertical integration began with the same firm manufacturing both the chassis and the engine. However, in the aircraft industry in the United States there was only one firm that developed both engines and airframes; and it is no longer in business. The essential reason vertical integration did not occur in the aircraft industry is that the industry has featured a higher degree of dynamic efficiency, so that a good engine has invariably been used by several aircraft manufacturers. By contrast, in automobile manufacturing the lack of technical progress, on the one hand, and much longer production runs, on the other, have made vertical integration a more attractive proposition.

On the other hand, there are three broad similarities between the evolution of the aircraft industry and the evolution of the automobile industry. First, the number of firms engaged in pioneering each industry was greater than the number of firms that survived. Second, it would not have been possible to predict later success on the basis of the firms that were initially most successful. Third, the major advances were brought about by highly interactive organizations. In the following discussion of piston-engine airplanes each of these points will be taken up. In concluding the discussion I will briefly take up Boeing's comeback in the field of commercial jets.

The Number of Firms in the Industry. In 1930, when the aircraft industry was in roughly the same state of evolution as the automobile industry had been in 1912, there were sixteen firms engaged in the development and production of commercial aircraft, and four firms in the development and production of aircraft engines—more than twice the total number of firms involved today. To be sure, the decline in the number of firms in the automobile industry was more dramatic. But it must be remembered that in the aircraft industry scale economies are not as important as in the automobile industry, and that the aircraft industry features a higher degree of dynamic efficiency.

Changing Fortunes of Firms, 1930 to 1940. Table 4 shows, for the period 1932-1940, the percentage of the total United States' fleet of commercial aircraft accounted for by those aircraft that enjoyed sales of ten or more. Almost as many more aircraft types were either produced in quantities of less than ten or were developed as prototypes and not produced. Nearly all of the aircraft in commercial use in 1932 were developed later than 1928. As Table 4 shows, the leading producers at the beginning of the decade were Boeing, Ford, Stinson, Fokker, and Fairchild. And the commercial fleet was composed of both trimotor and single-engine airplanes. If operated at high load factors, the trimotor airplanes had a significant advantage over the single-engine airplanes in costs per seat mile; according to Phillips's estimates, total seat mile operating costs (including depreciation) were about 20 percent lower.[32] But in 1932 the trimotors often carried no more than four or five passengers and operated at a cost disadvantage.

Cost differences, however, were not only a function of aircraft type (single engine airliners versus trimotor airliners). For particular types of airplanes, some firms were able to obtain better technical efficiency and lower costs than others. For example, according to Phillips's estimates, total operating costs per seat mile for the Boeing trimotor were about 35 percent higher than for the Ford trimotor and about 65 percent higher than for the Fokker trimotor.[33] Yet as of 1932, there were almost as many Boeing trimotors in the commercial fleet as Ford trimotors, and fewer Fokker trimotors than either Boeing or Ford trimotors.

How is the disparity between cost performance and the number of airplanes sold to be explained? Perhaps the Boeing airplanes had

Table 4. Aircraft in United States commercial fleet (by percentage of each plane in total fleet).

	Ford Trimotor	Boeing Trimotor	Fokker Trimotor	Stinson single-engine	Stinson Trimotor	Fairchild Pilgrim	Lockheed Vega	Fokker single-engine	Lockheed Orion	Boeing B-80	Condor transport	Boeing 247	Lockheed L-10	Vultee V-1-A	Douglas DC-2	Douglas DC-3	All others
1932	17	15	10	9	7	11	5	5	3	3	1	-	-	-	-	-	13
1933	13	10	5	5	7	3	5	4	6	3	6	16	-	-	-	-	16
1934	14	9	-	6	10	-	4	-	6	3	8	17	6	8	6	-	9
1935	7	8	-	1	13	-	4	-	5	1	6	18	10	8	18	-	4
1936	3	-	-	-	11	-	3	-	-	3	2	21	15	10	21	11	3
1937	-	-	-	-	4	-	2	-	-	-	-	20	16	-	21	32	5
1938	-	-	-	-	2	-	-	-	-	-	-	17	14	-	20	42	6
1939	-	-	-	-	1	-	-	-	-	-	-	15	13	-	17	52	3
1940	-	-	-	-	1	-	-	-	-	-	-	9	7	-	9	69	4
1941	-	-	-	-	-	-	-	-	-	-	-	8	5	-	4	79	4

Source: Almarin Phillips, *Technology and Market Structure* (Lexington, Mass.: D.C. Heath, 1971), pp. 151-158.

other advantages to compensate for their lack of cost effectiveness. However, my guess, like Phillips's, is not that competition took other forms than price competition; rather, due to a combination of government subsidies and special relationships between airline and aircraft companies, there was a lack of competitiveness in the development of commercial airliners. For example, the Ford Motor Company controlled Stout Airlines. Curtiss and Fokker had affiliations with airlines that required them to buy their planes. But the company that excelled in Type 4 entrepreneurship (entrepreneurship directed to controlling the environment) was Boeing. Although William Boeing, the son of a family that had made its fortune in the lumber business, was not keenly interested in bringing down operating costs, he did possess the talents of a financial organizer. He was instrumental in setting up an extremely profitable airmail operation in the form of the Boeing Transport Company, which, on the one hand, purchased its airplanes from Boeing and, on the other, was affiliated with United Airlines.

But the Air Mail Act of 1934 required companies competing for air-mail contracts to be completely separated from aircraft companies. Moreover, while the air-mail scandals did not result in criminal prosecutions, officials from some airlines resigned, including, among others, William Boeing. It is safe to assume that the Great Depression helped to introduce an element of cost consciousness into the aircraft industry, just as it did in the automobile industry. As was already pointed out, Trans World Airlines took the initiative in introducing more competition into the commercial airliner business when it asked several firms, including Douglas, to enter a design competition for an airplane whose performance would be equivalent to the Boeing 247 but whose operating costs would be a good deal lower. Douglas was not the only manufacturer to respond to the pressures for more economical airliners. In 1934 Lockheed completed the development of the L-10, a plane whose design was similar to that of the DC-2, but whose operating costs were 30 percent less.[34] But Douglas's DC-3, which became operational in 1936, had a 30 percent cost advantage over the L-10; and until the state of the art permitted four-engine airplanes it never had any real competitors.[35]

As a result, Douglas gained an even more impressive advantage from the DC-3 than Ford did from the Model T. As of 1922, every other car in the United States was a Model T. But as of 1941, almost eight out of every ten airliners was a DC-3.

Improved engines played a very important role in making possible efficient airliners like the DC-3 and the L-10. According to Robert Schlaifer's and S. D. Heron's *Development of Aircraft Engines and Fuels,* competition played more or less the same role in the evolution of air-cooled engines as it did in the development of commercial aircraft.[36] In the early 1920s there were three well-established American firms engaged in the development and production of aircraft engines: the Curtiss Aeroplane and Motor Corporation, the Wright Aeronautical Corporation, and the Packard Motor Car Company; and each had produced water-cooled engines during World War I. Their postwar strategy was to insist that the future market for aircraft engines be limited to the engine technology in which they already possessed expertise.

In addition, there were several small companies engaged in building experimental engines, including the Lawrance Aero-Engine Corporation, which, with a staff of five engineers, was engaged in the design and development of air-cooled engines. The feasibility of the air-cooled engine was established by development contracts from the Army and the Navy in 1918 for the development of small engines in the 30-40 horsepower range—as compared with the 400-horsepower water-cooled engines then available. And by 1921 Lawrance was engaged in the development of a 200-horsepower air-cooled engine. The three principal advantages of an air-cooled engine were, first, it required no radiator and coolant, second, it was lighter than a water-cooled engine, and, third, it was easier to maintain.

Following the success of this engine Curtiss became enthusiastic about air-cooled engines and developed one of about 400 horsepower. Not to be outdone, Wright purchased the Lawrance Company, and made J. Lawrance a vice-president. But the most successful engine of the period—the Wasp—was developed by a newly founded subsidiary of a New England machine tool firm: Pratt and Whitney Aircraft. The head of the firm was F. B. Rentschler, the former president of Wright, who claimed that his Wright board of directors would not give him a free enough hand in the development of air-cooled engines. Pratt and Whitney and Wright emerged as the two main contenders in the field of air-cooled engines. And after an intense competition in which both engines were test flown, the Wright 750-horsepower cyclone engine was initially chosen by Douglas for its DC-2.

In short, as in the case of the automobile, newly founded firms played a major role in maintaining the dynamism of the aircraft industry. Of the four major producers of commercial aircraft in 1930, only one, Boeing, survived as a major force in the industry; and of the three major engine producers as of 1920, only one, Wright, remained a major producer as of 1930. On the other hand, though Douglas had produced military airplanes since the 1920s it was a newcomer to the commercial aircraft field. And the firms that played major roles in the pioneering of aircraft engines—Lawrance and Pratt and Whitney—were newly founded firms.

Development of the DC-3. Like the Model T Ford, the DC-3 was developed in two stages. The first was the DC-2 (the production version of the DC-1), a simple and efficient airplane from a technical point of view. The second stage produced the DC-3, which was more efficient than the DC-2 from an economic point of view, and permitted airline companies to operate at a profit for the first time.

Although in earlier development programs Donald Douglas had played roughly the same role as Henry Ford had in the development of the Model T, as time went by he became more willing to decentralize decision-making. As a result, the DC-2 and DC-3 were developed by loosely structured teams that were given a relatively free hand. The DC-2 team included J. H. Kindelberger, who at the time was chief engineer at Douglas, Arthur Raymond, his assistant, Ed Burton, Lee Atwood, W. B. Oswold, Arthur L. Klein, and Fred Herman. Arthur L. Klein was a professor at the California Institute of Technology and a consultant to Douglas. According to Arthur Raymond, who was kind enough to furnish most of the material on which this section is based, Klein found a way to decrease the drag of the DC-1, an approach that was previously unknown to designers of low-wing monoplanes. Association between Douglas and Caltech began in 1928 when Arthur Raymond was asked to lecture at Caltech, because Robert Millikan, president of the school, wanted someone to teach the practical side of aircraft design to the prospective faculty of the newly formed Guggenheim Aeronautical Laboratory. And included in Raymond's first class were Clark Millikan and A. L. Klein.

The relationship between Caltech and Douglas provided mutual advantages. On the one hand, Caltech had one of the best aeronautics departments in the world, equipped with the most modern wind tunnels; on the other, Douglas provided an environment in which scientists could discover the real technical problems of commercial aviation, without which knowledge they could never have decided on the appropriate tests to be made in the wind tunnels.

The DC-1 combined for the first time several important advances: an improved type of engine cowl developed by the NACA, more efficient flaps, adjustable metal propellers, and the Northrop type of construction. Jack Northrop had left Douglas several years before to form his own company, which pioneered monocoque construction, but he returned in 1932 to head the Northrop Corporation, a subsidiary of Douglas. And the DC-1 utilized the Northrop approach to duralumin fuselages and cantilever wings.

The principal difference between Douglas and its competitors—Sikorsky and General Aviation—is that only Douglas was willing to propose a two-engine design. A two-engine airplane could be simpler and more economical. But there was considerable skepticism whether a two-engine airplane could meet the specified one-engine-out performance requirement. And Douglas received the contract only after Arthur Raymond was able to convince Charles Lindbergh, who at the time was TWA's technical consultant, that with the best available combination of technological inputs a two-engine design was feasible.

However, the success of the DC-1 and DC-2 was not merely a matter of basing the overall design concept on the appropriate combination of technological ingredients—of making the right "strategic" decision, so to speak. It was also a matter of making simplicity a theme of the detailed design. In 1951, Arthur Raymond gave the thirty-ninth Wilbur Wright Memorial Lecture to the Royal Aeronautical Society, in which he tried to explain the factors that made some Douglas aircraft development programs more successful than others. And one of the main points he emphasized was "excellence of detail design":

> Two aircraft designed to the same specification may differ widely in size, cost, and weight simply because of relative quality of detail design . . . In fact, much of the progress being made in the art consists in learning how to design a small, efficient aircraft to do the job previously done by a large complicated one. Not only does this hold true of the aircraft as a whole: it is also true of its components, down to the smallest parts. It is not always appreciated

> that a pound saving in weight empty may be compounded into ten or more pounds saving in gross weight in modern designs.[37]

And it may be assumed that the process involved in making aircraft simpler and more efficient is essentially dynamic, because it cannot be predicted how much engineers can simplify an airplane until they put their imaginations to work.

Another important factor in the success of the DC-2 and DC-3 programs was Douglas's ability to deal with unexpected events. When one is combining technological ingredients that have never been combined before, unforeseen difficulties do arise, as Raymond pointed out in his Wilbur Wright Memorial Lecture:

> When finally completed, the DC-2 was 30% overweight and would never have been able to meet its specification had it not been for two major and several minor developments which occurred during the course of construction and which were unforeseen at the time the contract was entered into.[38]

The specification in question was a safety requirement that the airplane be able to fly on a single engine at an altitude of more than 10,000 feet. The two unforeseen developments that saved the day were the variable-pitch propeller and an engine that delivered about 25 percent more horsepower than the one initially planned for the plane.

Was it then luck, and luck alone, that saved the DC-1? Or was the Douglas Company well prepared to deal with good and bad luck? This, of course, is the crucial question, and Raymond discussed it as one of the main points of his lecture under the general heading of "adaptiveness." After acknowledging that "often there is simply no way in which one can anticipate the course of events," he said: "The thing to do in such cases is to be on the alert to seize upon and use to advantage the favorable happenings and be prepared to take steps to minimize the effect of unfavorable ones."[39] Being better prepared for luck obviously requires sacrificing static efficiency for dynamic efficiency. However, the trade-off that was made in the early construction of steamboats—a sacrifice in durability to obtain higher performance— was not an appropriate trade-off in the case of aircraft and aircraft engines because it could jeopardize safety. So aircraft and aircraft engines were designed so that it would be relatively easy to incorporate new features. This required that in aircraft programs like the DC-2 and DC-3 sacrifices were made in highly predictable short-term benefits in order to be better prepared to deal with uncertainty. As Raymond made the point: "An aircraft designed for one particular type and model of engine, in such a way that the replacement of that engine by another of somewhat different size and characteristics can only be accomplished by major structural alterations, is in a highly vulnerable position if that engine fails to come through as anticipated. Nor can it take advantage of successive future improvements in power plant as they come along through the years."[40] Moreover, the sacrifice in static efficiency not only affects the design of the airplane, it also affects the tooling: "There has been considerable progress since aircraft were made by hand with little or no tooling. The correct middle course is to provide comparatively simple tools which can be augmented or duplicated if production is stepped up and which can be thrown away if the design is changed."[41]

Keeping designs simple and engaging in highly flexible planning are not very subtle ideas. Apparently, however, they are not very common ideas, for if they were, many more airplanes would have enjoyed the success of the DC-2 and DC-3. They are not very common because whereas flexibile planning requires a genuine willingness to make substitutions, to most engineers it is sinful to make major changes in the design of an airplane. Therefore, they tend to think in terms of rigid technological coefficients.

The DC-2 lived up to its promise of providing lower operating costs than the Boeing 247. As a result, soon after its development, which took about a year, United States' airlines ordered more than fifty DC-2s, and production of the Boeing 247 was discontinued. However, though the DC-2 cut the losses of airline companies, it did not allow them to make a profit. And it was William Littlewood, the chief engineer for American Airlines, who took the initiative when he proposed that with larger engines and a larger fuselage the DC-2 could be modified to carry twenty-four passengers (later revised to twenty-one) instead of fourteen, or a sleeper version could be built that could carry fourteen passengers. Moreover, American demonstrated its faith in the new concept by placing a firm order for twenty planes.[42]

The development team responsible for the DC-3 was somewhat different from that involved in the DC-2. Arthur Raymond, who succeeded J. H. Kindelberger as head of engineering when the later left Douglas to form North American Aviation, was responsible for the project. Franklin W. Collbohn, who later became head of the RAND Corporation, was added to the team. And William Littlewood, American's chief engineer, became an active associate. People from Douglas have argued that without the DC-2 it would have been impossible to have had a DC-3, and people from American Airlines have replied that without stretching the airplane it would have been impossible to have brought down seat mile costs from 4.8 to 3.4 cents.

However, as I suggested in the discussion of the Model T, the optimal organization, when it comes to making fast history, is one so interactive that the authorship of discoveries is unclear. And the DC-4E airplane, a four-engine commercial airplane developed later by Douglas under the direction of five airline companies, with each insisting upon particular features of the ultimate design, seems to confirm this proposition. When the airplane flew, its performance was so disappointing no one involved was willing to purchase it. The airplane ultimately was sold to the Japanese and is reported to have sunk in Tokyo Harbor.

Although with four-engine airplanes continued progress was made in extending the range of airplanes and in reducing flying times, operating costs were reduced more slowly after the DC-3. According to Phillips's estimates, the reductions in operating costs from the trimotor airplanes to the DC-3 (measured in constant dollars) were more than twice as large the reductions from the DC-3 to the four-engine airplanes.[43] And as dynamic theory predicts, with a decline in risk-taking less dramatic changes in market shares occurred during the post-World War II period (Figure 12).

It is not altogether surprising that with the slowdown of technological progress Douglas's share of the market declined. As we have already seen, the same happened to Ford's share of the automobile market during the 1920s. It is more surprising that Douglas remained a leader as long as it did. As Figure 12 shows, in the period 1947 through 1958 (after which the jet age began) Douglas's share of new sales of aircraft to domestic airlines fluctuated a great deal from year to year. But up until 1958 Douglas remained the leader. In its earlier successes with the DC-2 and the DC-3, Douglas's affiliation with Caltech was important. But more important to its later successes has been the solid reputation it developed for building good airplanes. Moreover, an airplane company in the happy position of selling airplanes to several airline companies is in a better

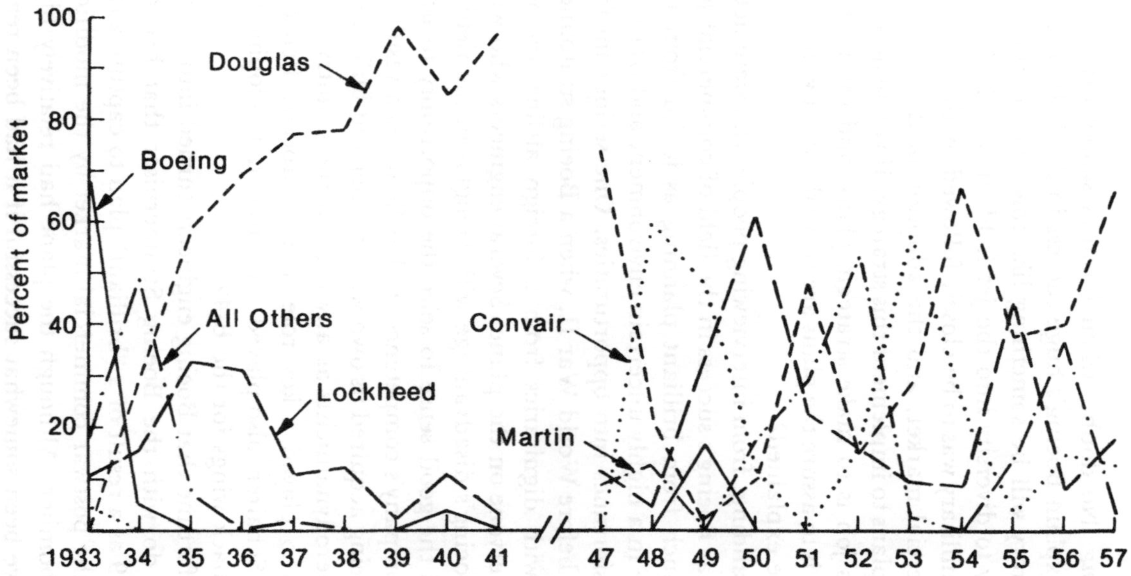

Figure 12. Share of market, major commercial aircraft developers, 1933-1941 and 1947-1957. From Almarin Phillips, *Technology and Market Structure* (Lexington, Mass.: D. C. Heath, 1971).

position to understand their problems. On the other hand, as will be seen in the next section, such a close association can also prove a liability when it comes to developing a new type of airplane.

The Rise of Boeing. No doubt, when business school experts on business strategy explain Boeing's huge success in the field of commercial jets, the story will be something like this: the adoption of a brilliant strategy to diversify into the jet field, in which the sale of bombers to the military was to be closely followed by the penetration of the commercial market, and the adoption of detailed and thorough tactical plans to implement this strategy. If you believe the top management's job is to make strategic plans, and the middle management's job is to assure the plans are carried out, how else can Boeing's success be explained?

But my understanding, from interviewing people who were actually involved, is that Boeing's success in the field of commercial jets resulted not so much from brilliant planning as it did from the necessity to survive in a highly uncertain environment and from the ability to turn misfortunes into opportunities. One serious misfortune occurred just before World War II, when a Boeing stratoliner, being test flown with dignitaries from a foreign airline aboard, crashed, killing everyone on the plane. Several engineers who were highly aware of Boeing's disadvantage with Douglas in the field of aerodynamics had the good sense to seize the opportunity to urge building up the company's competence in that field. As a result, in the early 1940s Boeing acquired its own wind tunnel and built up as good a group of aerodynamicists as any firm in the country. Two aerodynamicists who played a key role in this process, Benedict Cohn and George Schairer, also played a key role in developing the concept of swept-back wings for the B-47.

The second misfortune that Boeing engineers turned into an opportunity had to do with the Boeing Stratocruiser that became operational in 1949 as a result of a "brilliant" plan to capture a significant share of the postwar commercial market by the modification of the B-29 bomber. Although the plane had relatively high costs, it might have been somewhat successful if it had been ready for use before the appearance of the Douglas, Lockheed, Martin, and Convair transports. But since the production people insisted upon tooling for planes in the "modern" manner in which Boeing had operated during World War II, the Boeing 377 not only had higher operating costs than the Douglas DC-6, but it made its appearance three years later. Boeing is reported to have lost about 50 million dollars on this plane.

As a result of this fiasco, people in the middle management of Boeing were able to convince the top management that if the company hoped to survive in the commercial market it would have to become more seriously involved. As the argument was made to the top management, the company had become successful in the bomber business only as a result of possessing an intimate knowledge of the problems of the Strategic Air Command. And would it not have to do the same if it hoped to be successful in the commercial airline business?

To be sure, it was also recognized that the knowledge acquired in building bombers would be highly relevant for developing commercial jets. However, a plane like the B-47, which used drag chutes to slow it down while landing, was not likely to be suitable as a commercial airliner. Moreover, shortly after the B-47's first flight in December 1947, several Boeing aerodynamicists realized that a more basic uncertainty was involved in the development of an economical jet commercial airplane. The crucial uncertainty was the stalling speed of the airplane. It was known that the higher the stalling speed, the lower would be the certifiable weight of the airplane. It also was known that the lower the certifiable weight, the poorer would be the economic performance of the airplane: the payload would be smaller, and the required length of landing fields would be longer. And relatively small errors in estimating the stalling speed could lead to large errors in estimating the operating cost of the airplane, that is, in estimating its economic performance. On the other hand, it was not known what particular combination of physical characteristics was likely to keep the stalling speed low enough that the airplane would have a "satisfactory" economic performance (which, from the airlines' point of view, required no higher operating costs than with piston-engine commercial aircraft). The pertinent question, therefore, was—would the airplane end up with a satisfactory economic performance? Furthermore the uncertainty was compounded by the fact that for understandable reasons CAA certification requirements for commercial jet aircraft were not yet established; and there was no guarantee, therefore, that what was believed to be a safe stalling speed from a Boeing point of view would be a safe stalling speed from a CAA point of view.

The Boeing top management were finally persuaded. While genuine risks were involved in being the first American firm to pioneer the development of jet airliners, so were risks involved in being driven out of the field of commercial aircraft altogether. It was finally decided to build an experimental airplane with Boeing funds, which would be used as a prototype both for a commercial airplane and for an Air Force tanker. To keep other firms in the dark with respect to Boeing's intentions, a model designation was chosen to suggest it was working on a modification of the stratocruiser, and the entire project was placed under tight security wraps.

According to what I have been able to learn from one directly involved, the methods employed for dealing with uncertainty in designing and building the plane were much like those Raymond associated with the more successful Douglas programs. Benedict Cohn, one of those involved, insists that the test of a good engineer is his ability to deal with uncertainty rather than to avoid it, and that good engineers are aware that the price of optimizing projects for short-term benefits is a greater inability to deal with uncertainty.

In short, one of the factors that helped Boeing to become a leader in pioneering commercial jets was its competence in the field of aerodynamics; another was the adoption of strategy and tactics appropriate for dealing with uncertainty. And as a consequence of having a definite goal (operating costs no higher than piston-engine airplanes) and a diversity of ideas for reaching the goal, the 707 turned out to have lower operating costs than the DC-7 and, despite the earlier predictions that turboprops would have an economic advantage, lower operating costs than the Lockheed-developed turboprop airliner.[44]

Conversely, the Douglas Company's success with piston-engine aircraft helped to constrain its ability to become a leader in the field of jets. In the years 1953 to 1955, the position of the Douglas Company seemed to be very secure, indeed. After selling two hundred and seventy DC-6s to U.S. airlines (as compared with Boeing's total sale of fifty-five 377s), it became engaged in the introduction of the DC-7. And when good customers such as American Airlines had just placed substantial orders for DC-7s, why rush the introduction of the jets? Moreover, there was a good deal of agonizing whether to develop a turboprop or a turbojet. And, according to Arthur Raymond, Douglas was so committed to existing programs it had no excess capacity. As a result, not until June 1955 did work begin on the DC-8 jet, about a year after the first test flight of the Boeing prototype. But despite its late start, Douglas had no alternative but to enter the race. The mood within the Douglas Company is described by Arthur Raymond as follows: It was a big gamble. From that time on it became a real struggle and the tension was enormous. Gone were the days of the DC-3 monopoly and our overwhelming competitive advantage. We were depending on our reputation and our proven excellence in design to give us at least a share of the commercial market. We would probably have to settle for second place, but we were not out of the race."[45]

Nevertheless, Douglas managed to deliver its first jet for airline use in May 1959, or about six months after Boeing delivered its first 707. However, the people at Douglas felt that they were at a serious disadvantage in not having developed an experimental prototype. In the first place, although the Douglas people had hoped that the tanker competition would result in a production contract for both Douglas and Boeing, no doubt the prototype played a role in the award of the entire Air Force contract to Boeing. Second, the prototype helped Boeing to sign up American Airlines, Sabena, and Air France, all at a relatively early date. Third, because Douglas did not elect to take the prototype route, modifications were more expensive to make. As invariably happens, unexpected problems did arise. As Arthur Raymond points out: "We had a number of problems with the design, up to and including the flight test period before it went into service in late 1959. We were able to deal with all of them, but the final one was the worst. An incipient case of wing flutter was discovered that looked for a time as though a major change of the kind I had been dreading would be necessary. But we finally did find a solution and a fairly easy one at that."[46]

Furthermore, he recalls that cost escallation was a serious problem with the DC-8: "Cost estimates were skyrocketing way ahead of contract prices and actual costs were over-running estimates with shocking regularity."[47] No doubt the decision to concurrently develop and produce the airplane had a great deal to do with cost escallation. Even when relatively simple solutions to design difficulties are found, tooling changes can be very expensive. In other words, the economic advantage Boeing achieved from having developed a prototype was that to recover its initial investment it had to sell fewer planes. And according to Raymond, no one seems to have been more aware of Douglas's disadvantage in not having begun earlier with an experimental prototype than Donald Douglas, Sr.

Nevertheless, although the DC-8 was not the financial success it might have been, DC-8s were delivered to the airlines with no higher operating costs (including depreciation) than the DC-7. And in the period 1959 to 1965 Douglas sold almost as many DC-8s as Boeing sold 707s. However, the people at Boeing were quick to follow up the 707 with the development of the 720 and the 727. And as Figure 13 shows, from 1959 to 1965 Boeing's share of the market increased impresively.

Epilogue: The Case of Semiconductors

Is competition becoming more automatic, with uncertainty and competition playing smaller roles than they did in the development of aircraft and automobile technology? The search never ceases for some kind of heaven that contains no uncertainty. And I have found many people who believe that competition is being replaced by automatic progress.

Transistors, which were invented in 1948 by Bell Telephone Laboratories as an outgrowth of research begun during World War II, are one kind of semiconductor. The economic significance of semiconductors is that by providing a cheap and reliable replacement for electronic tubes they not only have improved existing products such as radios, television, and especially large computers, but have also made possible new products such as hand-held computers.

Like commercial aircraft and aircraft engines, semiconductor technology has received substantial support from the United States Department of Defense. And with equal justification, it can be said to be a science-based technology. Moreover, as Figure 14 shows, the rate of progress in improving the technology has been very impressive.

What role was played by competition in bringing about this progress? Although John Tilton's very interesting study *International Diffusion of Technology: The Case of Semiconductors* was more concerned with the international diffusion of technology than the role played by competition, it does contain a good deal of relevant information on the types of firms engaged in pioneering semiconductors.[48] In the early 1950s, several receiving-tube firms went into the semiconductor business, including General Electric, RCA, and

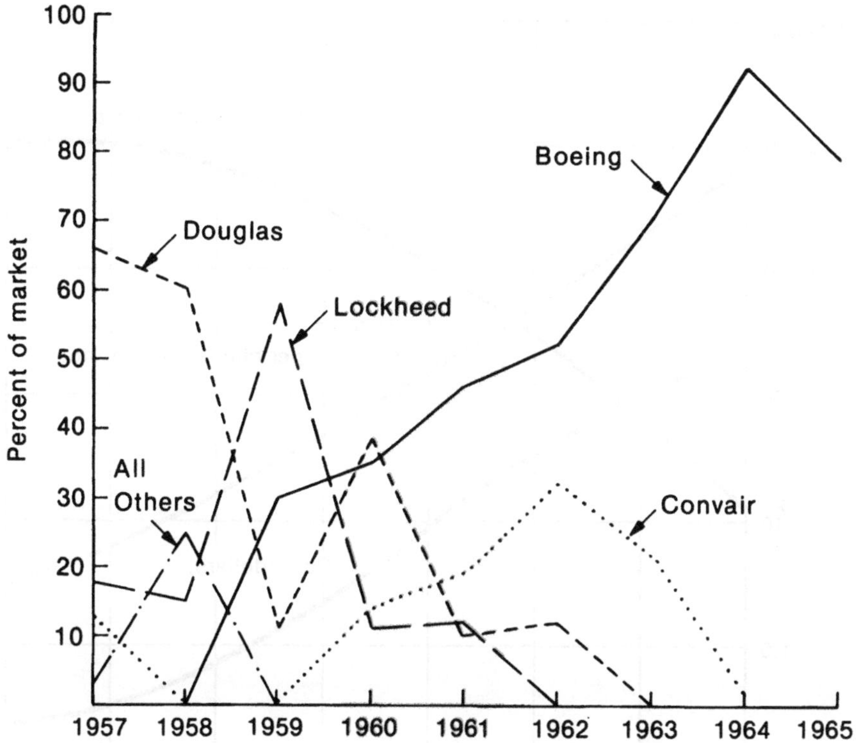

Figure 13. Share of market, major commercial aircraft developers, 1957-1965. From Almarin Phillips, *Technology and Market Structure* (Lexington, Mass.: D. C. Heath, 1971).

Sylvania. Although these firms did not play a major role in bringing about the crucial inventions in the semiconductor field, they nevertheless made important contributions to the evolution of the technology; their analogue can be found in the bicycle and carriage manufacturers who, by acting to prevent themselves from becoming victims of the process of creative destruction, helped to establish firms like General Motors.

The firms that played a more important role in the evolution of semiconductor technology were either small firms or newly organized subsidiaries of larger firms. For example, before becoming involved in the semiconductor business, Texas Instruments was a small research company with annual sales of about 6 million dollars. William Shockley, one of the inventors of the transistor, left Bell Telephone Laboratories to set up Shockley Laboratories, which was

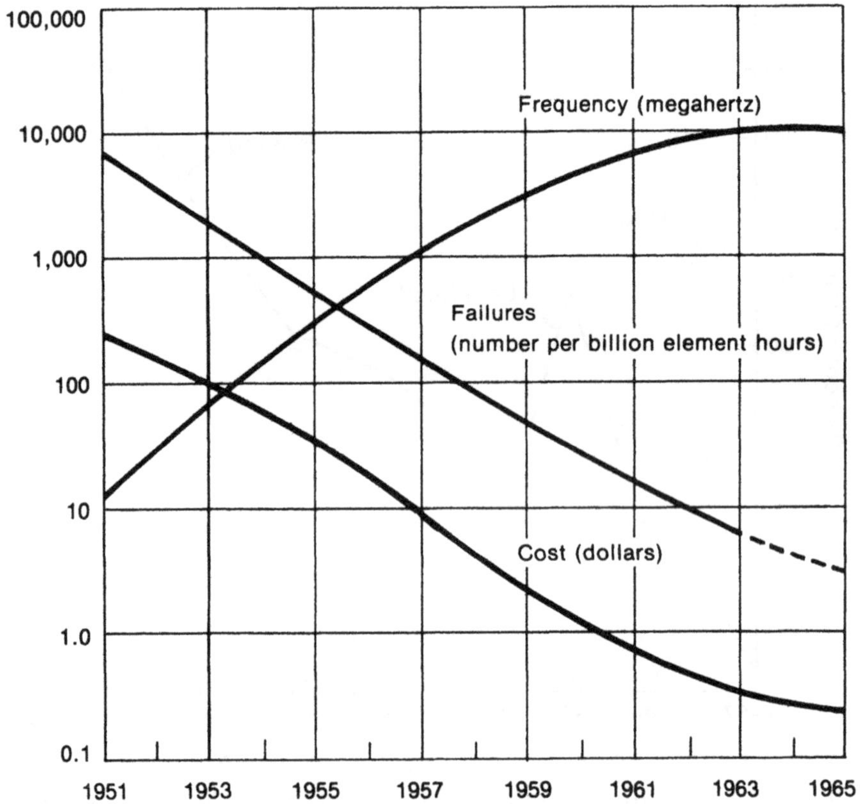

Figure 14. Transistor performance and costs in the United States, 1951-1965. From W. C. Hittinger and M. Sparks, "Integrated Circuits," *Bell Laboratories Record* 44:295 (October-November 1966). Copyright 1966, Bell Telephone Laboratories, Inc., used by permission.

financed by, and became a wholly owned subsidiary of, Beckman Instruments, a well-established firm in the field of scientific instruments. Shortly after Shockley Laboratories was established in 1954, a group of eight disgruntled young scientists resigned. These eight were convinced not only that they could reduce costs by one or two orders of magnitude but that Shockley was wedded to exploiting only the more expensive applications of transistor technology. Obtaining financing from Fairchild Camera, they successfully developed the planar process for lowering costs. So successful was their newly formed company that Fairchild Camera exercised its option to buy it. Some well-established electronics firms, including Hughes,

Motorola and IBM, also went into the semiconductor business by hiring solid-state physicists away from other firms.

Tilton concludes that one of the main reasons for the more rapid development of semiconductor technology in the United States, as compared with the countries of Western Europe and Japan, is the relative ease of entry in the United States.[49] In Western Europe and Japan, the receiving-tube manufacturers played a relatively larger role, and fewer new firms and new subsidiaries of other firms were established. Moreover, of the small firms established in Europe and Japan, Tilton was unable to find any successes comparable to Texas Instruments.

New firms were not only numerically more important in the United States; they also played a more significant role in enabling more or less continuous progress to occur. As Table 5 indicates, after 1955 new firms and newly established subsidiaries accounted for a significant proportion of the patents.

The fact that relatively new organizations played a major role in pioneering semiconductors suggests that the pioneering involved a good deal of uncertainty. Progress was not only "predictably unpredictable" in the sense that it was not possible to predict the next major advance; it was also unpredictable in the sense that it could not be predicted whether the advance in question would be brought about by one of the longer-established firms in the industry. Typically, newly founded firms are staffed with younger people than older, well-established organizations. And it is either the young and

Table 5. Percentage of semiconductor patents awarded.

	1952	1954	1956	1958	1960	1962	1964	1966	1968	Average 1952-1968
Bell Telephone Laboratories	56	46	26	17	21	12	13	10	10	16
Receiving-tube firms	37	38	54	50	38	31	38	41	40	40
New firms and subsidiaries	7	16	20	33	41	57	49	49	50	44

Source: John E. Tilton, *International Diffusion of Technology: The Case of Semiconductors* (Washington, D.C.: Brookings Institution, 1971), p. 57.

inexperienced, or the older highly experienced, entrepreneurs who are likely to possess the imaginativeness and flexibility of mind to deal with very strong uncertainties. When recently created organizations have played a major role in the evolution of a technology, this suggests an industry with a high degree of dynamic competition —competition whose basic purpose is to reduce uncertainty. And as Table 6 shows, the degree of competitive interaction, measured in terms of changes in market shares, has been high.

Table 6. Semiconductor market shares of the major firms, selected years, 1957-1966.

	Percentage of market[a]			
Type and name of firm	1957	1960	1963	1966
Western Electric	5	5	7	9
Receiving-tube firms				
General Electric	9	8	8	8
RCA	6	7	5	7
Raytheon	5	4	b	b
Sylvania	4	3	b	b
Philco-Ford	3	6	4	3
Westinghouse	2	6	4	5
Others	2	1	4	3
Subtotal	31	35	25	26
New firms				
Texas Instruments	20	20	18	17
Transitron	12	9	3	3
Hughes	11	5	b	b
Motorola	b	5	10	12
Fairchild	b	5	9	13
Thompson Ramo Wooldridge	b	b	4	b
General Instrument	b	b	b	4
Delco Radio	b	b	b	4
Others	21	16	24	12
Subtotal	64	60	68	65
Total	100	100	100	100

Source: John E. Tilton, *International Diffusion of Technology: The Case of Semiconductors* (Brookings Institution: Washington, D.C. 1971), p. 66.

[a]Market shares are based on company shipments and include in-house and government sales.

[b]Not one of the top semiconductor firms for this year. Its market share is included under "others."

It is impossible, of course, to compare precisely the degree of competition and uncertainty involved in pioneering semiconductor technology with that of pioneering automobile and aircraft technology. But there can be no question that, in all three cases, newcomers to the field played an important role in the subsequent evolution of the technology.

Dynamic Competition versus Automatic Progress

The empirical evidence presented in this chapter is by no means conclusive, yet it does call into sharp question some of the views expressed by Joseph A. Schumpeter in his *Capitalism, Socialism, and Democracy*[50] and by John Kenneth Galbraith in his *New Industrial State.*[51] As it happens, Schumpeter expressed very different views in his later writings than in his earlier works, so much so that one has the impression there were two Schumpeters: Schumpeter the revolter against determinism, and Schumpeter the determinist. Schumpeter's concept of entrepreneurship, as developed in his *Theory of Economic Development* (first published in 1909), is not a deterministic doctrine. Consider, for example, the following passage, in which it appears that Schumpeter anticipated the ideas of Thomas Kuhn:

> It is not only objectively more difficult to do something new than what is familiar and tested by experience, but the individual feels reluctance to it and would do so even if the objective difficulties did not exist. This is so in all fields. The history of science is one great confirmation of the fact that we find it exceedingly difficult to adopt a new scientific point of view or method. Thought turns again and again into the accustomed track even if it has become unsuitable and the more suitable innovation in itself presents no particular difficulties.[52]

And if entrepreneurship (whether in science, business, or politics) is described as an activity directed toward bringing about discontinuous change, then the entrepreneurship exhibited by Henry Ford and Donald Douglas and in the Boeing development of the 707 commercial airplane was entirely consistent with the ideas set forth in Schumpeter's *Theory of Economic Development,* which was initially written as his doctoral thesis.

Moreover, though Schumpeter believed that capitalism would evolve very differently in the future, in *Capitalism, Socialism, and Democracy* (initially published in 1942) his description of the role previously played by competition is in close agreement with the ideas contained in this chapter. For example, in contrasting the classical theory of competition with real-world competition, Schumpeter made two important points: first, "the problem that is usually being visualized is how capitalism administers existing structures, whereas the relevant problem is how it creates and destroys them,"[53] and second, "But in capitalist reality as distinguished from its textbook picture, it is not that kind of competition which counts but the competition from the new commodity, the new technology, the new source of supply, the new type of organization."[54] And when considering dynamic competition, whether in the automobile industry, the semiconductor industry, or the aircraft industry, both of these points certainly ring true. To ignore competition's role in the bringing about discontinuous change is to ignore its very essence.

On the other hand, Schumpeter believed that in the future the entrepreneurial function would become routinized. As he made the point: "Technological progress is increasingly becoming the business of teams of trained specialists who turn out what is required and make it work in predictable ways."[55] "Bureau and committee work tends to replace individual action."[56]

For his part, Galbraith has gone much further than Schumpeter with the proclamation that highly complex organizations are a necessary complement of modern technology. "More even than machinery, massive and complex business organizations are the tangible manifestation of advanced technology."[57] Moreover, according to Galbraith's second major pronouncement, the imperatives of technology require modern business firms to be even more able than the church in managing their demand. "From the viewpoint of the industrial firm, the regulation of total or aggregate demand is a matter of the highest urgency. Not only is it necessary that the public be persuaded to buy its automobiles, packaged cereals or household appliances in roughly predetermined volume but it is also necessary that people be able to do so."[58]

As evidence to substantiate his first proposition Galbraith points to the automobile industry, on the one hand, and to the military-industrial complex, on the other. However, the technology of the automobile industry can hardly be described as "modern" when, in fact, it was pioneered some fifty years ago. And while the organization of the automobile industry is extremely complex, it will be shown in the next chapter that complex organizations are not a result of modern technology, but rather a result of attaining a high degree of static efficiency. In other words, it will be shown that as a technological potential becomes more and more exhausted, more and more complex organizations are required to make the most of the remaining potential.

By contrast, military weapon systems tend to embody relatively new technology. And while the organizations are prone to be very complex, I shall argue in the next chapter that weapon systems developed by static military organizations cost *at least* twice as much as systems that embody a comparable degree of technological advance but utilize less complex organizations and procedures.

However, to appreciate that which is centrally wrong with Schumpeter's and Galbraith's argument, it is not necessary to become involved in a deep discussion concerning the nature of organizations. The first, principal problem with their argument is the tendency to associate entrepreneurship with a single individual, and assume that once it becomes a group activity progress becomes automatic. I doubt if many examples of entrepreneurship can be found that have not involved interaction among a number of people. This certainly was the case in all the examples cited in this chapter. And the reason should be clear: a highly interactive organization, in which hints for resolving problems can come from a variety of people, has a greater capacity for dealing with uncertainty than any single individual. However, unlike his earlier theory, Schumpeter's later discussions of entrepreneurship envisioned little or no uncertainty. Even before he wrote *Socialism, Capitalism, and Democracy,* Schumpeter had turned his entrepreneur into an innovator who put daring ideas into practice (as in the pioneering of the railroads).[59] However, because he could not explain why some entrepreneurs acted upon a good idea and others did not, his theory became, in effect, a theory in which those who reached great success were destined to do so, which is to say, it became a more deterministic concept of entrepreneurship than the one set forth in his doctoral thesis. And the only way to avoid this dilemma is to acknowledge that the type of organizational and social environment—whether highly interactive or highly structured—will make a great deal of difference in determining the extent to which Types 1 and 2 entrepreneurship are likely to flourish.

Outlawing uncertainty by imposing pompous preconditions on his subject matter is also a problem Galbraith has with his model, in which he replaces the closed system of classical equilibrium theory with a bureaucratically closed system: firms have no capability whatsoever to deal with unanticipated changes in their environments.

The second problem with the argument of Schumpeter and Galbraith is that there is no reason to believe any fundamental difference is to be found between the manner knowledge is generated today and the manner it was generated in, say, 1900. Sadi Carnot's theory (1827) on the efficiency of machines has never been repealed. And to bring about significant improvements in the efficiency of machines is quite as uncertain a business today as it ever was. Likewise, quite as much ingenuity is involved in overcoming scaling difficulties today as in the time of Galileo. And it hardly can be argued that engineers today are better able to deal with uncertainty than they once were.

To be sure, it might seem that because a highly disciplined organization like NASA can get an astronaut to the moon, engineers ought to be able to make discoveries on order. Indeed, if fifty billion dollars were made available there probably would be no technological feat that could not be made quite as predictable as traveling to the moon. The main reason technology is so unpredictable is the necessity of keeping within tight cost constraints. And from that point of view, the pioneering of the automobile involved a higher degree of unpredictability than did the journey to the moon.

The third problem with the Schumpeter-Galbraith thesis is a lack of evidence supporting the idea that the incentive provided by competition is being replaced by the institutionalization of progress in the technostructure. Now it is true that even if the degree of competitive interaction fell to zero some progress would still occur, because if the top management did not continue to swell the ranks of the technostructure by advancing people who have somewhat new ideas, it would risk having the technostructure take over control completely. Therefore, a positive rate of progress is an organizational imperative. But though the rate of progress during the Middle Ages was not zero, it was (as Oswald Merriman, my history teacher at Harvard, was wont to say), "Slow, slow, slow—almost unbelievably slow."

It is also true that there is no particular virtue in a higher rather than a lower rate of progress. For example, if the workers in the United States could somehow be persuaded to accept their lot and not to bargain for higher real wages, there would be no particular virtue in a higher rather than a lower rate of productivity-increase. Or if cleaning up the environment were as simple to accomplish as cleaning a room, the rate of progress in dealing with environmental degradation would be no serious issue.

If we grant that for the foreseeable future the rate of progress will matter, then how is it likely to be affected by the degree of competitive interaction? While by no means conclusive, the case studies presented here clearly indicate that the greater the degree of competitive interaction, the greater is likely to be the rate of progress (and vice versa). And although more evidence will be required to confirm my hypothesis, the only case I have been able to uncover to date that might be said to support the Schumpeter-Galbraith automatic progress hypothesis is AT&T, whose degree of competitive interaction with other telephone companies is probably close to zero. But as Figure 15 shows, measured in terms of rate reductions for long distance and international telephone calls, the rate of progress has been very impressive.

Now it can be argued that, since it takes the rate-making authorities a long time to reduce long distance and international rates in response to reductions in costs, the mechanism of risk internalization is at work, because the company has a special incentive to keep one step ahead of the ratemakers. And in support of this hypothesis it can be pointed out that, despite the fact that local calls constitute the lion's share of the business, Bell Telephone's main research emphasis has not been in improving the quality nor in reducing the cost of local phone services. Furthermore, it also can be argued that AT&T has faced competition in the fields of communications satellites and underseas telephone cables. But even though AT&T's progress has not been as automatic as it may seem, to my knowledge there is only one industrial laboratory that has long enjoyed the autonomy of Bell Telephone Labs.

In short, it is my contention that, statistically speaking, the degree of competitive interaction and the rate of progress are intimately related. Furthermore, I see no reason why competition should become a less important determinant of the rate of progress in the future than it has been in the past. Bringing about significant advances is just as uncertain a business as it ever was. And unless prodded by competitors firms are not likely to take uncertainty into account. Indeed, to assert that firms will act upon technological

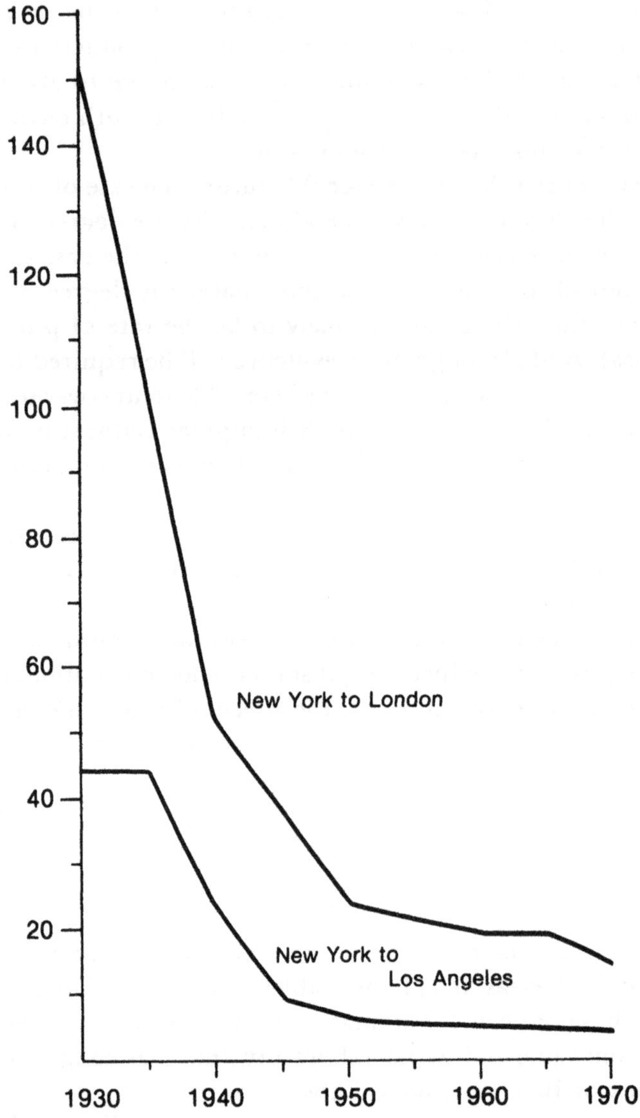

Figure 15. Long distance telephone rates (5 minutes, person to person), 1930-1970. From American Telephone and Telegraph Co., Statistical Reports Division, January 1974.

risks when there are no competitive risks is to declare there has been a change in human nature!

Of course, whether the argument of Galbraith and Schumpeter is right or wrong depends on how it is interpreted. If it is interpreted to mean that with no competition the rate of progress would be as it was during the Middle Ages then the argument is correct. On the other hand, if it is interpreted to mean that with no competition we can enjoy the rate of progress as occurred in the past, then both the evidence and common sense suggest it is wrong.

6. Microbehavior and Macroperformance

Suppose that an industry is in a dynamic equilibrium, in which the propensity for risk taking, as measured by the size of the advance sought, remains constant. And also suppose that firms in the industry have become fully adjusted to dealing with the uncertainty involved. In this chapter the relationship between the macroperformance of an industry (as measured in terms of the rate of smooth progress) and the corresponding ability of firms to deal with uncertainty (as determined by their internal characteristics) will be examined. To some extent this topic was anticipated in the previous discussion. In particular we have seen:

1. The rate at which firms demand progress from each other (by imposing large or small risks upon each other) is determined by the degree of competitive interaction.
2. The higher the rate of progress and the more emphasis on dynamic efficiency, the greater will be the degree to which entrepreneurial organizations will try to change technological environment (for example, as occurred during the pioneering stage of automobile technology); and the greater will be the degree of openness displayed in changing a technology.
3. The rate at which firms can supply progress is determined by the diversity of not only their people but also their internal interactions; and the more uncertainty that is involved, the greater will be the requirement for both types of diversity.

In order to more deeply understand the relationship between microbehavior and macroperformance there must be further clarification, on the one hand, of the relationship between uncertainty and openness from the point of view of conserving the ability of firms to more or less continuously adapt to new circumstances and, on the other, of the relationship between the optimal degree of openness and the optimal degree of organization from a statistical point of view. It is essential to think of organizations in statistical terms, because luck and luck alone can play a major role in making discoveries. And as will be shown, an organization "optimized for a high degree of uncertainty" is one in which outcomes are not highly sensitive to luck alone. How can it be known beforehand whether a particular organization is optimized for a high or a low degree of uncertainty? Though the science of measuring organizational characteristics is in its infancy, I will provide indicators of the degree of openness. And in the last part of this chapter I will point out the similarities and differences between my point of view and that taken by other authors who have found that the internal characteristics of firms are affected by the degree of uncertainty in their environments.

Two Kinds of Evolution

Generally speaking, there are two kinds of economic evolution: one involving major dilemmas (fast history) and the other involving minor dilemmas (slow history). The first takes the form of pioneering new technologies, for example, as automobile technology was pioneered in the period 1900 to 1925. And the second takes the form of making best use of an existing technology. In other words, whereas the first type of evolution is mainly (though not entirely) concerned with discovering and resolving dilemmas, the second is mainly (though not entirely) concerned with solving problems.

Therefore, to understand that these are basically different types of evolution it is essential to appreciate the difference between problems and dilemmas. As defined in the *Oxford Universal Dictionary,* a dilemma is a "choice between two (or, loosely, several) alternatives which are equally unfavorable; a position of doubt or perplexity." Now, if the entrepreneur could do nothing to change the alternatives in question, and had to choose one or the other, he would be faced with a "true" dilemma: a dilemma that could be resolved only by selecting one or the other alternative. For example, a person in a terminal state of cancer, who has to choose between an early death and having his life artificially prolonged, is faced with a true dilemma. On the other hand, there are many dilemmas that can be described as apparent (or seeming) dilemmas: the person in the dilemma need not take the initial two alternatives as givens and may resolve the dilemma with the discovery of additional alternatives. For example, a person who has to choose between a divorce and getting along with his mother-in-law may be dealing with an apparent, rather than a true, dilemma; the dilemma might be resolved by moving to another country.

When scientists and engineers speak of dealing with dilemmas, they have in mind apparent, rather than real, dilemmas. For example, a scientist who feels he has to choose between clinging to an unsatisfactory theory and changing his profession may be dealing with an apparent, rather than a real, dilemma; that is, he may be able to discover a theory that will make good predictions. And entrepreneurs, when they are trying to decide between the technological risk involved in making an ambitious advance that cannot be made on the basis of current knowledge and the competitive risk of having a market stolen away, often describe their plight as "being on the horns of a dilemma." But, again, this may turn out to be an apparent, rather than a true, dilemma: they may overcome the dilemma by finding a way to make a quite impressive advance. Dealing with a dilemma means not taking the initial alternatives as givens, but instead trying to devise a theory that will change the initial conditions.

Why do creative scientists and engineers say that dealing with dilemmas is entirely different from dealing with problems? A problem, as it is usually defined, is "a question proposed for solution." And when dealing with a problem the important factor is being able to arrive at an acceptable answer. On the other hand, when dealing with a dilemma, the important factor is explaining why an existing theory is not satisfactory. For example, when an aircraft developer asks why it is not possible for a competitor to obtain a larger reduction in costs, he is really asking why an existing theory is unsatisfactory. And in this activity, success is highly dependent on asking the right questions. Indeed, for this reason, creative scientists and engineers often say that more than half of the battle in overcoming a dilemma is understanding it. And no doubt Pasteur meant much the same when he said, "Chance favors a prepared mind." Once dilemmas are understood, fortuitous events can play a larger role in their resolution.

According to Freudian psychology, people's personalities and basic beliefs are formed to such a large degree during early childhood that they simply cannot interact with an environment to change both their ideas and the environment. Chance, according to Freud's famous experiments, can play no role at all in human development; and if troubled with a major dilemma, a person's only hope is to see his psychiatrist! However, influenced in part by biologists, a number of psychologists have begun to break away from Frued's highly deterministic doctrine. Abraham Maslow is generally regarded as one of the leaders in modern psychology, and his description of "self-actualizing" people should help to make clear that to display a high degree of openness in changing an environment people must have a good deal of self-confidence.

> It was found that self-actualizing people distinguished far more easily than most the fresh, concrete, and idiographic from the generic, abstract, and rubricized. The consequence is that they live more in the real world of nature than in the man-made mass of concepts, abstractions, expectations, beliefs, and stereotypes that most people confuse with the world . . . These people, it is true, are the intellectuals, the researchers, and the scientists, so that perhaps the major determinant here is intellectual power. And yet we all know how many scientists with high IQ, through timidity, conventionality, anxiety, or other character defects, occupy themselves exclusively with what is known, with polishing it, arranging and rearranging it, classifying it, and otherwise puttering with it instead of discovering, as they are supposed to do.[1]

Because people differ in their openness, their reference scales for judging the size of a particular discontinuity will not be the same. For example, to a specialist working with a well-defined scientific paradigm, a significant change in that theory will seem to involve a far more serious dilemma than it will to a novice in the field. In perhaps nine out of ten cases, the specialist has a lower degree of openness—that is the price one must pay to become a specialist. Indeed, differences in degree of openness, and hence in reference scales, may be the fundamental reason for Thomas Kuhn's observation that in science the outstanding contributions have mainly been made by newcomers: either by young scientists in their early twenties or by scientists who have changed fields.[2] What Kuhn calls "revolutionary science" is not so revolutionary to the scientists who bring about the revolutions as it is to those whose worlds have suddenly become shattered. Thus, what is revolutionary science to a specialist may be normal science to a Watson and Crick!

Organizations also differ substantially in their reference scales. For example, people in the Ford Motor Company speak of the Mustang as if it involved a technological revolution. On the other hand, to people in the computer industry an advance of this scale would seem quite insignificant.

Why have new technological paradigms come mainly from outsiders? Part of the reason is that the dominant firms in an industry exhibit a low degree of openness. They also may be more cautious about taking risks than outsiders. A low degree of openness and an unwillingness to take risks are associated characteristics.

What is the significance of a society's having people with a high degree of openness? Suppose that people could engage only in highly predictable types of evolution; suppose, for example, that for all people rational behavior consisted of becoming more and more specialized in terms of a given environment. In such a world, what capability would people have for dealing with new circumstances brought about by unexpected changes in their environments? For example, if they had taken their environment as a given, what ability would entrepreneurs in the automobile industry have had for dealing with the many changes in their technological and organizational environments that no one could have foreseen as of 1900? How, if the degree of openness were close to zero, would it have been possible to pioneer the development of commerical aircraft? And how are countries to deal with environmental degradation and rapidly increasing fuel prices if they have an almost zero capability to deal with new circumstances? Only by possessing imaginative entepreneurs, who can generate new ideological mutations, can societies hope to evolve in the face of new circumstances.

The discovery that man must be able to deal with quite unpredictable changes in his environment, if he is to make his future more predictable, is not new. In the nineteenth century, biologists commonly believed all evolution was Darwinian: that every species became increasingly specialized within a given environment. But today it is believed that evolution has given man an openness, the contrary of specialization, which enables him to deal successfully with changes in his environment. C. C. Darlington, a modern geneticist, makes this point as follows:

> Breeding varies . . . between the opposite poles of inbreeding and outbreeding. With inbreeding, heredity is all-powerful; determination is absolute: the group, the population, the caste or the race are invariable; they can be destroyed or removed but if they remain nothing can change them. With outbreeding heredity disintegrates; recombination produces unpredictable variability, endless innovation. Uncertainty, organized uncertainty, dominates not the organism but the population; determination in controlling evolution is transferred to the selective power of the environment. Between these two extremes, it now appears, every species of animal and plant is adapted to preserve some kind of balance.[3]

The seminal idea upon which modern biology is based was anticipated by several eighteenth-century intellectuals. As the following quotation indicates, Adam Smith himself was well aware of the limitations of specialization:

> The common ploughman, though generally regarded as the pattern of stupidity and ignorance, is seldom defective in his judgment and discretion. He is less accustomed, indeed, to social intercourse than the mechanic who lives in the town. His voice and language are more uncouth . . . His understanding, however, being accustomed to consider a greater variety of objects, is generally much superior to that of the other, whose whole attention from morning to night is commonly occupied in performing one or two very simple operations.[4]

Thomas Jefferson, a farmer, was more radical than Adam Smith. Unlike other writers during the Age of Enlightenment, he did not believe that man was so enlightened that no further enlightenment was possible. Consider, for example, his letter to William Green Munford, a student at William and Mary College:

> I join you . . . in branding as cowardly the idea that the human mind is incapable of further advances. This is precisely the doctrine which the present despots of the earth are inculcating, and their friends here re-echoing; and applying especially to religion and politics: "that it is not possible that anything better will be discovered than what was known by our fathers." . . . To preserve the freedom of the human mind and freedom of the press, every

> spirit should be ready to devote itself to martyrdom; for as long as we may think as we will, and speak as we think the condition of man will proceed in improvement.[5]

Moreover, although the Declaration of Independence proclaimed that all men were created equal, Jefferson's beliefs later changed. He ultimately concluded that in imaginativeness and willingness to face reality people were by no means equal. And to emphasize this point he made the distinction between the "natural" and the "artificial" aristocracy. Not surprisingly, Jefferson also believed that the test of democratic societies was the ability to evolve in the face of new circumstances. This is indicated in his oft-quoted statement on constitutions:

> Some men look at Constitutions with sanctimonious reverence, and deem them like the ark and the covenant, too sacred to be touched. They ascribe to the men of the preceeding age a wisdom more than human, and suppose what they did beyond amendment. I know that age well; I belonged to it and worked with it. It deserved well of its country . . . But I know also, that laws and institutions must go hand in hand with the progress of the human mind. As that becomes more developed, more enlightened, as new discoveries are made, new truths disclosed, and manners and opinions change with the change in circumstances, institutions must advance to keep up with the times.[6]

Perhaps the best statement about his theory of democracy is to be found in his essay *The Earth Belongs to the Living,* where Jefferson urged that each generation has the right to establish its own constitution. And in effect, he argued that a society that placed minimal constraints on freedom of choice when adjusting to new circumstances existed for the living; while a society in which the vested interests place a high degree of constraint on unpredictable behavior existed for the dead.[7]

What was to prevent societies from becoming so structured in terms of the past that they could not exist for the living? To keep societies sufficiently interactive and prevent that from happening Jefferson preached for a small revolution every twenty years. The role of a small revolution every twenty years was to prevent larger revolutions later, and to permit societies to conserve, more or less continuously, their ability to engage in unpredictable behavior, which is to say, their ability to adapt to new circumstances.

In brief, although the concept of an open system had not been discovered as of the time Jefferson wrote, it is apparent that Jefferson's theory of democracy was implictly based on that concept. The essence of an open-system concept of democracy is the recognition of a reciprocal relationship between individuals and a highly interactive society. On the one hand, this relationship fosters the development of the individual and encourages the discovery of new ideas. On the other hand, a society that can generate a diversity of new ideas is better prepared to deal with new circumstances. And it is not difficult to understand why Jefferson thoroughly appreciated this reciprocal relationship: no doubt, it was the type of democracy that flourished in America at the time we declared our independence from Britain.

It is important to keep in mind, however, that Jefferson's concept of democracy is not the concept that most people hold today. Rather, it is commonly assumed that democracy is associated with the right to vote. And the preferences in terms of which people cast their votes are taken as a given. In other words, the conventional theory of democracy assumes a closed system.

Which type of democracy is best? When there is no necessity to adapt to new circumstances, the conventional theory of democracy is best. On the other hand, if countries hope to deal with new challenges, Jeffersonian democracy is best.

Conservation of the Ability to Adapt to New Circumstances

Suppose that the rate of progress in an industry remains high over a period of years. What are firms in that industry conserving? They are conserving their continuing ability to deal with new circumstances. The individual discoveries that will be made are quite unpredictable. And some projects will turn out to be failures. But, if the industry as a whole continues to conserve its dynamic ability, it can be described as a predictably unpredictable system: you cannot predict how firms will resolve dilemmas, but you can predict that the dilemmas will be somehow resolved. To be sure, not every firm in the industry will display an equal degree of openness. But as long as one or another firm in the industry displays a high degree of openness, the industry will be able to do better than it could by having a revolution every twenty years: it will be able to conserve continuously its ability to adjust to new circumstances. And the scarce resource necessary for the industry to conserve its ability to engage in unpredictable behavior is people with a high degree of openness: Jefferson's natural aristocracy.

What, then, does it mean for a firm to conserve its ability to engage in dynamic behavior? As a result of a long-standing interest in trying to understand why some research-and-development organizations are more successful than others, I have found that the more successful ones defied what I had been taught about rational behavior. On the basis of classical theory, a rational planner would plan his system in detail from the beginning by taking care to make best use of existing knowledge. However, the more successful research-and-development organizations do not plan their systems in this way. Rather, they concentrate their attention on a few key features of the new system—and are very vague about the detailed optimization problems that systems planners are said to thrive upon. Indeed, the people involved insist that only amateurs start with detailed system designs. Professional planners do not make detailed initial plans, inasmuch as they assume that at close range all is not true; that is, they realize that everything they think they know is based upon an average of some kind, which can be proved wrong when applied to a specific situation.

Why do people who are engaged in creative activities proceed in this manner? If they had an unlimited ability to deal with uncertainty there would be no penalty involved in making the best guesses they could, and thence proceeding directly to the final design. But not only is the ability to deal with uncertainty limited. The closer a system is to a final configuration, the more expensive it becomes to make changes. Experimental models designed to facilitate learning about a few key uncertainties are obviously much less expensive to change than pre-production models. And if the system designer pretends that these uncertainties do not exist and goes directly to the final design, he will find that a favorable outcome of the project has been made not more predictable but *more unpredictable*. The most important fact about a world of strong uncertainties—a world in which there are no permanent truths—is that micropredictability and stability cannot be conserved. Only in a stable environment in which the probabilities remain fixed can micropredictability be conserved. Therefore, it is imperative to understand what is involved in the conservation of the ability to engage in dynamic behavior.

Organizations actually have a greater capacity for dealing with dilemmas than is acknowledged by Schumpeter's "hero entrepreneur." New ideas typically originate during arguments within a firm. Nevertheless, it can be safely asserted that as an organization is confronted with more and more uncertainty, its ability to deal with dilemmas will not only decline, but a point will be reached at which the organization will be overwhelmed.

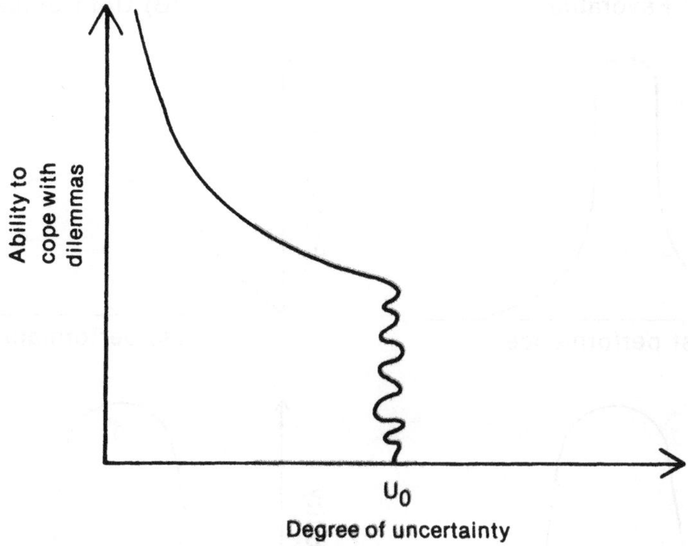

Figure 16.

Therefore, in order to survive, firms must conserve their ability to adapt to new circumstances. If a firm should decide to bring about minor advances when its competition is engaged in bringing about major advances it would risk going out of business. However, it also would risk going out of business if it failed to recognize that its ability to cope with uncertainty is limited.

What is involved in conserving a firm's ability to deal with unpredictability is the recognition of an uncertainty trade-off: the recognition that some aspects of a favorable outcome cannot be made more certain without making others more uncertain. Suppose that the outcome of research-and-development projects can be measured in terms of technical peformance, the time required to complete a project, and cost performance. Then it will be impossible to demand a high degree of certainty in any two of these characteristics without introducing more uncertainty into the third. For example, a firm might insist upon tight cost constraints and upon a reasonably definite date of completion. But, by doing so, the firm must be prepared for a high degree of uncertainty in the technical characteristics of the system (Figure 17 A). Conversely, if there is insistence upon freezing the design before it can be known which approach will be less costly, and if a very tight time schedule is imposed, then the cost estimates will be made more uncertain (Figure 17 B).

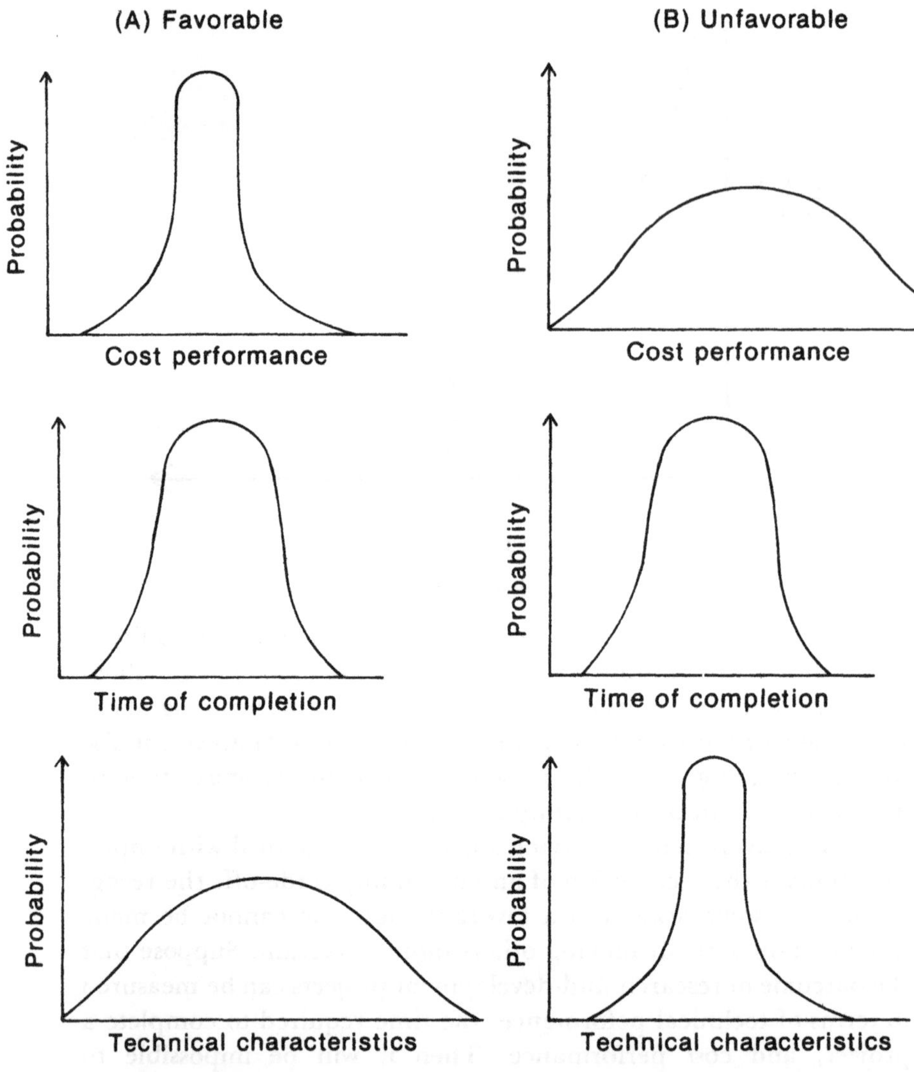

Figure 17. Outcomes with favorable and unfavorable incentives for risk-taking.

Now suppose that we observe a number of outcomes similar to those illustrated in Figure 17A. What can be said about the incentives of the firms in question? Obviously, in the industry in question a dynamic insurance policy was in operation, either because of a high degree of competitive interaction or because of other factors that have the effect of internalizing risks. As we already have seen, in the Ford Model T program there was a wide search for ways to reduce its cost. And the same occurred in the development of the Douglas DC-3 and the Boeing 707 jet. But engaging in a high degree of dynamic behavior to keep costs within narrow limits is not characteristic only of these particular programs; it occurs whenever the incentives strongly favor the internalization of risks. For example, Thomas Marschak has found that in the development of a large microwave-relay system Bell Telephone Laboratories imposed upon itself tight cost constraints from the beginning of the program; but at the same time, it was prepared for a high degree of uncertainty with respect to how costs could be held down.[8] And dozens of other examples could be cited.

Conversely, suppose that we observe a number of outcomes similar to those illustrated in Figure 17B. What can we say about the incentives? Obviously, such programs would have to be described as having incentives favoring the transmission of risk to others. A classic example is provided by military weapon-systems programs. Prior to the McNamara administration, the actual cost of weapon systems (including research and development, procurement, operations, and maintenance) exceeded earlier cost estimates by factors of 1.5 to 10.[9] And because contractor estimates of cost were regarded very suspiciously, the McNamara administration developed an in-house cost estimating shop for developing unbiased estimates. However, according to subsequent RAND Corporation studies, after adjusting for the degree of technical advance undertaken in weapon-systems programs, cost performance after 1960 was no better than it had been before.[10] But why should it have been any better? The best set of compromises can be determined only in the course of research and development. And no amount of top control over any bureaucracy can make up for poor internal incentives for dynamic behavior.

What makes for poor incentives is a form of risk aversion commonly known as the "requirements process." It consists of laying down elaborate technical and operational specifications before anyone can hope to know the cost of meeting these constraints. For example, trying to achieve the specified performance goals can make the problems of achieving a tolerable degree of reliability an order of magnitude more difficult, and triple the cost of maintaining the system in question. But whether or not an officer in charge of a weapon systems project gets promoted does not depend on how successful he is in minimizing costs five or ten years in the future. The type of behavior most likely to be rewarded consists of placing first priority on meeting the performance goals, no matter what additional costs might be incurred in the future.

Moreover, contractors have no incentive to keep costs down; quite the contrary. Once a two or three billion dollar commitment has been made to a weapon system program, they know the program will be very difficult to cancel. And since their profits are limited to 5 or 6 percent of total weapon-system costs, the more money the system costs, the higher their total profits. In other words, the making of large commitments has the effect of making all contracts into cost-plus contracts. And as a result of poor incentives, about three out of four weapon-system development programs consist of two phases: one to try to meet the requirement, and another to provide the system with a barely tolerable degree of operational reliability.

A good indication that incentives are poor with respect to cost performance is that practically every firm engaged in both military and civilian research-and-development activities carefully segregates these activities, and rarely permits the transfer of personnel from military to civilian work. Ask people engaged in, say, the development of commercial and military aircraft why these activities are segregated so completely, and they will tell you that making money in the civilian and military markets are two entirely different propositions.

How much does the requirements approach cost? Suppose that the initial commitments were for experimental prototypes, and additional commitments could not be made until these had been tested. And also suppose that the detailed requirement was left open ended, that is, to be determined in the course of development. How much money might be saved? Most economists whom I have asked this question estimate a 10 to 25 percent cost saving. However, the evidence I have examined strongly suggests that a very conservative estimate is 50 percent. As it happens, there have been some weapon-systems development programs that have met the two conditions set forth above. For example, whereas the Sidewinder missible (an air-to-ground missile developed by the Navy) met these conditions, the Falcon, which was developed for essentially the same mission under the requirements approach for the Air Force, did not. In this particular case the cost savings was larger than 50 percent. There also have been radar programs of comparable difficulty in which it was possible to make paired comparisons between those using the military requirements approach and those using the approach commonly employed in civilian research-and-development projects. And again it was found that the requirements approach more than doubled costs. In France, the firm of Daussault has developed fighters using a highly experimental approach, and comparing the cost of the Mirage series of fighters with comparable American fighter planes, much larger differences are found.

Over the years, some fifty paired comparisons have been made at RAND (part of which are reported in Thomas Glennan, Thomas Marschak, and Robert Summers in *Strategy for R & D*).[11] They strongly suggest that minimizing risk via the requirements approach has the effect of at least doubling costs.

Is the "requirements approach" to be associated only with military research-and-development activities, and its antithesis only with civilian research-and-development activities? It might so seem. But an examination of the evidence suggests a more basic distinction. For example, after World War II British military research and development was put under civilian control. Yet, in Britain, the requirements approach is even more stifling than it is in the United States. Conversely, when budgets were more austere in the United States during the 1930s, prototype competitions were commonly employed in the development of military airplanes. Moreover, in the Soviet Union, where military budgets are more austere and the threat of war is taken more seriously than in the United States, current military research-and-development practices are much like those employed in the United States during the 1930s, in the freedom given to designers and in the employment of competition as a common practice in development.[12] Indeed, because there has been little or no competition with the West in civilian technology, in the Soviet economy it is the military sector of the economy that supplies the dynamic element. And no doubt it is this contrast that made Nikita Khrushchev and others see the advantages of competition with the West.

In short, like other organizations, military organizations are strongly influenced by the risks they feel. To be more specific, let us suppose that the military services were somehow made to feel that prosperity is not right around the corner—that for the foreseeable future military budgets will remain as tight as they are today. And suppose that a law were passed that made it mandatory for the Secretary of Defense to cancel a project whenever the initial cost estimates were exceeded by 10 percent. Under such assumptions, there would be greater internal incentives to engage in risk-taking and a more rapid evolution towards the practices employed during the 1930s.

Conversely, what kind of behavior can be predicted in an industry if the degree of competitive interaction approaches zero? There is no reason to suppose behavior will be any different than it is in the military-industrial complex with respect to cost performance.

In short, for organizations to conserve their ability to deal with new circumstances there must be continuous pressure to internalize risks. Conversely, when the dynamic insurance policy that is provided by competition is withdrawn, we should expect in the civilian economy the same kind of cost performance observed in the military-industrial complex. It is impossible in a world of strong uncertainties to make some aspects of an outcome more certain without making others more uncertain.

The Optimal Degree of Openness

It should not be thought that an uncertainty trade-off exists only in research and development. *It exists in every activity in which there is uncertainty.* Consider, again, the matter of heart operations. It has been found that the successful recovery of a patient during the recuperation period can depend on a nurse's very quick decisions. In other words, if the patient's life is to be made more predictable the nurse must engage in some quite unpredictable action. A farmer desiring to increase his yields knows that if progress is to be more predictable his own life will have to be more unpredictable. When discussing the origins of the uncertainty principle in physics, Heisenberg recalled that during a walk with Bohr he managed to hit with a stone a telegraph pole a long distance away. Bohr's comment was: "If you had thought first about your aim, or about the correct angle of your arm and wrist, you wouldn't have had the least chance of scoring a hit."[13] Those who play golf are aware of the same phenomenon, and for the same reason: if the "correct" position is maintained at every moment of the swing there is no opportunity for making adjustments as the club approaches the ball.

The uncertainty trade-off exists even when there are only statistical uncertainties; but the necessity for unpredictable microbehavior becomes greater and greater as the degree of uncertainty increases. Take Mrs. Edna Blinker's macrostability objective, which is to live within her household budget and, if possible, put aside a little pin money (an entrepreneurial profit). Although her husband, Oscar, adjusts her budget to take into account changes in the average cost of food, there are large day-to-day variances. Because she continuously searches for hints about bargains, it can never be predicted what groceries she will buy on a given day. Consequently, she is a "predictably unpredictable system," subject to statistical uncertainties. Now, suppose Oscar truly loves microstability, and to insure that his own life will be made more predictable he adopts a "requirements" approach by insisting that his wife buy particular foods on particular days. He simply cannot demand more predictability in his life without introducing more uncertainty into the household budget.

What happens if Oscar's wages fail to keep up with the cost of living? Mrs. Blinker must be prepared for an even higher degree of unpredictable behavior (she must exhibit a higher degree of openness when searching for hints)—such as seasoning horse meat to taste like Irish beef stew. And what must happen if the housekeepers of the world are to keep up with inflation? They must cooperate with each other by competing to discover new recipes! Only in this way can they hope to deal with the risks of inflation.

What is likely to happen to wives if their husbands collectively adopt a "requirements" approach? They are likely to find that the stronger the uncertainties, the larger the cost of a particular type of constraint; because good new ideas are so scarce it is sometimes impossible to find an acceptable resolution for a dilemma. Therefore, if the husbands continue to add constaints they are likely to find they have driven their wives over the uncertainty precipice: driven them to the point that their ability to deal with uncertainty rapidly drops to zero.

On the other hand, it should be equally clear that if the wives impose no constraints upon themselves, neither will they be able to resolve any dilemmas. In order to make some quite unpredictable discoveries it is absolutely essential to impose a goal upon oneself that cannot be fulfilled in terms of today's alternatives. And such a goal can be regarded as a constraint.

A good way to describe the optimal degree of openness is as an optimal degree of constraint: sufficiently challenging so the person in question will be required to use his imagination, but not so challenging that he is likely to find himself bewildered by having to deal with too much uncertainty. And it should be apparent from the above example that the degree of constraint will depend upon the degree of uncertainty with which an entrepreneur must cope, as well as on his degree of openness. Thus, when the Mrs. Blinkers must live with a higher degree of uncertainty because their husband's wages fail to keep up with the cost of living, in the interest of preserving their macrostability objective they are forced to adopt a higher degree of constraint. On the other hand, it also can be assumed that to gain a higher degree of dynamic efficiency Mrs. Blinker has to give up something in the way of static efficiency. Therefore, there would be no point in imposing a higher degree of constraint if it were not necessary. Dealing with more uncertainty is not, so to speak, a free good. As we already have seen, it always involves a cost in terms of static efficiency.

To pursue further the matter of the optimal degree of openness (or, in other words, the optimal degree of constraint) let us consider a highly oversimplified illustration in which the uncertainty trade-off has only two dimensions: time performance and cost performance. Now, *if* the entrepreneur knew the uncertainty trade-off beforehand his problem would be relatively simple. Suppose that the uncertainty U associated with a favorable outcome of the dilemma A facing the firm is:

$$U(A) = KU(x_1)\,U(x_2)$$

where K is a constant (which depends on initial conditions) and x_1 and x_2 are the factors upon which A depends. For example, x_1 can represent the initial cost goal and x_2 the initial time goal for building the airplane. On the basis of this assumption the trade-off between $U(x_1)$ and $U(x_2)$ would be "smooth":

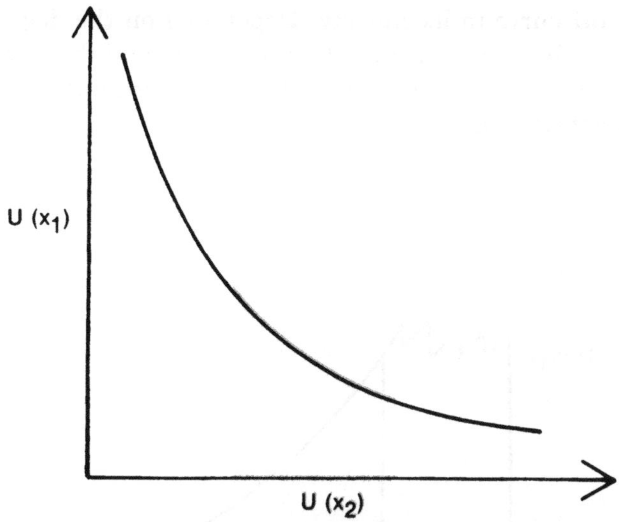

Figure 18.

The entrepreneur would only have to decide how much "time" was worth to him. However, while the trade-off shown resembles the one described in the uncertainty principle in physics, once humans are brought into the equation strong uncertainties are introduced, which is to say, life becomes more complicated. That the trade-off cannot be smooth where humans are concerned can be illustrated by the example of a contractor who desires to save time during the construction of a building, and thinks he knows the trade-off between his cost and time uncertainties. The contractor believes that with the addition of more and more workers his initial cost estimates will be made more uncertain, because the men will impede progress by getting in each other's way. In fact, he understands that, if enough workers are added, a point will be reached in which the outcome of their work will be totally unpredictable. He will have people hitting each other with shovels—a situation that can be described as an infinite amount of motion, but no movement. What the contractor does not know is *just when in the course of adding more and more workers the process will become totally unpredictable*. The world social scientists observe is a world of *strong uncertainties*.

When the uncertainties are strong, the entrepreneur cannot see the trade-off curve in its entirety. Depending on the degree of uncertainty involved, he is in a position to understand the implications of the trade-off between time and cost uncertainty only within rather ill-defined limits:

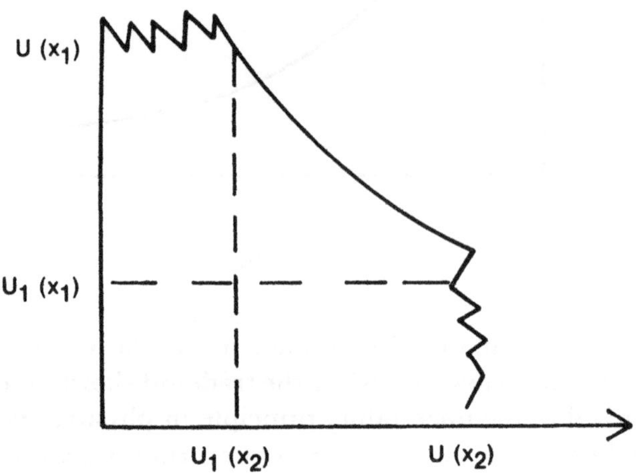

Figure 19.

Now, an entrepreneur engaged in developing a computer obviously sees a smaller portion of the trade-off curve than an entrepreneur who is trying to save time on a construction project. But regardless of whether the portion is small or large, the entrepreneur cannot, by placing artificial constraints on his freedom of choice, demand less uncertainty than U_1 (x_2) in his initial time goal or less uncertainty than U_1 (x_1) in his initial cost goal. If it is assumed that U_0 (x_1) is the maximum uncertainty in costs with which the entrepreneur can cope, and U_0 (x_2) the maximum uncertainty in time, then:

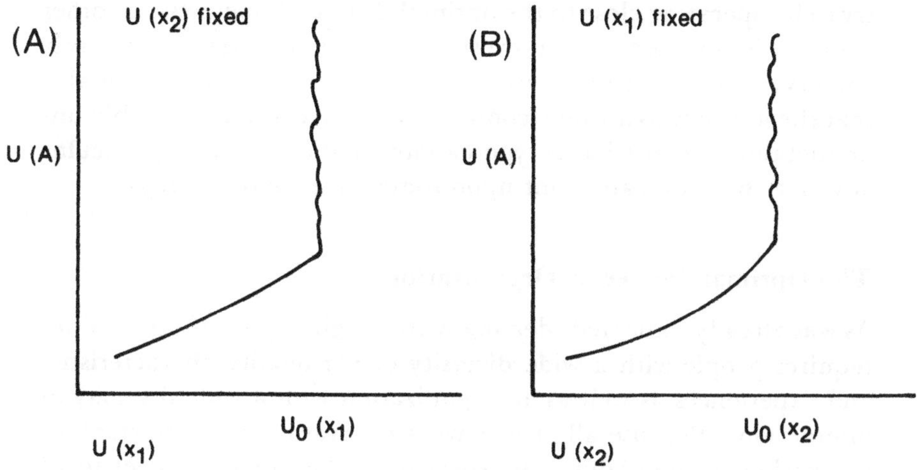

Figure 20.

It appears that the process of minimizing *U (A)* defines an upper and lower boundary for the optimal uncertainty in the cost goal and the time goal. Hence, a successful optimization process requires that:

$$U_1 (x_1) < U(x_1) < U_0 (x_1)$$

and

$$U_1 (x_2) < U(x_2) < U_0 (x_2)$$

However, it is important to keep in mind that the optimal degree of openness depends upon the degree of uncertainty. The larger the degree of uncertainty, the smaller will be the portion of the trade-off curve the entrepreneur can see; the smaller the degree of uncertainty, the larger the portion. Only in the limiting case of weak uncertainties will he be able to see the curve in its entirety. And while rational behavior does not consist of imagining less uncertainty than there really is, neither does it consist of giving up any more static efficiency than is essential to deal with a given degree of uncertainty.

This is not to say, of course, that at each moment every firm in an industry will be operating at the optimal degree of openness. Rather, it is highly probable that after a discovery has been made the discovering firm will suffer a decline in openness. For progress to be steady it is only necessary for one or another firm in the industry to be operating close to the optimal degree of openness. In other words, it is not essential that every firm in the industry continuously conserve its ability to deal with unpredictability. What is essential is that the industry as a whole continue to behave as a predictably unpredictable system (that is, you cannot predict the next particular advance, but you can count upon some advance occurring).

The Optimal Degree of Organization

As was already indicated, dealing with a high degree of uncertainty requires people with a wide diversity of personality characteristics and experiences as well as an organization with a wide diversity of interactions. Because all of us have a natural tendency to think of the world in terms of our own experiences, the wider the diversity of experiences represented, the greater the capability of an organization to deal with uncertainty; the narrower the diversity, the smaller the ability. For example, a university headed entirely by professors of Greek would have a poor capability to deal with uncertainty. And the cavalry survived three revolutions in military warfare only because the top leadership of the army was drawn mainly from cavalry officers.

An organization featuring quite unpredictable interactions is required to make good use of human diversity. It obviously is impossible to know beforehand just when a particular type of expertise might come up with a valuable clue. Therefore, the more constraints imposed on the internal interactions, the smaller the probability the organization will be able to generate a diversity of clues. This is not to say, of course, that organizations have not existed in which all the ideas came from one man. My argument is that, given the complexity of modern technological systems (for example, the automobile, the airplane, the computer) a wide diversity of people and internal interactions greatly increase the probability of discoveries.

On the other hand, it should also be apparent that an organization optimized for a high degree of dynamic efficiency cannot be optimized for a high degree of static efficiency. In static organizations the guiding principle is Adam Smith's principle of specialization, in which complex operations are broken down into relatively simple functions (for example, drawing the wire and cutting the heads in a pin mill) in order to minimize labor costs. And in a statically efficient operation not only is a wide diversity of people not needed, it is not wanted. An organization with a wide diversity of people will contain a good deal of conflict, which, while highly productive in a dynamic organization, is counter-productive in a static organization. In a dynamic organization people thrive on conflict. But in a static organization it is essential, above all, to keep up morale. Once the tasks are well-defined it is imperative that conflict be minimized, because a happy team is needed, with each person doing his or her part. And because it is important for morale, people in static organizations tend to dress alike and sing company songs. For example, visit executives in an automobile company and you will find less difference in habits of dress than you will find in a computer company. But this was not the case with IBM before it went into the computer business. Then, when its business rested mainly on a technology developed about the time of World War I, executives dressed alike and sang the company song, "Onward and Upward."

Another important difference between organizations optimized for a high degree of dynamic efficiency and those optimized for a high degree of static efficiency is that the former tend to contain more trust than the latter. This occurs because the role relationships are looser—and the looser the role relationships, the wider the latitudes in which people trust each other. In fact, all inventive behavior can be regarded as an externality that depends upon trust. And it should be apparent that if relationships are tightly structured to achieve results no worse than can be achieved in a zero-sum game, the results are unlikely to be any better. Conversely, when trust is present inventive behavior is more likely. Consider, for example, the playful and innovative whales of San Diego's Sea World. If a whale said to itself, "One unpredictable move and I will eat that man," if his trainer said, "One unpredictable move and I will kill that whale," the whales would never learn a repertoire of tricks.

It must be emphasized, however, that for trust to exist an organization must have a genuine sense of mission—for example, as people in the aircraft and automobile industries had when fast history was being made. It is the sense of mission that permits trust to exist and conflict to be of a highly impersonalized nature.

Conversely, in organizations that feature mainly static efficiency the relationships between the members of the bureaucracy must be more precisely defined, with the almost inevitable result that trust is always in short supply; that is, people trust each other within very narrow limits. This is not to say that many firms go as far as the Ford Motor Company did in the 1930s by way of setting up an internal security system. But organizations engaged in making slow history do expect obedience from their members. A company in the automobile industry today that featured the same kind of relationships found in the Ford Motor Company when the Model T was being developed would quickly go out of business. And the type of relationship that develops between the individual and the organization when slow history is being made is a reciprocal relationship in which the organization tries to protect the individual from change and the individual in turn tries to protect the organization from change.

To be sure, such a relationship may preserve the microstability of an industry at the expense of the macrostability of the nation. But, nevertheless, such behavior is highly rational: highly specialized people cannot easily adapt to new circumstances, nor can organizations composed of such people and of highly specialized equipment.

To sum up this discussion: If organizations are to deal with a high degree of uncertainty they must possess a high degree of openness. And the corresponding state of organization is the state of organized disorganization: a state in which the sense of mission provides the organizing element, and many quite unpredictable interactions supply the disorganizing element. On the other hand, if organizations are to be optimized to deal with a low degree of uncertainty and a high degree of static efficiency, they must possess a degree of openness approaching a semi-closed system in the limiting case. The corresponding state or oganization is one that features more methodical people and a type of organization in which the interactions are highly constrained.

It should not be assumed, however, that there are only two types of organizations: one optimized for a high degree of dynamic efficiency, the other optimized for a high degree of static efficiency. Rather, in terms of their ability to engage in dynamic behavior there is a continuum of organizations, from those possessing a high degree of openness to those whose degree of openness is just above zero. To make this point more clear, let us assume that a diversity-of-people index can be constructed on a scale from zero to one. When the index approaches one, the organization possesses a very high diversity of people, in terms of both their openness and their backgrounds. On the other hand, when the index approaches zero, we have an organization in which the people think exactly alike. They will differ in their tastes, but ask them for the best combination of inputs to maximize profits and they will all come up with exactly the same answer.

Let us also assume that a diversity (randomness)-of-interactions index can be constructed on a scale from zero to one. When the index is zero, the interactions are entirely constrained and the organization behaves as if it were a single person. When the index is one, we have chaos: all sorts of interesting ideas but no sense of mission.

On the basis of the foregoing discussion we can say in very general terms that the rate of progress (ΔE) is a function of the diversity of people index (D_p), the diversity of interactions index (D_i) and Luck (L), or

$$\Delta E = f(D_p, D_i; L)$$

Now, what happens to the organization's dynamic capability as it becomes more structured and, consequently, a higher degree of constraint is imposed on its interactions? If the D_i index were 1, the interactions would be completely unconstrained (that is, in an unorganized state of organization, *UO*). In this case, since only luck could bring order out of chaos, the organization's dynamic capability would be close to zero. At the other extreme (D_i only slightly above zero), it would have no dynamic stability, because only luck could save it if its environment changed in an unpredictable manner (the state of organized organization, *OO*). Thus the peak of the curve occurs when the organization is in the state of organized disorganization (*OD*):

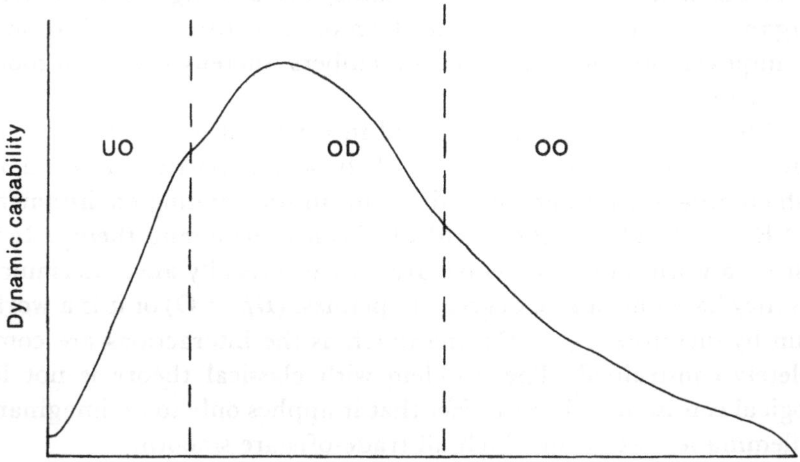

Figure 21.

The state of organized disorganization corresponds to the optimal degree of openness, because in this state there is so much randomness in their communications that the members cannot distinguish luck from any other hint! And it was probably this state of organization that Pasteur had in mind when he said "chance favors a prepared mind."

As the degree of uncertainty decreases, the optimal state of organization becomes more structured. If he were in the state of total disorganization (or unorganized organization: *UO*), a person who had lost his keys would impose no constaints upon his search party; that is, he would tell the searchers that the keys might have been lost anyplace in the world. And under such an assumption, the probability of finding the keys would be close to zero. A person in the state of organized disorganization would impose a higher degree of constraint on his search party: he would try to retrace his steps—but allow for some absentminded detours. On the other hand, a person in the state of completely organized organization would take a military requirements approach and tell his search party: "I lost them on this very spot; and don't stop digging until you have gone down a thousand feet." And again, under the assumption of strong uncertainties, the probability of finding the keys would be close to zero, because if the organization were so tightly constrained, it would have almost no dynamic capability. It is not surprising that an organization that imposes a very high degree of constraint on its members will behave in precisely the same way as a tightly structured organization. The basic purpose of a more structured organization is to impose more constraints on its members, thereby making it more predictable.

What can be said about a world in which all entrepreneurs can give very precise instructions to their search parties: a world in which organizations are optimized for an unchanging environment (ΔE = O)? This is the world of classical economic theory. It is either a world in which people are only technically alive, inasmuch as they have only a zero degree of openness (Dp = O) or it is a world run by dictators (D_i = O), inasmuch as the interactions are completely constrained. The problem with classical theory is not its logical consistency, but the fact that it applies only to an imaginary dilemma-less world in which all trade-offs are smooth.

Indicators of Dynamic Behavior

How can it be known if firms in a particular industry are exhibiting a high degree of openness? And what evidence suggests a significant decline in the degree of openness? Two good indicators are interactions with universities and subcontractors. When technological revolutions are at their peak, firms searching for ideas will interact with university departments in, for example, aerodynamics, chemistry, or computer technology. When the revolutions are over, however, the firms will become more businesslike; the university departments will become more academic; and within a year or two the interactions will come to a standstill.

Firms with a high degree of openness not only tend to do more subcontracting, they also tend to change subcontractors more often. Therefore, a decline in openness may be revealed either by more routinized subcontracting or by a decline in subcontracting. The underlying reason is, of course, a shift from dynamic to static efficiency.

Let us turn to the internal characteristics of firms. The assumption that "openness" and "creativity" are highly correlated corresponds with the findings of a number of post-Freudian psychologists. Their measure of openness is "tolerance of ambiguity." And they have found that while intelligence (as measured by the standard intelligence tests) matters up to a certain threshold (which is different for each profession), beyond the threshold, tolerance of ambiguity is a better predicator of creativity.[14] Not surprisingly, people with a high tolerance of ambiguity tend to have had parents who moved several times when they were young. They also tended to be people who were relatively late in deciding which field to enter.

It also has been found that in two highly dynamic firms tolerance-of-ambiguity tests were better predictors of who would make it into middle management than the standard intelligence tests. And again, the people in question tended to have had varied experiences.

It can be assumed, therefore, that when fast history is replaced by slow history, the more imaginative and flexible people in the leadership of the firm will be replaced by people who are more methodical, more prompt, more efficient in the usual sense of the word, that is, by people who have a lower tolerance of ambiguity.

As far as organizations are concerned, the best available indicator of dynamic behavior is the randomness of communications. Organizations that excell in dynamic behavior tend to be like New York City under La Guardia: you never could predict whom he would be seeing next. On the other hand, in slow-history organizations, the communications tend to be more predictable—going mainly up and down the organizational hierarchy. It can be predicted, therefore, that when history slows down, communications will be much less random.

There are also other indicators of a slowdown in dynamic behavior. Rarely in an organization that has lost its ability to engage in dynamic behavior will people say "I don't know." Conflict on how to achieve the broad goals of the organization tends to be replaced by a more personalized form of conflict. Being good at company politics tends to be more important if a young man hopes to be promoted. Humor tends to be replaced by politeness. What is important, above all, in a slow history organization is that people look busy.

Other Recent Studies in Organization Behavior

How do my conclusions on organization behavior differ from other studies completed over the past fifteen years? The highly static work of Richard M. Cyert and James G. March in the field of organization behavior has led others to conclude that organizations optimized for a high degree of uncertainty are not the same as organizations optimized for a low degree of uncertainty, which is, of course, a correct observation. But why are some economic environments more uncertain than others? The primary reason is the degree of competitive interaction, the imaginativeness of the people involved, and the ways they interact. Indeed, it is impossible to define an economic environment without reference to the people involved and their interactions. And the principal difference between my conclusions and others that will be cited is that whereas organization experts tend to take the rate of change in an environment as a given, I do not. I regard the primary driving force to be the degree of competitive interaction.

The Cyert and March Model. The following are some of the important characteristics of the firms observed by Cyert and March; they used the characteristics to develop their theory of the firm:[15]

1. The president talks only to the board of directors, his staff assistants, and vice-presidents. Vice-presidents talk only to their staff assistants, the president, and division managers. For many purposes the standard organization chart is viewed as a rule for commication.[16]
2. Our studies, however, lead us to the proposition that firms will devise and negotiate an environment so as to eliminate the un-

certainty. Rather than treat the environment as exogenous and to be predicted, they seek ways to make it controllable.[17]

3. Search is based initially on two simple rules: (1) search in the neighborhood of the problem symptom and (2) search in the neighborhood of the current alternative.[18]

In my terms, such firms would possess a degree of openness approaching a semiclosed system; and they would be characterized by so little randomness in their communications that they would be optimized for an unchanging environment. Apparently, the technological environment of the three firms Cyert and March studied—a large heavy-manufacturing firm, a medium-sized construction firm, and a medium-large manufacturing and retail firm—is changing very slowly. If firms in the computer industry had displayed a similar behavior, the computers that Cyert and March used for their simulation models would never have been made!

In short, the Cyert and March model is in the tradition of the highly deterministic organization model established by Max Weber.[19] An excellent example of Weber's ideal organization is provided by Swiss chocolate companies, which, before they diversified, were so structured that joining them was said to be like joining the Church. However, by stimulating sociologists, economists, and psychologists to ask of themselves whether all firms are like those they studied, Cyert and March have made a very important contribution.

The Burns and Stalker "Mechanistic" and "Organic" Firms. Tom Burns and G. M. Stalker selected twenty firms for study, some of whose technological and market environments changed very slowly, and others whose environments changed both rapidly and regularly.[20] Included in the former group were firms from a variety of industries. Included in the latter were mainly electronics firms. Not surprisingly, Burns and Stalker found that the management practices pursued by the two types of firms were quite different. The firms optimized for very slowly changing environments were described as "mechanistic"; some of their features were the following:

1. In mechanistic systems the problems and tasks facing the concern as a whole are broken down into specialisms. Each individual pursues his task as something distinct from the real tasks of the concern as a whole, as if it were the subject of a sub-contract.[21]
2. The technical methods, duties, and powers attached to each

functional role are precisely defined. Interaction within management tends to be vertical, i.e., between superior and subordinate.[22]

3. Management, often visualized as the complex hierarchy familiar in organization charts, operates a simple control system, with information flowing up through a succession of filters, and decisions and instructions flowing downwards through a succession of amplifiers.[23]

These observations closely correspond to my description of a firm possessing a high degree of internal structure and a small degree of openness. On the other hand, their description of "organic firms" suggests organizations with more openness:

1. Organic systems are adapted to unstable conditions, when problems and requirements for action arise which cannot be broken down and distributed among specialist roles within a clearly defined hierarchy. Individuals have to perform their special tasks in the light of their knowledge of the tasks of the firm as a whole.[24]
2. Jobs . . . have to be redefined continually by interaction with others participating in a task. Interaction runs laterally as much as vertically.[25]
3. Communication between people of different ranks tends to resemble lateral consultation rather than vertical command. Omniscience can no longer be imputed to the head of the concern.[26]

My main difference with Burns and Stalker is that whereas they describe two quite different types of firms, I think it is more useful to think in terms of a continuum—from those optimized for a rate just above zero to those optimized for a high rate of change. For example, I have read descriptions of French Canadian and Indian firms that make them seem even more mechanistic than those described by Burns and Stalker—more mechanistic because of the special constraints provided by the social environments in which they exist.

On the other hand, I have observed a type of research-and-development organization that is more "organic" than any described by them. This is an organization commonly known in America as a "skunkwôrks"—an organization in which the leaders operate on the basis of rough drawings (instead of detailed designs) and interact freely with general machinists (rather than production departments). The general theory of a skunkworks is that new hardware is not developed as it was originally designed, but rather it is developed on the basis of the knowledge gained from testing it. To be sure, it is necessary to start with a reasonably imaginative design. But the more time taken to design the system, the more complicated it is likely to be, the more difficult it will be to develop, and the more costly it will be to procure. Hence, the rush to get hardware into test at the earliest possible moment.

Skunkworks seem to be more "organic" than the firms described by Burns and Stalker. In the first place, such organizations are characterized not only by lateral consultation, but by an interaction between the top and bottom echelons of the organization. At one moment the chief engineer on an aircraft project will be arguing with some machinists. At another time he will be talking to one or another of the four or five people mainly responsible for the project. And at still another time he can be seen giving instructions on spot welding to some new workers. In the second place, skunkworks are probably characterized by more conflict and more crises than the organizations described by Burns and Stalker. One skunkworks director was asked, "When do you do your long-range planning?" His answer: "At seven o'clock every morning."

The term "skunkworks" was coined by Kelly Johnson, an aeronautical engineer who was responsible for the development of the U-2, and more recently of the SR-71 airplane that flew across the Atlantic in less than two hours. However, skunkworks existed long before Kelly Johnson. They represented the common method for developing aircraft during the 1930s. Being almost the direct antithesis of the research-and-development organization associated with the current automobile industry, the organization that pioneered the Model T was a skunkworks. And even earlier, as far as Thomas Edison or Charles Kettering were concerned, the skunkworks method of operation was standard operating procedure.

It also seems likely that if Burns and Stalker had looked into the pioneering of radar during World War II they would have found more "organic" organizations than those associated with the electronics industry after World War II. As we have seen, the greater the degree of uncertainty, the greater the degree to which individuals must perform their tasks in the light of changes in knowledge. And because there must be some driving force if the generation of a diversity of ideas is to be highly productive, the greater the advance, the more will be required of people of vision, that is, people who can somehow find ways to turn a challenge into an opportunity.

Lawrence and Lorsch: Managing Differentiation and Integration. Paul R. Lawrence and Jay W. Lorsch undertook their study in the light of the Burns and Stalker findings, which meant they assumed from the beginning that dealing with a rapidly changing environment requires a different type of organization than dealing with a slowly changing environment.[27] They selected firms in which the rate of change in the environment was quite different. The plastics industry was selected as a case of rapid change, the packaged-food industry as a case of moderate change, and the container industry as a case of slow change. The purpose of the study was to ascertain how two organizational functions—differentiation and integration—were affected by the rate of environmental change. Differentiation occurs when activities (such as sales, production, or design) are organized in quite separate units, and it occurs because of the advantages provided by specialization. However, each of these units tends to develop its own point of view. Hence the need for an integration function if the firm is to be successful.

It should be apparent, however, that the need for integration arises only because the outside environment is changing in quite unpredictable ways. Obviously, if the environment never changed, or if it always changed in ways that could be predicted, each unit could continue to operate as if it were a separate firm. Therefore the need for integration arises only when the environment changes in quite unpredictable ways and when the tasks of the individual units must be redefined.

In the following respects the Lawrence and Lorsch findings are similar to those contained in this book: First, they found there is a conflict between the degree to which the differentiation function is carried and the task of integration (in my terms the organizational counterpart of the conflict between static and dynamic efficiency): "The more differentiated an organization, the more difficult it is to achieve integration. To overcome this problem, the effective organization has integrating devices consistent with the diversity of the environment. The more diverse the environment, and the more differentiated the organization, the more elaborate the integrating devices."[28] Second, they found that the "more unpredictable and uncertain the parts of the environment, the lower in the organizational hierarchy" must be the "locus of influence to resolve conflict." This finding is in agreement with my finding that the greater the uncertainty in the environment the greater must be the diversity of the interactions.[29] Third, their findings with respect to the types of people needed in more or less uncertain activities are similar to mine: "Those in the plastics organization seemed to prefer more independence and had a greater tolerance for ambiguity, while those in the container company were perhaps better satisfied with greater dependence upon authority and were more bothered by ambiguity."[30]

On the other hand, there are two important differences between the position taken by Lawrence and Lorsch and my own. In the first place, I believe that the difficulty of integration depends not only upon the degree of differentiation in an organization, but also upon the diversity of people in the various units of the organization. For example, assume that the only people in a firm interested in what their competitors are doing are the people in sales. Quite obviously, the integration function will be more difficult in this case than in a firm in which several departments are keenly interested in their competitors' activities. In other words, the more specialized each of the departments, the more difficult integration will be. The second and more important difference between their position and mine is that whereas Lawrence and Lorsch tend to take the degree of change in an environment as a given, I regard the rate of change as a function of the degree of competitive interaction, as well as of the openness of people involved and the randomness of their interactions. The fundamental reason firms in some industries are better organized to deal with uncertainty than firms in others is that they have more reason to be concerned about the actions of their competitors. For example, I would assume that changes in market shares tend to be more pronounced in the plastics industry than in the container industry.

Alfred D. Chandler: Diversification and Multidivision Firms. Alfred D. Chandler, a historian, in his *Strategy and Structure*,[31] deals with the change in organization behavior after the pioneering of a new technology has been more or less completed. The firms he has studied in depth include DuPont, Standard Oil (New Jersey), General Motors, and Sears, Roebuck. In addition, he has examined some fifty other firms to see whether his conclusions apply to them. The general thesis of his book is that the strategy of the firm determines its structure. When the automobile industry began making slow history in the 1920s, General Motors was already a highly diversified automobile manufacturer, inasmuch as it was competing in all price categories. Moreover, General Motors was also characterized by a high degree of decentralized decision-making. In fact, as we have already seen, Afred Sloan, the chairman, had increased the degree of centralized control. On the other hand, as of 1900 DuPont was almost entirely in the explosives business, and, managed as a family business, it had a higher degree of centralized control. However, beginning about 1908 DuPont began to diversify by going into the artificial leather business, not on the basis of research and development activities carried on at DuPont, but rather by purchasing one of the leading firms in the field, the Fabrikoid Company. Then, in 1913, DuPont went into the pyroxylin business by building a plant, but because the technology had already been established the risk was relatively small. Following World War II, DuPont found itself with an enormous amount of excess capacity, and again there were pressures for diversification. This time DuPont went into the dyestuffs business, again using an established technology. It also went into the paint and varnish business, mainly by converting existing facilities.

In Chandler's terms, decisions to diversify a company's activities are "strategic" decisions. On the other hand, following diversification it was found that DuPont's decision-making structure was too centralized for such diverse activities. So a multidivisional structure was set up in 1921, with explosives, dyestuffs, pyroxylin, paints, and other products organized into separate divisions, much like the structure adopted about the same time by General Motors. Chandler has found this pattern of diversification, and the setting up of a multidivisional structure, to be characteristic of a number of companies.

In one respect, my conclusions are entirely consistent with those of Chandler. If a firm wants to continue to grow after it has become a static organization, continued growth can come about only as a result of acquisition. However, while it is true that the decision to diversify has an impact on the structure of business firms, it is also true that the structure of business firms has an impact on their strategy. Obviously, if firms remain dynamic they continue to grow mainly as a result of their own discoveries; for example, as the commercial aircraft and the computer industries have continued to grow. But even DuPont, which is more research oriented than most of the other firms Chandler studied, seems to have grown mainly by acquisition. And I suggest that it is the structure of firms that constrains them to engage in such a strategy. As in the case of countries, a relatively poor ability to deal with problems at home leads to empire building. For example, firms in the steel industry are currently diversifying by acquisition of data-processing firms.

Another difficulty I have with Chandler's argument is the sharp distinction he makes between "strategy" and "tactics." The top echelons of the multidivisional firms are said to be involved in broad strategic decisions, and the operating divisions in tactical decisions. The sharp distinction between "strategic" and "tactical" decisions goes back to theories of public and private administration developed during the nineteenth century, according to which the functions of making policy and implementing policy can be sharply distinguished. Thus, elected officials are said to be in charge of making policies, and civil servants are said to be in charge of carrying them out.

However, in practice it is never possible to sharply distinguish between the strategic or policymaking functions, on the one hand, and the tactical or implementative functions, on the other. For example, Napoleon's decision to put his artillery in front of his infantry can be regarded as a strategic decision because it changed the entire history of warfare—and it brought about Napoleon's defeat when the British adopted his strategy. On the other hand, it also can be regarded as a tactical decision, because, unless Napoleon's experiments with this new strategy had proved successful, it is unlikley he would have adopted such a strategy. The more general point, however, is that making good strategic decisions does not only depend upon understanding the big picture. The fact of the matter is that understanding the big picture is often crucially dependent on understanding a few, easily overlooked details.

The assumption that strategic and tactical decisions can be sharply differentiated is also inconsistent with the conclusions reached by Lawrence and Lorsch. Obviously, under such an assumption there is no need for integration. Integration is, in part at least, a function of bringing strategic and tactical considerations into harmony with each other.

Finally, still another difference between Chandler's position and mine is that whereas he tends to regard the survival of large firms as the survival of the fittest firms—"fittest" in the sense of being most efficient—in my view, firms can survive although they are efficient neither from a static nor from a dynamic point of view: they can survive by possessing a superior ability to manipulate their environments. Indeed, I suggest that the main scale-economy has to do neither with production nor research and development but rather with influence. Influence includes advertising and various activities to affect political decisions, for example, lobbying for higher tariffs or for loopholes in the tax laws.

Conclusion

As far as this book is concerned, understanding organizational behavior as a function of the degree of uncertainty associated with an environment is not an end, but only a means to understanding the relationship between microbehavior and macroperformance. So let us return to that theme.

First, the higher the degree of competitive interaction, the more uncertainty there is in the environment of firms; the more uncertainty, the more favorable the incentives for risk-taking; and the more favorable the incentives, the greater the need for openness, and the more rapid the rate of progress.

Second, if firms are to take advantage of the uncertainty trade-off, and conserve their ability to adapt to new circumstances, there is an optimal degree of constraint (and an optimal degree of organization) corresponding to every degree of uncertainty. The more uncertainty involved, the lower the degree of constraint efficient organizations will impose on their members; the less uncertainty, the higher the degree of constraint.

Third, when the degree of competitive interaction declines, firms will almost automatically become more structured, which will make them less able to cope with uncertainty. And the more structured organizations become, the more difficult it will be for them to become unstructured, so they can again deal with a higher degree of uncertainty. In other words, while not completely irreversible, movements towards a greater degree of structure are not easy to reverse.

Fourth, once there has been a decline in the macrostability of an industry, there is no automatic hidden hand for restoring its ability to deal with new circumstances. And only because of the creation of new firms and new industries have economies remained dynamic. However, sooner or later a stage of evolution will be reached in which the forces resulting in microstability will become dominant.

7. An Explanation of the Mysteries

The Trade Paradox

Why did the United States, during the period 1900 to 1965, trade with the rest of the world by specializing in the export of goods with a relatively high unpredictability content (newly developed technologies) and the import of goods with a relatively high predictability content (older technologies and raw materials)? For such a pattern of trade to occur, the United States had to have a relative advantage in organized disorganization, that is, in Type 1 firms that had a genuine sense of mission and, by virtue of being highly interactive, were able to generate quite unpredictable advances. Conversely, it must be assumed that the countries with which the United States traded had a relative advantage in Type 2 firms, that is, in "borrowers" that exhibited a lower degree of openness and a higher degree of internal structure. In other words, just as trade takes this form within a country, because there are advantages in firms being specialized in terms of the degree of uncertainty, so does trade take place between countries.

The 1900 to 1965 pattern of international trade was, however, very different from that described in the classic theory of competition. According to the classic theory of international trade, the basic character of nations is predetermined and cannot be changed by the trade in which they engage (an idea originally proposed by Rousseau in the eighteenth century and widely accepted by nineteenth-century economists and biologists). However, by accelerating the discovery of technological knowledge, the United States not only made possible higher living standards, by promoting the concept of consumption for the masses, but also advanced industrial democracy. To put the point very bluntly, had it not been for competition between new and older ideas—for creative destruction in the broadest sense of the term—in all probability, Type 4 rationality (the rationality associated with feudalism) would have become dominant. The British Industrial Revolution promoted democracy as well as economic progress by breaking up older forms of feudalism on the continent of Europe, and the United States did the same for roughly half a century by breaking up newer forms of industrial feudalism in Europe and Japan. This point is made by J.-J. Servan-Schreiber in *The American Challenge.*[1] However, the American challenge has had its strongest impact not on England or France but on Germany and Japan. In the latter countries, firms are far less authoritarian today than they were before World War II; and it may be assumed that competition with American firms played no small role in this development.

It is interesting to note that, shortly after the turn of the twentieth century, Louis D. Brandeis not only appreciated the relationship between competition and progress, but came close to predicting that the United States would lead in the promotion of industrial democracy. As far as Brandeis was concerned, the essence of competition was that it brought about progress: "Competition consists in trying to do things better than someone else; that is, making or selling a better article, or the same article at a lesser cost, or otherwise giving better service."[2] And he saw in competition that generated a diversity of ideas a way to introduce into industry Jefferson's concept of democracy: "It remains with this century and perhaps with America to prove that as we have in the political world shown what self-government can do, we are to pursue the same lines in the industrial world."[3]

The fundamental reason other countries had no need for antitrust legislation for many years is that competition from relatively unstructured American firms performed this task splendidly. American firms not only increased the degree of risk-taking in other countries, but, by widening the diversity of consumer goods, they also had a very profound effect upon history. Paradoxical as it may seem, although Americans only recognized that their country was a great technological leader and a world power after World War II, the United States' influence on the rest of the world was undoubtedly more pronounced when it was a so-called isolationist country. The explanation for this paradox is that, whereas competition in ideas provided a wide diversity of interactions with other countries, a foreign-policy establishment intent upon civilizing other countries in terms of its system of values can only succeed in isolating itself from the rest of the world. In other words, a nation can influence others only as long as it retains a relative advantage in openness.

The Growth Paradox

Why did seven-eighths of the economic growth of the United States, as measured in constant dollars, occur as a pure productivity increase: an increase that cannot be directly attributed to land, labor, or capital? Since many discoveries cannot be patented, and since the inventor seldom has the foresight or the bargaining ability to fully internalize the benefits, productivity gains represent, in large measure, a positive benefit or externality for society as a whole. In other words, such productivity gains indicate that capitalism is operating at a profit! And there can be no question that this externality is generated by dynamic competition—competition which, by generating new knowledge, can provide better results than can be achieved in a zero-sum game. To be sure, if one thinks of competition in static terms, the difference between a competitive and noncompetitive economy is equivalent to no more than a 10 percent, once and for all, increase in the GNP. Actually, A. C. Harberger has estimated that the loss of GNP due to monopoly would be closer to 1 percent than to 10 percent.[4] More recently, however, A. Bergson has produced a higher loss estimate than Harberger's, namely, 7 percent.[5] To be charitable to classical theory, I am willing to stretch the figure to 10 percent; in any event, the gains from improving all allocative efficiency of the economy are so small they are hardly worth worrying about.

On the other hand, unless one thinks of competition in dynamic terms, it is virtually impossible to imagine costs declining by an order of magnitude in a decade or two (as they did in the automobile, commercial aircraft, and semiconductor industries) without competitive pressures to internalize risks. And it is impossible to imagine that the United States' economy would have remained dynamic for sixty-five years if new industries had not replaced older ones when, in the latter, fast history was succeeded by slow history.

In short, from 1900 to about 1965, the United States led the world in dynamic behavior, with competition supplying the driving force. What is sorely needed is a good deal of historical research on how competition began in the United States, and how it spread from industry to industry. My guess is that the concept of technological competition is very deeply rooted in American culture. For example, in the letters that Thomas Jefferson, while ambassador to France, wrote to James Madison, he raised questions as to why the United States could not surpass European countries in various technologies. However, with relatively few exceptions, Jefferson's concept of progress did not seem to flourish until the Civil War, at which time there was a great deal of rivalry in agriculture: witness the county fairs and local newspapers. And because at that time a farmer had to be a jack of all trades, entrepreneurship flourished on farms. As result, beginning about 1880, cities and industries were able to grow by attracting entrepreneurs from the countryside. Thus, Jefferson's fascination with agriculture does not seem to have been entirely misplaced. Industries like the automobile industry were pioneered mainly by the sons of farmers.

During the period 1900 to 1965, the American economy not only featured more dynamic competition than other countries, but it undoubtedly led the world in subcontracting. Subcontracting has important advantages not only for static efficiency, but also for dynamic efficiency. The smaller the units in which competition can take place, the easier it is to enter an industry; and with easier entry, competition is more likely to thrive. Conversely, when subcontracting is replaced with vertical integration, the cost of entry rises, and competition is likely to be less effective. For example, in American aircraft production, the proportion of value added represented by subcontracting is almost twice that in British aircraft production. And no doubt this is one reason there is more competition in the American aviation industry. However, it should also be kept in mind that the British are at a real disadvantage when it comes to subcontracting. For subcontracting to develop, a good deal of trust is required. However, in Britain, manufacturers probably know each other too well to provide the appropriate degree of trust; that is, they tend to be so critical of other firms that they are unwilling to depend on them to deliver the needed component at the right time. And this disadvantage is likely to remain until British firms become willing to negotiate with subcontractors in other European countries.

Granting that dynamic competition and subcontracting go hand in hand, what, then, provided the United States with a relative advantage in imaginative, flexible, and practical entrepreneurs? For one thing, it can be taken for granted that the thirty-five million Europeans who emigrated to the United States during the nineteenth century possessed a greater sense of adventure than those who chose not to leave the old country, and that they consequently contributed greatly to the United States' genetic diversity. For another, the westward movement exerted an entrepreneurial drain on the more settled parts of the country. And it is no accident that the major technological revolutions in America tended to follow the frontiers. During the late nineteenth century, when the Midwest was seething with industrial revolutions, New England had already become known for its predictability. And later, when movies and airplanes brought the industrial revolutions to California, the Midwest was making slow history. Thus, the macrostability of the United States as a whole was maintained, because some regions specialized in more unpredictable behavior than others. And trade within the United States took place in terms of such specialization.

Moreover, the immigrants to the frontiers, whether from Europe or the eastern part of the United States, brought with them values that were highly propitious for a competitive society; they did not place as much emphasis on social position as upon actual performance.

It can be seen, then, that if dynamic competition is to flourish, risk-takers are required. And the United States became endowed with a plentiful supply of risk-takers by, first, the millions of nineteenth-century immigrants, and, second, the westward movement, which exterted an entrepreneurial drain on the more predictable sections. Finally, if a dynamic process is to occur, favorable initial conditions are required. These were provided by cheap land.

The Stability Paradox

What, then, is responsible for the worsening dynamic performance of the United States' economy, that is to say, for the loss of technological leadership and for the relatively poor showing in productivity? In manufacturing the United States' rate of productivity-advance has declined today to one-half that of Britain (see Chapter 1). And how is the stability paradox to be explained? According to classical economic theory, a more predictable economy is a more stable economy. Yet during her Victorian Age, when the British economy was more predictable and less dynamic than it had been during the period 1800 to 1870, Britain developed a chronic balance-of-payments problem because her rate of productivity-advance became the lowest of any major industrial country. At the same time, the British economy acquired a chronic inflation problem—chronic, in the sense that inflation could be cured only by unemployment. More recently, the British economy has been afflicted with simultaneous threats of inflation and depression. And now that the American economy has entered its Victorian age, by featuring the lowest rate of productivity-advance of any major industrial country, thereby becoming the most predictable major economy, it seems to be developing the same afflictions that are plaguing the British economy.

However, the stability paradox is a paradox only for those classical economists who steadfastly refuse to acknowledge the difference between earthly and heavenly stability. Once the logic of dynamic theory is appreciated—once it is appreciated that quite unpredictable discoveries made in the process of dealing with business and technological dilemmas pave the way for smooth progress—then the mystery disappears. More specifically, it is relatively easy to understand why: (1) there is a trade-off between "dynamic competition" and "unemployment" as an economic stabilizer: the lower the degree of competitive interaction, the more unemployment will be required to keep inflation within particular limits; and (2) with business firms and labor unions optimized to deal with a lower degree of uncertainty, the economy will not only be less able to deal with inflation and recession, it will have a lower capacity to deal with new circumstances in general. For example, an economy less able to bring about impressive gains in productivity is an economy less able to deal with environmental degradation or continuing shortages of fuels.

The Slowdown. Why has the dynamic performance of the United States declined? One important reason is the slowing down of the postwar industrial revolutions and the very profound impact this slowdown has had on the internal character of business firms. That technological revolutions tend to come in bunches is not a new finding. A number of distinguished economists, including Schumpeter, Abramovitz, and Kuznets, have given this as one of the main explanations for the long cycles observed in economic activities. The post-World War II industrial revolutions have been the most widespread in American history, involving synthetic fibers, plastics, television, microwave relay stations, underseas telephone cables, communications satellites, computers, computerized machine tools, semiconductors, jet aircraft, an entire array of new pharmaceuticals, and major advances in medicine. These and other advances have played a major role in the unprecedented period of prosperity the United States has had since World War II. Many people now look back on the period 1960 to 1965 as an economic golden age, when prosperity flourished without inflation. However, the point that seems to have escaped the attention of many economists and policymakers is that this golden age occurred when the postwar industrial revolutions were at their peak. President Kennedy notwithstanding, the country was moving very fast. And if my argument is correct, this golden age was primarily the result of a highly competitive economy generating a wide diversity of ideas.

To be sure, some of the advances in technology made during World War II (jet engines, computers, nuclear energy) helped to pave the way for the postwar industrial revolutions. However, more important than the technological inheritance from World War II was the people inheritance. The wartime Office of Scientific Research and Development, which played a leading role in developing not only nuclear weapons but also radar and the proximity fuse, was organized disorganization at its finest. And institutions like the Radiation Laboratory at the Massachusetts Institute of Technology, through their expertise in discovering and exploiting new technological potentials, helped train people to become leaders of American industry. One of these business leaders, Russel Varian, once confessed to me that the only other way a person could witness for himself the advantages of organized disorganization was by working on a farm—where life is also filled with surprises.

The fact that technological revolutions have been clustered in history does not, of course, explain why they eventually slow down. It is certainly conceivable that as rapidly as older technologies run into diminishing returns, new ones are discovered. But new firms play a major role in the discovery of new technologies—and there is no invisible hand to assure that they will be created as needed. For example, new firms certainly played a major role in the dynamism of the post-World War II economy. If our postwar prosperity had depended on the firms that existed prior to World War II, there probably would have been a major postwar depression—either that or much larger public deficits. However, while much of the dynamism of the present economy is to be found in relatively small firms and farming, new firms are not playing the significant role they did in the period 1945-1960; and it seems safe to assume that the primary reason is the shortage of risk capital. While I do not share the belief of some of President Ford's economists that a general shortage of capital exists, there certainly is good reason to suspect that risk capital for small firms is not as plentiful now as it was shortly after World War II. Risk capital for new firms has always come from private investors and not from the capital markets. And private investors seem to possess neither the liquidity nor the faith in the future of the American economy that they did in the late 1940s and early 1950s.

The dynamism of the American economy is highly dependent upon new firms, because the slowing down of the industrial revolution has had a marked impact on the character of those firms that participated in the postwar advances in technology. A decline in openness has caused large firms to become more structured and, as such, less able to deal with risk. Moreover, the change in internal incentives results in the selection of managers with quite different personality characteristics. And there is a good deal of evidence that imaginative scientists and engineers are being replaced by business school graduates and lawyers, that is, by people who perform the same function in modern societies as did genetic inbreeding in feudalistic societies. Once the relationship between microbehavior and macroperformance is understood it is relatively easy to infer changes in microbehavior from the macroindicators: lower risk in the environment of the firm indicates that the internal incentives will favor administrative managers, whose expertise consists of preserving the firm's history, rather than entrepreneurs, whose expertise consists of making new history. Observations by John Ruskin on the Victorian Age provide a somewhat more colorful description of the type of mentality involved in administrative capitalism: "In a community regulated by laws of demand and supply, but protected from open violence, the persons who become rich are generally speaking, industrious, resolute, proud, covetous, prompt, methodical, sensible, unimaginative, insensitive, and ignorant."[6]

Unfortunately, Ruskin could never bring himself to recognize that the type of person who succeeded during the Victorian Age was not necessarily the type who succeeded during the Industrial Revolution. Indeed, if the entrepreneurs of Birmingham, Manchester, and Nottingham had been as unimaginative as the types who succeeded them during the Victorian Age we can be quite sure that the Industrial Revolution never would have occurred.

What independent evidence is there to substantiate my claim that with the advent of the New American Victorian State, business firms no longer possess as high a degree of openness? One piece of evidence is the declining degree of interaction between business firms and universities. Beginning in the late 1960s, the deans of engineering in a number of universities began to worry about this trend. And for awhile they thought the problem was one of human relationships which somehow might be patched. But it is now generally recognized that when there is a mutual advantage in interacting, people will interact; and when there is no longer a mutual advantage, they will stop. Apart from the field of computers, the interactions are not nearly as intensive today as they were fifteen years ago. People in industry blame the universities for having become too academic; and people in universities blame business firms for no longer offering graduates exciting problems. And both groups are right.

Another piece of evidence suggesting less risk-taking in American industry is the fact that, since 1969, the number of scientists and engineers engaged in research and development has been declining. As Table 7 shows, while the increase was somewhat above 10 percent a year during the period 1957 to 1969, from 1969 to 1972 the total number employed declined by 10 percent. True, there was a modest increase in 1973, but this was almost entirely in the electrical-equipment industry, where rapid progress is still being made in computers and missiles.

Of course, a decline in the number of scientists and engineers does not in itself indicate a lower propensity for risk-taking. For example, the number could decline as a result of the weeding-out of less creative people. However, the evidence indicates that the decline was accompanied by increased internal rigidity and that

Table 7. Number of research-and-development scientists and engineers, by industry.

Industry	Number (in thousands of full-time equivalents)[a]					
	1957	1969	1970	1971	1972	1973
Chemicals and allied products	29.4	40.3	40.2	42.8	41.4	42.0
Petroleum refining and extraction	6.9	10.0	9.9	9.2	8.2	8.1
Rubber products	4.7	6.3	6.8	5.9	5.9	5.8
Stone, clay, and glass products	—[b]	4.2	4.6	4.1	3.8	3.9
Primary metals	5.1	6.2	6.3	6.3	6.0	5.7
Fabricated metal products	8.4	6.6	5.9	6.9	6.8	7.1
Machinery	24.9	39.4	41.4	40.5	41.1	42.7
Electrical equipment and communication	42.9	101.6	102.4	95.2	87.7	93.0
Motor vehicles and other transportation equipment	13.6	25.0	25.1	27.8	29.5	29.6
Aircraft and missiles	58.7	99.9	92.6	78.3	72.7	74.3
Professional and scientific instruments	10.2	15.1	14.8	15.1	14.8	15.8
Other manufacturing industries	} 24.6[c]	17.4	17.8	19.1	18.5	18.8
Other nonmanufacturing industries		15.1	16.3	15.6	15.9	15.7
Total	229.4	387.1	384.1	366.8	352.2	362.5

Source: National Science Foundation, *National Patterns of R&D Resources: Funds and Manpower in the United States, 1953-1974,* NSF 74-304 (Washington, D.C.: U.S. Government Printing Office, 1974).

[a]Excludes social scientists.

[b]Data included in the "other manufacturing" group.

[c]For the years 1957-1960, other-manufacturing and nonmanufacturing are combined. Other manufacturing industries include food and kindred products; textiles, apparel; lumber and wood products; paper and allied products; tobacco products; printing and publishing; leather products; and miscellaneous manufacturing.

recruitment of graduating scientists and engineers has been drastically curtailed.

There is also evidence that research and development has become a more controlled activity aimed at highly predictable advances. For example, a study by Edwin Mansfield, John Rapoport, Jerome Schnee, Samuel Wagner, and Michael Hamburger of research and development in the chemical, petroleum, and ethical-drug industries indicates, first, that during the 1960s firms in these industries became more and more loath to undertake research projects without calculating the estimated rate of return.[7] To be sure, research managers often regarded such calculations as window dressing. But they do indicate a growing distrust of researchers by the top management. A research manager in a large electronics company (not included in the above study) described his problem to me as one of mutual distrust between people at the top and those at the working level. The latter feel that the top management is failing to do its job by not giving them a good picture of the problems faced by the firm; and in lieu of the top management doing a good job, more and more controls are imposed upon the lower echelons. On the other hand, the top management feels that the working scientists and engineers are interested in projects more for their technical interest than their economic payoff. Second, and related, the authors found evidence of a low propensity to engage in risk-taking. For example, in the nineteen laboratories they studied, the probability of technical completion of a project was better than fifty-fifty; risky projects were not often being undertaken.[8] However, even more disturbing evidence from my point of view is the finding that in forty-nine projects there were large cost overruns (in the later 1960s, before serious inflation began) with the average overrun equal to 1.8 times the initial estimate and the overruns for more ambitious projects running to 2.3 times the estimate—about 70 percent as large as cost overruns on military projects.[9]

How are such overruns explained? According to Mansfield and associates, when the size of advances in commercial research and development approximates those in military research and development, the cost overruns should be the same.[10] However, inasmuch as more uncertainty presupposes a wider range of choices, there is no reason to associate large cost overruns with a higher degree of uncertainty. For example, because there was a great deal of uncertainty in the Model-T program, ways could be found to bring the cost far below the initial estimate. To be sure, in military development programs, cost overruns have been largest when the most ambitious advances have been attempted. But as we saw in Chapter 6, this occurs because the greater the degree of uncertainty involved, the greater will be the cost of applying technical constraints.

It may well be that in the ethical pharmaceutical industry constraints are applied to minimize health hazards rather than costs. However, while in this particular case there may be special reasons for not engaging in risk-taking that would reduce costs, generally speaking, cost escalation should be regarded as evidence of a low propensity to engage in risk-taking. And I have no doubt that investigation of other industries will yield similar findings.

In a more recent study of sixteen drug firms, Mansfield and Wagner found that research managers are often so preoccupied with the technical success of their projects they pay little attention to economic factors.[11] More specifically, they found that the probability of economic success is likely to be greater if (1) economic considerations are taken into account at a relatively early date in the program; and if (2) there is a high degree of integration between the marketing and research divisions. If we assume an industry with a significant degree of competitive interaction, these findings are entirely consonant with the major arguments of this book. In my terms, the entrepreneur acts as a marriage broker between what is economically desirable and technologically possible. And highly interactive firms are required to perform the entrepreneurial function. If they are to be successful, research people must understand the problems facing their firm. However, unlike Mansfield and Wagner, I doubt if the rate of technological change can be significantly increased simply by exhorting firms to be more interactive. To my way of thinking, such advice is more or less equivalent to urging a monopolist to lower his prices. And their findings that firms experience real difficulty in integrating technical and economic considerations suggests an industry in which competition is in the process of dying out.

To discover firsthand what has happened to risk-taking in large American firms, one only need visit a dozen or so firms that a few years ago were highly dynamic. A recently retired vice-president in charge of research of a large chemical company confided to me that only after reflecting for several months following his retirement could he admit that with as litle risk-taking in research as there is today, the revolution in synthetic fibers would not have been possible. "Suppose you had been more alert to the decline in dynamic behavior. What are the danger signals to which you would have paid more attention?" I asked him. His reply: "When everyone started to be so damn polite!" In another chemical company the former president was an entrepreneur of the old school: he believed chemists can discover changing needs only if they interact with society. But in that company this spirit reigns no more; now the research division has hired a team of psychologists to manipulate consumer tastes.

But, while I find such evidence of microbehavior is highly consistent with the changes in the macroindicators that have occurred since 1965, Mansfield does not. In fact, on the basis of the evidence he has collected, Mansfield has criticized me, among others, for having exaggerated the degree of risk-taking associated with civilian research and development.[12] And from the perspective of an equilibrium economist, he is entirely correct: conduct suggesting a low propensity to take risks is "normal" behavior. However, from my perspective, an economy with as little risk-taking as Mansfield observes is one that possesses a minimal degree of dynamic stability; that is, the quest for microstability is so great that firms retain little ability to adapt to new circumstances.

What would be the consequences for the economy as a whole if particular industries were to avoid taking risks? In an economic system in which the degree of interdependence is low, for example, in the United States as of 1900, the average degree of openness would be lower than it otherwise might be, and opportunities would be diminished for productivity gain and economic expansion. In other words, the effect would be the same as if an economy were threatened by oversavings. And to argue that the low propensity for risk-taking that favors the stability of the firm in an uncompetitive industry also favors the stability of a nation is to commit the same fallacy-of-composition error as in arguing that savings habits that favor the stability of an individual necessarily favor the stability of the nation.

In 1900, however, the American economy was less interdependent than it is now; that is, making substitutions was accomplished more easily because facilities were not as specialized for specific inputs as they are today. As a consequence, adjusting to new circumstances, whether by overcoming specific shortages of one kind or another, or by anticipating new types of consumer and business needs, did not have the ramifications as adjustments today. For example, today oil refineries are often so specialized in the type of crude oil they can use that merely changing the mix can cause serious problems. But not only are economies more interdependent. The new circumstances to which we must adjust—fuel shortages and environmental degradation—by their very nature will call for more general adjustments than those made in the past. Indeed, as a consequence of both the greater interdependence of the economy and the nature of the new circumstances, there is hardly any sector of the economy that is exempt from making adjustments. And if, under such circumstances, two or three large industries should be unwilling to engage in genuine risk-taking, they will jeopardize the macrostability of the entire economy.

An Example: The Automobile Industry. In Chapter 5 we saw how the automobile industry once contributed to the macrostability and, thereby, to the prosperity of the United States. But that occurred when the industry was highly competitive and risks had to be taken. What evidence is there of a further decline in risk-taking in the automobile industry, that is, beyond that which took place during the 1930s; and in what ways can the quest for stability, narrowly defined, threaten the achievement of stability, broadly defined? The following discussion is based on Lawrence White's book, *The Automobile Industry Since 1945,* and on interviews with people from the automobile industry.[13] Not only were those interviewed very frank in answering my questions, but they were very anxious to understand for themselves what was happening to the industry.

We have seen how price competition in the early 1900s was replaced by quality competition in the 1920s. Then, during the 1930s, when economists were busily engaged in writing about product differentiation, the theme of price competition was reintroduced, with not only Ford, Chevrolet, and Plymouth competing in the low-price field, but several other manufacturers as well. However, during the postwar period, what price competition there has been has come mainly from foreign manufacturers. And just as the steel industry introduced price leadership when it feared nothing more than unpredictability, so does price leadership in the automobile industry evidence a strong aversion to risk-taking.

However, according to the evidence gathered by White, price leadership in the automobile industry does not necessarily take the familiar form of the largest firm in the industry seizing the initiative and the others following suit.[14] Rather, it is a type of price leadership in which, while General Motors may not always have the first word, almost invariably, it has the last. For example, in September 1956, Ford was the first to raise its prices, and the average increase was 2.9 percent—with the largest increases on the low-priced models. On October 15 of the same year, Chevrolet announced price increases of 6.1 percent, but with lower increases than Ford on the low-priced models. One week later, Ford brought its increases into line with those of Chevrolet by lowering its prices on the lower-priced cars and raising its prices on the more expensive ones. A second example: In the fall of 1965, Chrysler took the initiative by announcing an average increase of $72.94. Shortly afterwards, General Motors and Ford announced increases averaging $58.68 and $67.88, respectively. As of December 1, 1965, however, Chrysler initiated a wholesale rebate program, which essentially removed the difference. A third example: Early in 1966, Ford anounced price increases averaging $107. A few days later, Chrysler announced a $92 average price increase, and General Motors followed with an increase of $56. Within a week of the announcement both Ford and Chrysler cut their prices, though Ford, in the process, made items like clocks optional instead of standard equipment. A fourth example: In the fall of 1967, Chrysler announced an increase of $147.94. Ford and General Motors followed with more or less equal increases: $115.28 and $119.97. Within a week Chrysler revised its initial announcement to make the average increase $115.82.

This type of price behavior is relatively easy to explain. Although Ford and Chrysler products are usually a few dollars more expensive than those of General Motors, larger differentials could be maintained only by shifting the burden to dealers, which in the longer run would jeopardize effective dealer organizations. On the other hand, neither would it pay to start a price war with General Motors—a war in which General Motors could outlast them. Hence, it really pays to allow General Motors to have the last word on price increases.

What can be said about competition other than price competition? The leaders of the automobile industry seem to believe that it is now quite as competitive as it ever was. And in a sense they are right: price and quality competition have been replaced by competition in "style." Alfred P. Sloan, Jr., the former president of General Motors has described this new trend as follows:

> In the course of time the product engineer raised the state of his art so high that he produced not only a superb creation but also a mature one, so far as the present type of gasoline-powered car is concerned. Now he devotes much of his skill to solving the prob-

> lems created by the stylist. The consumer recognizes this today by taking for granted the varied engineering excellence of all competitive makes of cars, and so his shopping is strongly influenced by variations in style. Automobile design is not, of course, pure fashion, but it is not too much to say that the "laws" of the Paris dressmakers have come to be a factor in the automobile industry —and woe to the company which ignores them.[15]

As evidence that Sloan is absolutely right about the plight of firms that ignore style considerations, consider the price paid by Chrysler when it ignored a new trend. In 1953 and 1954, when the trend in the industry was towards longer cars and larger tail fins, Chrysler made its cars short and boxy. And Chrysler sales declined from about 20 percent of the market to 12 percent. Then, in 1958, after having almost recouped its position by adopting the largest tail fins in the industry, Chrysler suddenly found that the new look featured cars that were larger on the inside and smaller on the outside. And its sales dropped from 18 to 14 percent of the market.

What the people at Chrysler failed to recognize is that once the designers think in terms of style, they appeal to consumers who are highly averse to risk. To be sure, a daring dress design can have unique buttons or a more plunging neck. But style-conscious consumers will not wear long dresses when the trend is toward shorter dresses (and vice versa). And firms in the automobile industry were not long in learning this lesson. Now, it is said, firms use helicopters to spy upon each other's test grounds. And when it is found that their designs are too far out of line, last-minute changes, often expensive, are made to bring them into conformity. In any event, a type of leadership has emerged in which General Motors generally has the last word in products as well as prices. For example, Ford anticipated the trend toward sports cars when it brought out the Mustang and Thunderbird. But when General Motors followed with larger "sports" cars, the Mustang and Thunderbird were made longer and longer. And the striking resemblance between the Cadillac Seville, the Chrysler Cordoba, and the Ford Granada evidences an unwillingness to take risks that is rivaled only in politics.

As might be expected, competition, as measured by changes in market shares, has declined since the 1920s and 1930s. As Figure 22 shows, in the period 1927-1941, Chrysler boosted its share of the market from 10 percent to over 30 percent, while Ford's share de-

Figure 22. Share of market, major automobile producers, selected years, 1927-1941 and 1946-1974. From *Automotive Industries Annual Statistical Issues* (Detroit: R. L. Polk and Co., 1927-1974), reprinted with permission.

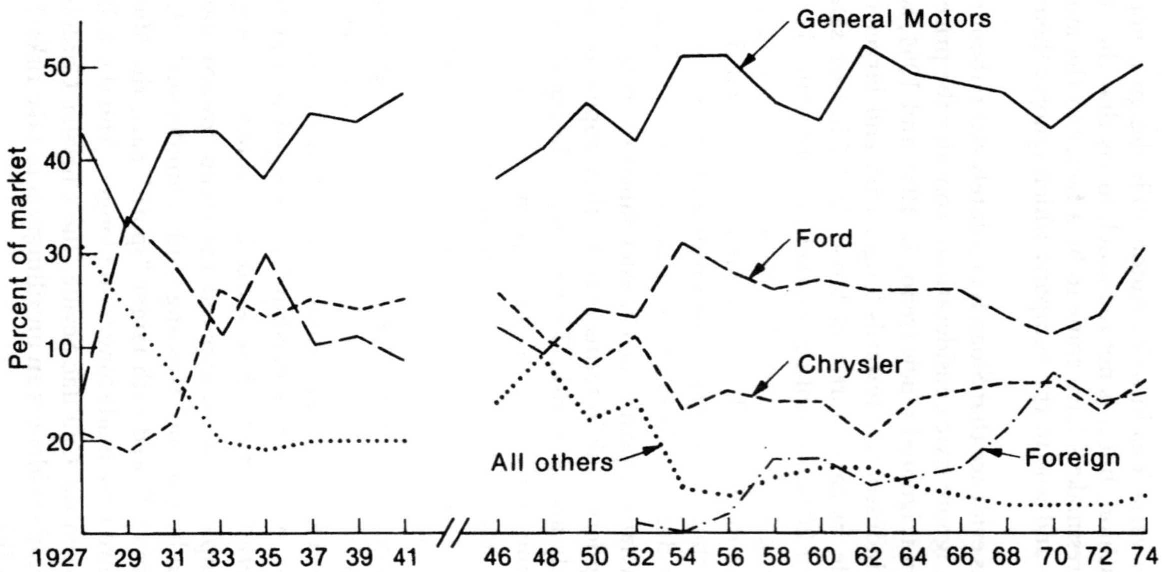

clined to a low of 20 percent. And there were some quite impressive changes in market shares during the early postwar years: as a result of being more style conscious Ford gained at the expense of Chrysler, and all but one of the independent producers disappeared. Why? According to conventional wisdom, the economies of scale favor the giant firm. But the emphasis on style also favors the giant firm: it can charge retooling and advertising expenses against larger production runs. Conversely, these costs may help explain why foreign auto producers do not change models as often as American firms do. The American independents were unable to make cars that were either inexpensive enough or distinctive enough to forfeit the model changes, so they became victims of "style" competition.

The name of the game now seems to be well understood. And as Figure 22 shows, since the late 1950s the market shares of the three major firms have been remarkably constant. Even with no risk-taking by the big three, some minor changes in market shares occur due to unanticipated changes in consumer demand. But as Figure 23 shows, the market shares of ten leading automobiles have changed within very narrow limits. There have been no changes comparable to the 1930s, when Plymouth sales surpassed those of Ford. The main evidence of competition is not to be found in serious rivalry among the big three, but rather in the increasing share of the market held by foreign firms. In the late 1950s, the foreign market suddenly rose to 10 percent, but the introduction of American compacts drove it down to 5 percent. Although in the late 1960s a combination of public and private measures helped to arrest a steeply rising trend, they could not prevent imports from acquiring almost 20 percent of the market. And though in 1976 there was a decline in the sales of foreign cars, it nevertheless appears that while we may be winning the battles, we are losing the war.

Why have consumers shifted to buying foreign cars? The rise in foreign car sales was once blamed by people in the industry on "those crazy people from California." But beginning about 1972, consumer surveys indicated that shifts to smaller cars—American or foreign—were occurring mainly in the better-educated families. Indeed, it was even found that some automobile executives living in Ann Arbor, Michigan, were driving smaller cars. And how did American automobile firms deal with this dilemma? They "competed" by designing practically all of the larger cars to look like the German Mercedes. In this way, style continues to be the dominant

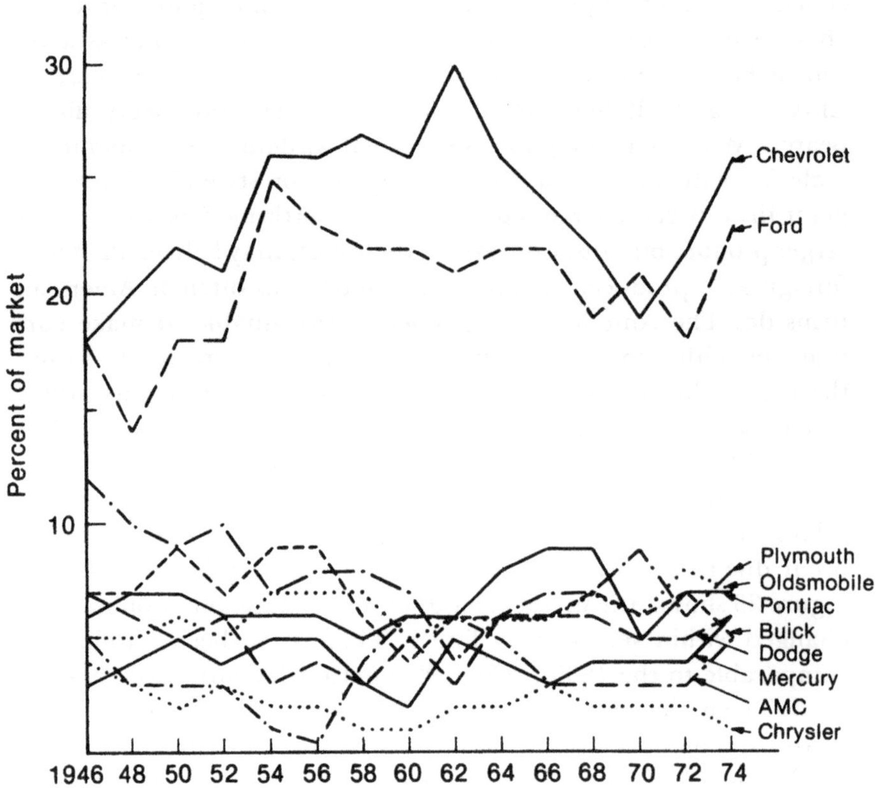

Figure 23. Share of market, ten leading United States automobiles, selected years, 1946-1974. From *Automotive Industries Annual Statistical Issues* (Detroit: R. L. Polk and Co., 1946-1974), reprinted with permission.

theme of the industry, and as cars shrink in size they become more expensive. In short, whether it is possible to fool most of the people most of the time remains an open question.

It can be seen, therefore, that firms in the automobile industry exhibit remarkably parallel behavior with respect to both products and prices—behavior similar to that of the trusts of the late nineteenth century.

What can be said about the dynamic capability of firms that engage in such behavior? Before turning to this question it will be useful to distinguish between two types of flexibility: one associated with static efficiency and the other with dynamic efficiency. The first may be defined as "Stigler flexibility," because George Stigler has shown how a plant that operates on a flatter cost curve rather than on a steeper cost curve (thereby sacrificing something in the maximum degree of static efficiency attainable) can be made better able to deal with fluctuations in demand.[16] It should be noted, however, that this is a completely static type of flexibility: permissible changes in demand are taken into account in the initial conditions. On the other hand, as we have already seen, dynamic flexibility is required to deal with new circumstances. For example, firms that were very quick to introduce superior hand-held computers evidenced a high degree of dynamic flexibility.

During the post-World War II period, the automobile industry discarded a policy of producing automobiles at the lowest possible cost in favor of a policy of "Stigler flexibility." As we have already seen, Henry Ford's policy for producing automobiles at minimal cost consisted of making them exactly alike. But today's production lines do not require cars to be exactly alike. A typical assembly line can assemble four intermediate cars—from the Chevrolet Chevelle to the Buick Special—with the basic body shell alike, but with almost every car coming down the line having different options. This type of tooling policy permits the automobile companies to shift the product mix with respect to both more and less prestigious models (for example, Buicks versus Chevrolets) and with respect to options (for example, conditioning, size of engine, citizen band radio). But "Stigler flexibility" does entail additional scheduling and inventory costs.

But more important is the cost of this static type of flexibility in terms of stifling dynamic efficiency. During the 1930s, the automobile companies were able to achieve a modest degree of dynamic efficiency because, subject to the constraint of achieving reasonable earnings, division heads (such as the heads of the Pontiac and Chevrolet divisions of General Motors) were given a high degree of autonomy in choosing designs. Moreover, General Motors and Chrysler had stock-option plans to make their executives feel they had a genuine stake in the success of the enterprise. Now, however, with the same basic body being used to build an entire range of intermediate cars, there is no longer any need for divisional autonomy, and decision-making has either been centralized or made a committee responsiblity. Thus, at Ford, engineers talk about having escaped from the tyranny of Henry Ford only to have a new managerial revolution imposed upon them in the form of thirteen echelons of decision-makers, with decisions going up and down. And at General Motors, engineers talk about a state of affairs in which everyone has a voice in everything but no one is responsible for anything. Nevertheless, Ford engineers claim that they are at an advantage. They say if they undertake a project without clearing it with one of the vice-presidents, they will be fired if the project is unsuccessful. But they also say that if the project is successful, occasionally Henry Ford II will back them; and they insist that with somewhat better incentives for heroes this provides them with a real advantage over engineers at General Motors.

With decision-making responsibility either so diffuse or so centralized, stock options obviously cannot play the role they once did as a reward for risk-taking. In fact, nearly everyone I interviewed insisted that risk-taking was no longer rewarded; on the contrary, they say, higher rewards come to those whose expertise consists of protecting the organization from risk. What evidence is there for such a reward system? They point to a system of fringe benefits that every year makes leaving a particular firm more expensive. And it must be acknowledged that such a system of rewards encourages obedience rather than risk-taking.

This discussion should make clear that insurance against fluctuations in demand costs something in terms of dynamic efficiency, because it limits the scope for individual initiative. This is but another illustration of the proposition that anything that makes the environment of the firm seem more certain will dull incentives for risk-taking. Nevertheless, it would be wrong to attribute the trend to more centralized decision-making entirely to the adoption of a policy of static flexibility. As contrasted with price of quality competition, style competition not only lends itself to centralized decision-making, it demands a high degree of centralized authority, whether in the world of automobiles or of fashion. The style decisions are obviously decisions of the highest importance which must be made at the top echelon of the company; and if the delicate balance of power is to be maintained, engineers must be kept under tight control. Furthermore, with competition in style rather than in terms of cost or quality, it is easier to differentiate strategic from tactical decisions. The top command can ask for long fenders or shorter bodies, as the case may be, and expect their orders to be carried out.

Returning now to the subject of flexibility, several automotive industry engineers I talked with knew that I had worked for

McNamara when he was Secretary of Defense. So during the course of our conversations, the policy of flexibility followed by the automobile industry was likened to the policy of flexibile response initiated by McNamara: the policy of flexibility in the automobile industry was designed to meet well-defined uncertainties, as was the strategic policy of flexibile response, which was intended to prepare the United States to fight *either* a nuclear or a nonnuclear version of World War II. However, the Pentagon's policy of flexible response did not provide the dynamic flexibility required to deal with new circumstances, such as those encountered in Vietnam.

What limits the dynamic capability of large structured organizations, whether in the automobile industry or in the Defense Department? The basic problem with such organizations is that, while they can be programmed to say "yes" or "no," they cannot be programmed to say "maybe." In large-scale military engagements, the top military leadership seldom assumes that it is possible to change strategy on the basis of what is learned in combat. To become convinced, the top generals must be led to believe that the new plan does not have a single blemish associated with it.

And no less than military planners, automobile planners think in yes and no terms. Consider, for example, the Ford development of turbine engines for trucks—a program begun in 1968 to provide an alternative to diesel engines. According to people from the engine division at Ford, when the turbine engine program began there still remained some serious unresolved technical problems; but it was very difficult to communicate problems to the higher echelons at Ford. In the top management, an engine is either a promising bet or it is not a promising bet. Moreover, experienced hands in the automobile industry will tell you that if a person wants to succeed he must never say "I don't know." Be that as it may, the turbine episode has made it quite evident that Ford is not programmed for saying "maybe." It is programmed for making ponderous production decisions. In Toledo, Ohio, a Ford production facility was converted to manufacture the turbine engine, and some 15 million dollars was spent on machine tools. Over two-hundred turbine engines were produced before the project was canceled at a cost to the company of 150 million dollars. What went wrong? Very serious problems were encountered in making regenerator discs and seals—problems that sent the cost of seals spiraling from $150 to over $700, and resulted in a doubling of the cost estimates for the engine. In short, the turbine engine as it was developed did not turn out to be an attractive alternative to the diesel engine. And the cost of obtaining this information was at least five to ten times as much as it should have been.

The principal difference between the automobile industry and the Defense Department is the latter's advantage in resources. Consequently, it is possible to recite many examples of expensively abandoned projects—from a nuclear bomber program that involved building special airfields before the problems of reactor development had been overcome, to cruise missile programs in which production and development were undertaken concurrently to save a few months lead time, to fighter airplane programs that could not be abandoned because too much money had already been spent. Indeed, it is a matter of common knowledge that given the way the military market for new ideas operates, it is easier to obtain a billion dollars for a weapon system program than 10 or 15 million for an exploratory development program. In the automobile industry and in the Defense Department, the underlying bureaucratic problem is much the same: a substantial unwillingness to live with ambiguity.

Such unwillingness helps explain why, at the present time, an intensive program is not underway to develop alternatives to the internal-combustion engine. The internal-combustion engine was not developed to meet the double constraints of low fuel-consumption and low emissions. And there is no reason to suppose that in the future better alternatives cannot be discovered. Shortening cars will have a marginal impact on lessening fuel consumption; to achieve concurrently a 50 percent increase in gasoline mileage and a 50 percent reduction in emissions, new types of propulsion schemes will have to be found.[17] Automobile industry spokesmen claim they would be willing to go ahead with an expedited program in engine technology if the federal government would underwrite the cost of development. And given the way the automobile industry does research, it is understandable why federal assistance is felt to be necessary. However it is not only the inability of the automobile industry to undertake ambitious advances that constitutes an obstacle. A more serious constraint is their fear of undertaking significant advances because the balance of power might be upset. The engineers engaged in engine development do not have to be lectured on the fact that a wider number of technological choices will permit smoother adjustments when dealing with an uncertain future. Occasionally, money is obtained for exploratory development projects. But according to the engineers, projects are undertaken mainly as low-cost insurance against another firm obtaining a lead.

It is really the aversion to risk-taking that explains why selling new ideas is so difficult. Were there a higher degree of competitive interaction, the internal incentives would be different.

Suppose that antitrust action is required to strengthen competition in the automobile industry. What would be the appropriate action? From the perspective of static economic theory, the answer is quite clear. The industry would be broken down into as many firms as possible without jeopardizing economies of scale. White, for example, favors breaking the industry down into ten vertically integrated firms, which, according to his calculations, could be done with no loss of static efficiency.[18] They would be vertically integrated to permit a higher degree of static efficiency; that is, White makes the argument that with vertical integration there can be a better coordination of the production process, and less risk from either strikes or exploitation by a supplier.[19]

However, I am not impressed with the reasons usually given for vertical integration. A more important reason, it would seem, is that firms possessing a minimal ability to deal with uncertainty have to control their environments. Business firms cannot manage their effective demand à la Galbraith. But they can use vertical integration to insure themselves against the risk of creative destruction.

From the point of view of dynamic theory, what is the appropriate action? Perhaps there is room for more than four American firms to engage in the business of producing bodies and assembling automobiles. But the main need is to have quite separate companies engaged in the development and production of automobile engines. With such a separation there would be greater incentives to take risks in engine development because of the possibility of selling engines to foreign automobile companies. As matters now stand, two American automobile firms will be buying engines made in Europe. However, with the design of American cars becoming more like that of European models, there is no reason to not look upon the United States and Europe as one market. Moreover, having to weigh the risks of other automobile firms—either European, Japanese, or American—adopting better performance engines, automobile companies would become more receptive to new ideas. In fact, their enchantment with vertical integration is that, with it, such risks do not have to be compared. Nevertheless, what is good for General Motors is not necessarily good for the country.

The main topic to be emphasized, however, is the stability paradox rather than antitrust policy. According to conventional wisdom, when firms engage in quite predictable decisions they promote stability. But as we have already seen, quite unpredictable discoveries, made in the course of overcoming dilemmas, contribute to smooth progress in the real world. For example, when Ford, by changing initial conditions in quite unpredictable ways, made the Model T a more reliable and less expensive automobile than the alternatives then available, it not only contributed to smooth progress in the automobile field, but, more broadly speaking, it contributed to the prosperity of the United States.

But when automobile firms insist upon avoiding risks they contribute just the opposite: they conserve their microstability at the expense of preventing smooth adjustments to new circumstances. Moreover, nowadays, entrepreneurship in the automobile industry does not consist of trying to bring about major, nonincremental changes in the product or prices when business is slack. It consists, rather, of urging the government to reduce taxes to stimulate the demand for automobiles. To be sure, in Keynesian models, the degree of risk-taking is taken as a given. The new type of entrepreneur, however, has been unwilling to subscribe to this aspect of modern Keynesian economics. On the contrary, it is now believed that it is the government's responsibility to make up for private risk-taking. And the larger the industry, the more influence it can hope to have on economic policy. Keynes declared that when you owe the bank one thousand pounds the bank owns you, but when you owe the bank one million pounds you own the bank. And being a large firm in an industry whose output is equal to about one-half of the gross national product of Australia is equivalent to owning the bank.

So what can the government do to escape from the current dilemma in which measures to stabilize the economy are self-prophesying—by weakening the incentives for private action they increase the need for government action. Obviously there is only one way to escape from this vicious cycle. When the performance of an industry becomes so poor as to threaten the macrostability of an entire economy, the government must find ways to bring about more risk-taking. The very essence of a democratic society, according to Thomas Jefferson, is its ability to evolve in the face of new circumstances. And unless ways can be found to stimulate risk-taking when it is sorely lacking, it will be impossible to preserve this concept of democracy.

This is not to say, of course, that risk-taking is now as frowned upon in all American firms as it is in the automobile industry. After all, the revolutions in the automobile industry did occur many years ago. However, several factors have substantially reduced the time required to establish bureaucratic routine in a business: the rise of business schools, the use of the computer as a substitute for imaginative behavior, and greater familiarity with the practices associated with preserving a way of life. And it seems reasonable to assume, therefore, that what happened to automobile firms between the 1920s and today will happen to other firms within a period of five to ten years, that is, if there is no dramatic change in government policies.

One of the indications that other large business firms may not be far behind the automobile companies in finding ways to insure themselves against risk is the growth in mergers and conglomerates. Although the data needed for comparisons are not plentiful, based upon fragmentary information, I would guess that over the past ten years the United States has witnessed quite as large a movement towards mergers and conglomerates as occurred during the 1920s. For firms that have lost their ability to deal with uncertainty, mergers and conglomerates provide an entirely rational method to protect themselves from risk. However, they also supply evidence of an economy entering a period of stagnation.

In one respect my argument is similar to that Schumpeter set forth in *Capitalism, Socialism, and Democracry,* and to a very similar argument advanced earlier by Thorstein Veblen in *The Engineers and the Price System.*[20] The main question Schumpeter had in mind when writing his book was: Why did it take so long for the United States to recover from the Great Depression? Others, like Alvin Hansen, had stressed the vanishing of investment opportunities. But not Schumpeter; he stessed the replacement of the entrepreneurial organization by the type of organization Max Weber had described as "the psychology of the salaried employee working in a bureaucratic organization."[21] To be sure, in the same book Schumpeter also presented his automatic progress theory; but my interpretation is that Schumpeter was consoling himself that in a highly bureaucratic society progress would not cease altogether.

Veblen had come to much the same conclusion when trying to explain the slowdown that occurred in the period 1900-1920 (when, according to Kuznets' estimates, the rate of increase in output per worker declined by about 50 percent).[22] Veblen, who was perhaps the keenest observer of economic reality since the time of Adam Smith, can be credited with having discovered the phenomenon now known as the "Phillips curve": the coexistence of substantial inflationary pressures and unemployed resources. Describing the economic situation in the United States at the end of World War I, Veblen wrote: "Workmen are being laid off and an increasing number of those workmen who have been serving in the armies are going idle for want of work . . . And all the while all these peoples are in great need of all sorts of goods and services which these idle plants and idle workmen are fit to produce."[23] How could this phenomenon be explained? Like Schumpeter, Veblen argued that the explanation was a shortage of risk-taking. Veblen quite correctly pointed out that the captains of the British Industrial Revolution were inventors who were replaced by financiers who avoided risk-taking. And when the rate of progress began to slow down in the United States, Veblen attributed the change to the replacement of technological entrepreneurs by financial entrepreneurs, who sought in various ways to preserve the integrity of their organizations. Moreover, although Veblen was not nearly as polished a writer as Schumpeter, he understood quite well that a decline in risk-taking would not lead to economic stability:"Advertising and maneuvers of salesmanlike spell-binding appear to be the only resource to which the country's businessmen know how to turn for relief from the tangle of difficulties into which the outbreak of business-like peace has precipitated the commercial world."[24]

As it turns out, both Schumpeter's and Veblen's arguments were proven wrong by the appearance of new crops of technological entrepreneurs. Firms founded after World War II, such as Varian Brothers, were almost the exact antithesis of the highly structured organization portrayed in Schumpeter's automatic progress model. And during the 1920s, the pioneering of radios and movies for the masses represented the antithesis of Veblen's thesis. Yet by associating tightly structured bureaucracies with periods of stagnation they both had discovered a fundamental truth.

In the past, whenever stagnation threatened it was sooner or later averted by the creation of new products and new industries. However, an economy cannot remain dynamic forever by creating new organizations. A day of reckoning must come in which there are so many constraints on unpredictable behavior that the economy simply cannot recover from periods of stagnation as it has in the past. And the United States' economy seems to be approaching that day.

The Dynamics of Inflation. When competition dies out of an economy what happens to the rate of inflation? Let us assume, first, that workers will want continuing increases in their real incomes. For anyone who has a large home, owns two cars, and spends his or her vacations in Europe, it is easy to become cynical about an overly affluent society. However, people who have never owned their own homes feel differently. It is reasonable to assume, therefore, that they will continue to bargain for higher money wages as a means of increasing their real incomes.

Second, if inflation is to be avoided, money wages cannot increase more rapidly than productivity. In manufacturing, about three-quarters of all costs consist of wage payments. Therefore, if wages increase at a significantly more rapid rate than productivity, there will be either a decline in profits or an upward pressure on prices. But although everyone dislikes inflation, business firms seem to prefer a price rise to a profit squeeze. And if the monetary authorities are sufficiently cooperative, prices can rise without a squeeze on profits or on wages.

Third, as we already have seen, when firms impose significant risks upon each other, competition acts as a dynamic stabilizer because it provides an incentive for productivity gains—which, when looked upon as isolated events, are quite unpredictable—and a deterrent to wage and price increases. Competition provides an incentive for productivity gains, because firms are motivated to search for ways to keep within tight cost constraints (either to increase their share of the market or to prevent it from declining). Competition provides a deterrent to wage and price increases because firms that allow wages to increase more rapidly than productivity face penalties in the form of reduced profits and reduced employment.

It is true that with industry-wide bargaining the role of competition in keeping wage increases in line with productivity increases is somewhat diminished. Indeed, industry-wide bargaining probably began as a response to firms trying to shift the entire burden for dealing with uncertainty from the firm to the worker. However, while industry-wide bargaining makes wage rates more rigid, it by no means eliminates the incentive to keep wage increases in line with productivity increases. As long as the demand for a product is somewhat elastic, and as long as firms in the industry differ in productivity and profits, the poorer performers will still have an incentive to improve their productivity more rapidly and to restrain wage increases. And it is only when firms stop competing for a share of the market that this incentive disappears.

Dynamic competition depends not only on the degree of risk firms are willing and able to impose upon each other to bring about productivity gains, but also on the degree of constraint imposed on productivity gains by labor unions. In several important industries, notably construction, trucking, and printing, American labor unions have imposed a degree of constraint typically associated with their British counterparts. However, the degree of constraint they can impose depends on the degree of competition in the industry: the more competitive the industry, the greater the incentive for union leaders to be modest in their demands—and the lower the degree of competition, the more uncompromising they can afford to be. Thus, the absence of competition in a given industry goes hand in hand with restrictive practices on the part of labor unions.

What kind of price behavior can be expected when competition dies out not only in the United States, but in other countries as well? Thorstein Veblen's suggestion that more and more stability at the microlevel will be accompanied by more and more instability at the macrolevel was absolutely right. If my basic argument is correct, with a smaller and smaller degree of risk-taking there will be less and less uncertainty in the environment of business firms and labor unions; and with less and less uncertainty, more and more unemployment will be necessary to keep inflation within tolerable limits. Conversely, if countries try to keep unemployment at some predetermined rate (such as 4 percent), they will find that the rate of inflation will become greater and more unpredictable.

In industries with little or no competition, unemployment provides a stabilizing factor in dampening inflationary pressures: in slack times union leaders display a higher propensity to engage in risk-taking by being more modest in their wage demands, and business leaders display a higher propensity to take risks by searching for ways to cut costs. However, in two important respects "unemployment" is an inferior substitute for "competition" as an economic stabilizer. In the first place, competition will result in a higher rate of productivity gain. Secondly, the smaller the proportion of the economy in which risk-taking is featured, the higher will be the cost of restraining inflation, as measured by the rate of unemployment and the degree of unpredictability with respect to prices.

Competition generates a higher rate of productivity gain because it provides both positive and negative incentives: firms that bring about significant reductions in costs can substantially increase their share of the market. By contrast, an economy in which firms have a low capacity to deal with unpredictability, and dare not provoke their competitors to become more adventurous, does not provide strong incentives for advances in productivity. For example, it is no accident that the long-term rate of productivity-gains in the British economy is lower than in any other major industrial country: the British economy has featured relatively little dynamic competition. Evidence of a low propensity to engage in risk-taking is to be found in the unwillingness of British industrial firms to exploit advances brought about in British laboratories. In a number of instances, including jet engines and computers, advances made by British laboratories were more quickly exploited by American firms than British firms. Evidence of a low propensity to take risks is also to be found in the degree of constraint imposed on productivity gains by British labor unions. And, if my analysis is correct, without a resurgence of competition it is quite unlikely that productivity gains will be accelerated in the United States.

The essential reason unemployment plays a zero role in curbing inflation in an economy featuring rivalry in all industries is that in such an economy firms that raise prices and wages more rapidly than their productivity gains will jeopardize their market position. In such an economy, prosperity and recession occur simultaneously; that is, the more successful firms in an industry will experience prosperity while the less successful will experience recession. And when it is apparent to a firm that by its own actions prosperity can be turned into recession, entrepreneurs are likely to exhibit a high degree of cost consciousness, and labor leaders, a high degree of economic statesmanship.

To be sure, there will be frictional unemployment in a competitive industry: relatively short-term unemployment between the time workers are laid off in firms suffering from recession and the time they are hired by firms experiencing prosperity. But frictional unemployment can occur and has occurred while total employment in an industry is rapidly expanding; and it plays no role whatsoever in restraining wage and price increases. It is competition, rather than the level of unemployment in an industry, that keeps wage rates from increasing more rapidly than productivity gains.

In several important respects, slow-history industries differ from fast-history industries. In slow-history industries, "prosperity" and "depression" are not as pronounced. Neither employment, production, nor wage rates rise as rapidly. However, because a minor recession for a fast-history firm is a major depression for a slow-history firm, there is likely to be the same pressure to keep wage rates in line with productivity gains. For example, during the period 1925-1940, competition in the automobile industry was not as robust as it had been in the period 1900 to 1925. Nevertheless, price competition did not disappear; and there was a good deal of pressure to keep wage increases in line with productivity gains.

In short, in a fully competitive economy, competition plays a dominant role in restraining inflation. And although there is frictional unemployment in such an economy, it plays no role whatsoever in restraining inflation.

What happens when there is a decline in risk-taking? Figure 24 shows the trade-off between the degree of dynamic competition, on the one hand, and the inflation rates associated with particular unemployment rates, on the other. *A* shows an economy with risk-taking in all industries; and in such an economy we can observe only a close cluster of points relaing to frictional unemployment. *B, C, D,* and *E* show economies with less and less risk-taking. In other words, Figure 24 is a representation of the trade-off between macro- and microstability: as we move from *A* to *E* we are moving from an economy with a high degree of macrostability to an economy with a zero degree of macrostability and 100 percent microstability.

In order to explain why, as competition declines, particular unemployment rates will be associated with higher and more unpredictable rates of inflation, let us assume that even in a highly dynamic economy a small percentage of GNP will be accounted for by industries whose firms can be described as "slackers": they know no

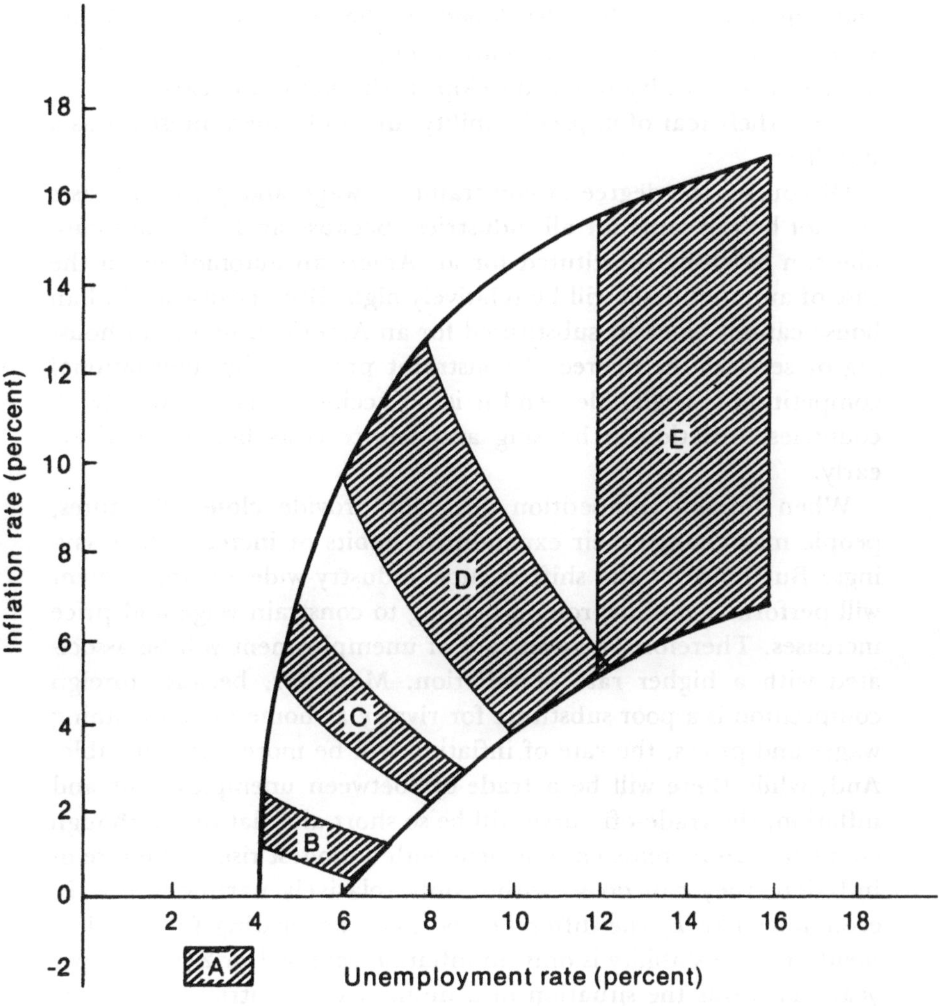

Figure 24. The dynamics of inflation. (*A*) Rivalry in all sectors of an economy (high degree of openness). (*B*) Rivalry in most sectors with no change in rivalry in the rest of the world. (*C*) Slackers in most sectors with no change in rivalry in the rest of the world. (*D*) Worldwide decline in rivalry. (*E*) A world of slackers (zero degree of openness).

worse fear than the fear of unpredictability and they engage in consonant behavior with respect to products and prices (Types 3 and 4 firms). Under these circumstances, wage and price increases will be constrained by foreign competition. But this constraint will not become operative until the foreign share of the market has increased and unemployment has developed in the home industry. Why? Were domestic firms to anticipate foreign competition, rather than merely react, rivalry would develop in the home industry. So, because of their fear of unpredictability, unemployment must act as a stabilizer.

Of course, the degree of constraint on wage and price increases will not be the same for all industries. Because an Italian automobile can be easily substituted for an American automobile, in the case of automobiles it will be relatively high. But because an Italian house cannot be easily substituted for an American house, in housing or services the degree of constraint provided by international competition is negligible. And it is no accident that, in nearly all countries, inflation in housing and service costs begins relatively early.

When foreign competition does not provide close substitutes, people may change their expenditure habits or increase their savings. But however the shift occurs, industry-wide unemployment will perform a positive role in helping to constrain wage and price increases. Therefore, a given rate of unemployment will be associated with a higher rate of inflation. Moreover, because foreign competition is a poor substitute for rivalry at home in constraining wages and prices, the rate of inflation will be more unpredictable. And, while there will be a trade-off between unemployment and inflation, the trade-off curve will be so short and flat that although countries can increase employment with a modest rise in the rate of inflation, they can do so within only relatively narrow limits. In economies like *B,* the difference between advocating full employment or price stability is only an inflation rate of 1 or 2 percent per year. This was the situation in a number of countries during the period 1955 to 1965. Although the British rate of inflation was higher than that of Germany, Japan or the United States, in all four countries during the period 1955 to 1965, as Table 8 shows, there was a fairly close relationship between wage increases and productivity gains, which indicates that competition was doing a good job in its role as an economic stabilizer.

Next, let us assume a case of almost no rivalry in a particular country, but a high degree of rivalry in the rest of the world. In this case, the situation will be shown in *C* on Figure 24: the cost of restraining inflation, as measured in terms of the level of unemployment, will become greater. Substitution of a poorer set of con-

Table 8. Wage rate increases versus productivity increases in manufacturing, 1955-1965.

	Average annual increase in wage rates (percent)	Average annual increase in productivity (percent)
Britain	4.1	2.0
Germany	5.5	4.0
Japan	6.9	6.7
United States	3.8	2.2

Source: Bureau of Labor Statistics, March 1975.

straints will make the trade-off curve steeper and the rate of inflation more unpredictable.

In short, it is no accident that the Phillips curve trade-off was appreciated in Britain before it was in the United States and most other countries. Apparently, British industry features so little rivalry that only foreign competition can act as a constraint on wage and price increases. But even so, until 1967, at which time the British government began its policy of devaluing the pound in order to maintain full employment at home, the British price index for manufactured goods increased only about twice as rapidly as the world price index for manufactured goods (2.2 percent annually as compared with 1.1 percent annually).[25] In other words, though foreign competition is a poor substitute for rivalry at home, it nevertheless provides some degree of constraint on wage and price increases.

Next, suppose that the decline in risk-taking in America results in less uncertainty in the environment of firms in other countries and, consequently, in less powerful constraints on wage and price increases. In this case, we can expect to observe in many countries that the curve will shift upward and to the right; and worldwide inflation will become greater and more unpredictable, with unemployment playing a larger and larger role in restraining inflation. This is *D* on Figure 24.

Finally, if rivalry disappeared completely in all countries, (that is, 100 percent of world output was accounted for by slackers) the Phillips curve would become vertical, as in *E* on Figure 24: a situation in which a single round of wage increases could lead to endless inflation throughout the world. *E* represents a world in which dynamic competition plays no role whatsoever as an economic stabilizer; therefore inflation can be restrained only by controlling the money supply and fiscal policy. However, trying to keep the rate of inflation at some predetermined figure is likely to make the unemployment rate highly unpredictable. To be sure, if a country that does not trade with the rest of the world (or pursues a foreign exchange policy that isolates it from the rest of the world) starts from a "no inflation" position, it can control inflation by keeping the unemployment rate so high that labor union leaders will not be willing to risk bargaining for higher wages. But once inflation is under way, the cost of monetary and fiscal constraints, in terms of the unemployment rate, is highly unpredictable. In this situation, wage rates become adjusted to the rate of inflation, and there are no constraints on wage and price increases.

As it happens, *E* closely corresponds to Milton Friedman's concept of the "natural rate of unemployment": a rate that cannot be exceeded without changing expectations with respect to the future course of prices and without running the risk of galloping inflation.[26] And it is no accident that in Friedman's model of the world, dynamic competition is permitted to play no role whatsoever as an economic stabilizer. Friedman explicitly assumes either a Walrasian general-equilibrium model or some variant in which firms move toward a predetermined equilibrium.[27] In such models, firms do not compete for markets. And if they do not, there can be neither any stimulus to productivity gains nor any deterrent to wage and price increases.

In fact, in terms of the monetarists' position, instability in the economy can result only from inflexible wages and by the monetary authorities' failure to keep the money supply stable. Therefore, if the economy ever strays from the path of a blissful equilibrium (as it did during the Great Depression) the villains are either the monetary authorities or the labor unions. Indeed, for this reason the monetarists have renamed the Great Depression "the Great Contraction."

Nevertheless, it is my contention that Milton Friedman has performed a very valuable service for the economics fraternity. He has demonstrated, in effect, that an economic system composed of classical firms, which have no ability to deal with unpredictability, is inherently unstable. Because the menu of alternatives is taken as a given, the only type of flexibility in a classical world is price flexibility. And once the labor unions have taken away that type of flexibility the entire system is unstable. Fortunately, however, we do not live in a classical world in which firms have a zero capability to respond to new circumstances and the economy has a zero degree of dynamic stability. If we did live in such a world, raging inflation would have begun many years ago—either that or we would never have recovered from the Panic of 1834.

However, the monetary theorists are not the only ones oblivious to the workings of a modern dynamic economy. So are those Keynesians mainly concerned with macroanalysis, who believe that both productivity gains and wage rates are determined by exogenous factors. For example, according to some Keynesian economists the remarkable price stability in the United States during the period 1960 to 1965 was a result of the wage and price guidelines established by the President's Council of Economic Advisors. But not all Keynesian economists believe this. For example, I regard myself as a Keynesian who is merely trying to remove Keynes' artificial assumption of a completely static Ricardian world. To my way of thinking, a Keynesian economist is one who is unwilling to assume that mismanagement of the money supply is the sole cause of economic instability.

However, many of his followers have become far more doctrinaire than Keynes himself. And as a result, neither the doctrinaire views of the monetarists nor the doctrinaire views of the Keynesians appeal to more earthly economists. According to the monetarists, the only alternative to more and more unemployment is raging inflation. And according to the doctrinaire Keynesians, the only alternative to serious inflation is either wage and price controls, superior economic statesmanship, or prayer.

Surely there must be some point of view that is better than either of these. And I suggest that the principal shortcoming of both the doctrinaire monetarist models and the doctrinaire Keynesian models is that they contain people who are only technically alive; that is, people who are utterly incapable of dealing with increased risk in their environments. But once it is granted that people do have imaginations that they can put to work when confronted by risk, it should be apparent that the Phillips curve can shift, either to make the rate of inflation greater and more unpredictable or to make it smaller and more predictable, depending on the degree of risk in the environment of firms and labor unions. The only real difference between the old and the new Keynesian economics is this: According to the old Keynesian economics, during periods of prolonged depression, when firms and individuals are faced with more uncertainty than they can cope with, the government should act to increase the level of effective demand. And according to the new Keynesian economics, the prescription for dealing with prolonged depression is exactly the same. But during periods of prolonged inflation the government should cooperate with firms and labor unions by injecting more uncertainty into their environments, because, unlike serious depressions, during periods of stagflation there is an acute shortage of negative feedback.

To return to the main argument, the growing rate of inflation is merely another indicator of the macroinstability that can be expected when competitive rivalry becomes weaker and weaker. During the period 1955 to 1965, unemployment in the United States averaged 5.3 percent of the labor force, and the consumer price index increased less than 2 percent annually. During the period 1970 to 1975, an average unemployment rate of 5.9 percent was associated with an average annual increase in the consumer price index of about 10 percent, with greater unpredictability in the rate of inflation. And growing worldwide inflation is a grim reminder that countries cannot hope to conserve their microstability.

This is not to say that the war in Vietnam did not contribute to inflation in the United States and other countries as well. Nor is it to deny the impact of increasing fuel prices on inflation. My argument does not assume inflation can occur only as a result of a decline in competition. It does assume that a permanent upward shift in the Phillips curve has occurred. And if my argument is correct, without measures to promote competition or otherwise encourage risk-taking, there will be no significant downward shift in the Phillips curve.

Moreover, when business firms and labor unions lose their ability to cope with uncertainty, the economy not only becomes more vulnerable to inflation, it also becomes more vulnerable to depression. Indeed, the very inability to engage in unpredictable behavior is the cause of a "stagflationary" economy: an economy requiring continuing large deficits to keep the unemployment rate as low as 6 percent, while at the same time experiencing a growing inflation rate annually. Our political leaders notwithstanding, prosperity is not to be found right around the corner.

8. Public Policy Trade-Offs

If it is acknowledged that we live in a stagflationary economy, highly vulnerable to both inflation and depression, what are the public policy trade-offs? According to conventional wisdom the only available choice is between a policy of restraint, as followed by President Ford's administration, and a policy of regulation. Though the former fosters a substantial amount of unemployment, it seeks to dampen inflationary pressures by restricting demand. A policy of regulation would place major emphasis on employment and growth and would seek to suppress inflationary pressures through wage and price controls. However, if my argument is correct, the first alternative will turn out to be so ineffective that in the longer run the question will not be whether to engage in regulation but, rather, which form of regulation to engage in: regulation to promote competition or regulation to control monopoly?

Competition requires regulation because there is no automatic mechanism to assure a satisfactory rate of progress. This is not to say, of course, that there is anything wrong with the argument for deregulation. For example, as was already pointed out, deregulation of the airline companies to permit competition in rate-setting is likely to strengthen incentives for risk-taking. However regulated industries are not the only ones that constitute a vexing problem. Indeed, if my basic argument is correct, the real danger facing the United States is that in a relatively few years industry in general will be acting like the nineteenth-century trusts; that is, as in the steel, petroleum, and automobile industries today, prices and products will be alike. Therefore, some form of "regulation" is needed to ensure that in the future the United States will escape from stagflation: positive measures must be undertaken to encourage more risk-taking.

Associated with the policy goals of regulation to promote competition, and regulation to control monopoly, are two fundamentally different concepts of "stable growth": macrostability and microstability.

Macrostability: Stable growth is equated, first, with achieving the right mix between industries engaged in making fast and slow history, and second, with facilitating the discovery of new technologies (for example, obtaining a replacement for the internal combustion engine) whenever smooth progress is jeopardized. In other words, stability at the macrolevel assumes a good deal of dynamic behavior at the microlevel. According to this model of growth, human beings are regarded as open systems who can interact with their environments to change them. Therefore, whenever the dynamic stability of the nation is threatened the problem is looked upon as one of strengthening the incentives for risk-taking.

Microstability: Stable growth is equated to each industry engaging in a highly predictable form of growth. Output expands because workers are provided with more and more capital, or because of gradual improvements in knowledge, the rate of which cannot be accelerated. But output cannot expand as a result of dynamic behavior brought about within the economic system. According to such models of economic growth, the entrepreneur is regarded as a passive agent—as a puppet who can only respond to changes in his environment. Therefore, the only available policy instruments are wage and price controls or fiscal and monetary restraint.

In other words, the choice facing the American people today is between the type of economy we have had in the past and the type of economy Britain has long had, namely, a highly regulated economy that features microstability at the expense of macrostability.

The Promotion of Competition versus the Regulation of Monopoly

As we already have seen, a policy of restraint is likely to prove ineffective in dealing with the basic cause of a chronic inflation problem because it cannot restore the incentives associated with a highly competitive economy. Thus, whereas in a dynamic economy the penalty for failing to engage in risk-taking can easily be a 25 percent drop in sales (and employment), it would be politically impossible for any political party to accept a 25 percent unemployment rate as a means of stabilizing the economy. And whereas in a highly competitive economy the reward for engaging in risk-taking can easily be a 20 percent return on capital, it would be politically impossible to provide tax incentives to assure such a return. Moreover, there is real doubt whether the usually recommended incentives—reduced corporate taxes or more liberal investment credits—would have any incentive effect in promoting genuine risk-taking, that is, the type of risk-taking associated with a policy of macrostability. On the contrary, tax measures that provide an incentive for replicating the types of capital facilities now in existence provide a disincentive for discoveries.

It is my conclusion, therefore, that given the present aversion to risk-taking, a policy of restraint will not have any noticeable effect in bringing about a downward shift in the Phillips curve; that is, whenever the unemployment rate falls as low as 5 or 6 percent we can look forward to an inflation rate in the neighborhood of 5 to 10 percent annually. Therefore, if America is ever to have prosperity without inflation again, ways must be found to increase the propensity for risk-taking.

To be fair, however, it must be acknowledged that the policy of restraint subscribed to by President Ford's administration did not have as its objective the promotion of risk-taking. According to the President's Council of Economic Advisors' official explanation of inflation, "cost-push" inflation can occur when wages rise more rapidly than productivity. Or it can occur when a foreign cartel increases the price of oil. Inflation can also occur because the growth in the money supply outstrips the growth in real output. But it cannot occur because domestic firms engage in the same behavior as foreign cartels; it cannot, that is, unless such behavior is accompanied by an overt agreement to limit competition.[1] In other words, just as many economists and politicians in 1931 desperately adhered to the belief that no profound change had taken place in the economy and prosperity was right around the corner, so many want to believe the same today.

Inasmuch as a policy of restraint will not suffice to deliver the economy from inflation, the longer-run alternatives will consist of measures to either promote competition or regulate monopoly. From two points of view, regulation has real advantages over the promotion of competition. In the first place, such a policy has an obvious appeal to the politicians. To be reelected, a politician must project the image of being the voter's lawyer in Washington: the man he can count upon to regulate business in his interest. Second, if action must be taken, direct controls are generally preferred by business leaders in well-established firms. George Stigler goes too far when he asserts that regulation is actively sought by business.[2] But nevertheless, there is an important germ of truth in his argument: when the incentives to internalize risks are so weak that some public action is likely, more often than not direct controls will be preferred to changes in incentives. For example, I recently had occasion to talk to a number of people from the automobile industry about an environmental tax to encourage more rapid progress in developing smog-free engines as an alternative to direct regulation. The working engineers, with relatively few exceptions, preferred the tax to direct regulation. In fact, they told me it was essential to make profits depend on performance if more rapid progress was to be made in dealing with environmental degradation. On the other hand, higher officials in the firms took the view that "we can live with regulation." And as far as they are concerned, it is an eminently rational position.

As Marshall pointed out many years ago, the leadership in well-established firms has an obvious interest in perpetuating itself; and because regulation has the effect of minimizing the degree of uncertainty in the environment of the firm, what better way is there for an artificial aristocracy to perpetuate itself?[3] It seems to be no accident, therefore, that except in the underdeveloped and socialist countries, the degree of economic regulation practiced in Britain is unmatched. What better way to form a cartel than under the auspices of the government?

Nor should anyone underestimate the benefits of being regulated by the United States Government. Becoming regulated is something like losing a war to the United States: it will look after the security of the regulated firm forever. For example, consider the lengths to which the government goes to maintain full employment in defense firms. Or consider how, by preventing competition in fares and by restricting entry, the Civil Aeronautics Board operates a cartel for the benefit of the airlines. Or consider what the Federal Communications Commission has done to limit competition in the communications field, for example, by protecting existing broadcasting companies from the competition of pay television.

What is the cost of economic regulation? The cost will be calculated in a quite different manner depending on whether one takes a static or a dynamic point of view. In static terms, the cost of regulation is measured in terms of a misallocation of resources. For example, the "Averch-Johnson effect" results in a misallocation of resources because regulation provides artificial incentives for capital intensive projects.[4] The "Stigler effect" results in a misallocation of resources because the regulators restrict entry in the regulated industry.[5]

Similarly, according to conventional wisdom, the cost of wage and price controls is to be measured in terms of a misallocation of resources. However, while wage and price controls do have this cost, they also have a potential benefit: the possibility of restraining inflation with less unemployment. To be sure, there are real questions as to how wage and price controls might be made more effective in controlling inflation than they were under the Nixon administration. Nevertheless, it is an open question whether the cost of economic regulation, as measured in terms of a misallocation of resources, would exceed the benefits, as measured in terms of higher employment levels.

However, it is also not a very interesting question, because just as static economics underestimates the benefits of competition, it also underestimates the cost of regulation. From a dynamic point of view, the cost of regulation in bringing about a misallocation of resources is relatively trivial. The more important cost is a reduced rate of progress. And as we already have seen (Chapter 2), regulation will result in a slowdown in the rate of progress, because by making the environment of the regulated industry seem highly certain incentives for risk-taking will be dulled (as has happened in the regulation of railroads and defense firms—and as is happening now to the airlines).

How does such an environment develop? According to Stigler's theory of regulation, the regulatory agency is captured by the regulated industry. And if his theory is correct, business firms take the initiative in making their environments more certain, for example, by prevailing upon the regulatory authorities to prevent entry of new firms into the industry.

Inasmuch as it involves a conspiracy between the regulated

agency and the regulated industry, Stigler's theory of regulation is much like President Eisenhower's theory of the military-industrial complex. And what is wrong with such conspiratorial theories is the failure to recognize that, more often than not, the regulatory agency and the regulated firm have common interests. For example, the military agencies like to impose elaborate requirements on new weapon systems because the requirements process minimizes bureaucratic risk (just as taking four times as many clothes as are needed on a vacation trip provides a way to minimize social risk). And because defense firms' profits in relation to sales are strictly limited, it pays to cooperate with the armed services by developing weapon systems with high unit cost. In short, no conspiratorial theory is needed to explain the relationship between regulatory agencies and regulated industries. Above all, regulatory agencies desire an environment with little or no uncertainty. And such an environment is ideal for firms whose main quest is microstability.

Anyone who has studied regulatory agencies is surely aware that military organizations are not the only ones highly intolerant of uncertainty. For example, on the basis of the evidence I have seen, the Environmental Protection Agency is, in its intolerance of uncertainty and unwillingness to take risks, more militaristic than the Defense Department. In its various monitoring activities it does not necessarily give first priority to those hazards that might represent the greatest risk to health, but rather to those nuisances that are easiest to detect (backyard trash burning, commercial incinerators, dense smoke). The air and water quality standards that are laid down are quite as arbitrary as military requirements. And the Environmental Protection Agency is no more receptive to modifying its requirements on the basis of current knowledge than is the Defense Department.[6]

It is my belief that nearly all regulatory agencies evidence the same intolerance of ambiguity and the same unwillingness to take risks. For example, Stigler suggests that regulatory agencies restrict entry in order to make it possible for existing firms to earn monopoly profits. However, my hypothesis as to why the Civil Aeronautics Board has not allowed a single new trunk line to be established since 1938 is quite different: once having promulgated a set of regulations, bureaucratically speaking, the CAB simply could not tolerate the uncertainty associated with allowing a new member into the club. Or to consider another case, the railroads. Inasmuch as rail innovations come about rather slowly, and knowledge of alternatives changes slowly, railroad regulation represents about as favorable a case for regulation as anyone can hope to find. Yet it can be argued that in a number of respects the railroads have not even kept up with current alternatives. Nor have the railroads regarded the achievement of a modest degree of dynamic efficiency as important. This is indicated by the fact that shortly after the Interstate Commerce Commission was established several of the largest railroads appointed lawyers as their presidents.

Suppose that the regulatory agencies were not intolerant of uncertainty and possessed a genuine willingness to take risks. How might they behave? Quite obviously, if a regulatory agency is not to become a prisoner of its environment, it must possess a good knowledge of current technological possiblities. How does it acquire such knowledge? As Louis Brandeis once suggested, the Interstate Commerce Commission might establish its own equivalent of the agricultural experimental stations to reveal alternatives not revealed by the railroads. And rates might be set on the basis of the best available alternatives. In other words, the government might impose more risk on the railroads by going into competition with them. Or to take another case, during the 1920s and the 1930s the Army and Navy did "regulate" aircraft and aircraft engine firms by sponsoring competition to determine which firm could come closest to meeting their technical and cost requirements.

In other words, under conditions of strong uncertainties, competition is the best form of regulation. Without imposing risk, how can the best available alternatives be found? And without a knowledge of the best available alternatives, how can a regulatory agency prevent itself from becoming a prisoner of its environment?

With relatively few exceptions, however, regulatory agencies do not operate on the premise that competition is the best form of regulation. And the reason, of course, is that, like other public bureaucracies, they operate to minimize bureaucratic risk; that is, the fewer alternatives a bureaucracy reveals, the less subject it is to outside criticism and bureaucratic strain. Moreover, from a bureaucratic point of view, it is an eminently rational way to operate. Why employ the competitive model when you, the bureaucracy, do not have to worry about the actions of your competitors?

A reasonable model of regulatory behavior should also include the constraints imposed upon dynamic behavior by the United

States Congress. For example, people in the armed services claim it is the difficulty of selling ideas to Congress that has caused so many exploratory development projects to be undertaken as weapon systems projects. In fact, a colleague of mine at Caltech, Morris Fiorina, a very able political scientist, argues that basically it is Congress and not the bureaucracies that is responsible for the behavior we observe.[7] However, I suggest that the behavior is again the result of a genuine partnership, arising out of the common interests involved in playing pork barrel politics and minimizing bureaucratic risks.

For the purpose at hand, however, it is unnecessary to determine to what extent the unwillingness of regulatory agenices to take risks is determined by bureaucratic imperatives and to what extent by congressional constraints. In either event, the effect is much the same: regulation makes the environment seem more certain, and with a more certain environment regulated firms have less incentive to engage in risk-taking. But not only does regulation weaken the incentives for risk-taking, it perverts incentives for the generation of a diversity of ideas; that is, firms are provided with an incentive to pursue identical technological approaches in order to get the regulations relaxed. For example, why did the entire American automobile industry concentrate on one smog control device—and why did the main elements of diversity come from foreign firms (Honda and, more recently, Volvo)? Quite obviously, the American automobile firms have an incentive to get the regulations relaxed. And their best strategy is to concentrate on one device, thereby putting up a united front to the Environmental Protection Agency and Congress. Conversely, foreign automobile firms are encouraged to take risks, because they have reason to believe that in the enforcement of the Clean Air Act, American firms are given preferential treatment. In other words, air quality standards actually provide better incentives to foreign automobile firms than to American automobile firms!

To be sure, if dynamic competition is working well in a regulated industry, and if firms are able to conceal ideas for advances from the regulatory agencies, then, of course, regulation will not reduce the rate of progress. On the other hand, if it is working poorly, regulation will create perverse incentives by reducing the degree of uncertainty in the environment of the regulated firm and, even in an industry in which technology improves as slowly as it does for the railroads, it can result in large costs in terms of a reduced rate of progress. In short, regulation works best when it is not needed.[8]

If we assume that the opportunities for progress are not exhausted in the United States, it is apparent that, in terms of the theory just sketched, the cost of wage and price controls is not to be measured in terms of a mere misallocation of resources. Rather, the cost is to be measured in terms of a further weakening of the incentives to engage in risk-taking and an increase in the demand for more and more controls. Indeed, it is by no means clear that the economy has recovered from the last experiment with wage and price controls. Bringing about a constant rate-of-productivity increase in an industry requires a continual search for new ideas. And it is easier to stop such a progress than it is to start it.

On the other hand, if we assume a Keynesian model—a model than contains no explicit provision for progress that is accompanied by unpredictable microbehavior and regards finding jobs for the expanding labor force as the sole purpose of economic growth—then the case for regulation is much stronger. As we have just seen, regulation involves a minimal cost under conditions of weak uncertainties. And, if the only purpose of growth is to provide more jobs, it really does not matter if regulation results in perverse incentives with respect to productivity.

Therefore, the more basic question is: given the challenge facing the United States today, which policy is more likely to be successful—a policy of microstability or a policy of macrostability?

Microstability versus Macrostability

Until about 1950, when, under the banner of "stable growth," American policymakers sought to rival the Soviet Union in the degree of security provided to citizens, the ethic of America was "progress," and economic growth was regarded as a by-product of progress. Moreover, as far as the liberal politicians were concerned (generally speaking, those who were strongly influenced by Jefferson's philosophy), progress was the accepted paradigm for making decisions on matters of public policy. For example, the argument made by Louis D. Brandeis against the trusts was not that they would result in a misallocation of resources—but rather that they would stifle progress.[9]

Today, however, economic growthmanship has become the religion of America, and unlike the goal of progress, which is to produce better alternatives, cheaper alternatives, or alternatives intended to widen the diversity of our pleasures, economic growthmanship has become an end in itself. To be sure, like any other religion, it means different things to different people. To Keynesian economists—Republican or Democrat—growth means a sufficient annual expansion of output so that resources are not wasted. There are, of course, differences of opinion as to how much unemployment should be tolerated in an inflation-prone economy. Nevertheless, on one matter all static economists are in solid agreement: business firms are closed systems—and as such are quite predictable. Therefore, the economic and political environment in which they function cannot impair their ability to deal with new circumstances.

On the other hand, to business firms, the growth religion means something quite different. To a General Motors' executive, stable growth means the ability to plan on a 6 percent growth in sales annually. And according to Keynesian economics for executives, it is the government's responsibility to act as an automatic stabilizer whenever automobile sales falter. To be sure, determining the mix of Chevrolets and Buicks, deciding whether they should be longer or shorter and whether they should comply with emissions and safety standards are regarded as matters of private responsibility. But whenever the overall demand for automobiles lags, the appropriate remedy is not to find ways to make them less expensive to own and maintain. Rather it is to increase consumer buying power.

Few industries have the nationwide economic impact as the automobile industry. But the Congressman who hopes to be reelected is not concerned only about unemployment in the country as a whole. He is concerned with assuring that business firms in his district enjoy stable growth. For example, he may be against a general increase in defense expenditures; but not going ahead with a defense contract in his own district is quite another matter. From his point of view, stable growth does not mean having his constituents threatened with adversity.

To be sure, this is not the first time business firms have turned to politicians as an alternative to dealing with business bureaucracies. In the past, however, only local politicians specialized in the granting of favors; with the notable exception of the regulated industries, Washington politicians were in a relatively poor position to dispense favors. However, as a result of the large growth in public expenditures, and the emphasis given to maintaining near full employment everywhere, Tammany Hall politics has moved to Washington. And the main difference between the two great political parties is that whereas one is concerned with exempting big corporations and wealthy individuals from risk-taking, the other is concerned with insuring that the common man will not have to engage in risk-taking. In short, the goal of American politics is a society of politicians in which no one need use his imagination.

It would be wrong, however, to place the entire blame for the trend towards microstability on big business, labor unions, full employment, and politics, for in almost every enterprise in American society there has been a steady decline in risk-taking: in the universities, in local governments, in public schools, and in federally supported research-and-development activities. Nor is it difficult to explain this decline in risk-taking. No matter what activity they are engaged in, the newly established middle classes know no worse fear than the fear of unpredictability, and they desire, above all, to conserve their microstability.

In short, the United States is headed towards an economy like Britain's: an economy in which every person has the right to his existing job and no firm has the right to be a failure. To be sure, the planning mechanisms have not been completely established; but it is not difficult to predict what they will involve: they will involve doing for the unregulated industries what the government is now doing for the regulated industries. "Planning" in the New Victorian State will require industries to grow at approximately the same rate, with each firm acquiring a constant share of the market. Of course, a foreign power or a group of foreign powers might shut off our supplies of this or that raw material. However, while we cannot completely isolate ourselves from the rest of the world, the goal of such planning would be to ban unpredictability.

What is wrong with such an argument for a "planned economy"? According to conventional wisdom, many of our freedoms would be curtailed. However there is nothing wrong per se with giving up freedom. For example, traffic signals involve giving up a personal freedom. But relatively few people would propose abolishing traffic lights to protect our freedoms. Indeed, there are a number of instances in which it is quite rational for people to give up a little of their desire for adventure in order to protect their desire for security.

Freedom is a valuable commodity mainly because we live in an uncertain world. Why do many people who live in dictatorships crave freedom? It is not necessarily because they love freedom for its own sake. Rather, it would seem that they know from their own experiences that a society that imposes many constraints upon its members, so it can remain highly predictable, is a society whose members have a poor ability to deal with uncertainty.

The basic question about a society—planned or unplanned—whose goal is microstability is not whether personal liberty must be surrendered so the members of society can collectively insure themselves against risk and uncertainty. It is, rather, a question of the degree of uncertainty facing the society, because that will determine what must be given up to acquire a high degree of microstability. A dynamic, competitive society is not an end in itself, and the utility of such a society can be determined only with reference to the importance of making further progress.

As far as the United States is concerned, a strong case for a dynamic, competitive society cannot be made, because of the need to multiply indefinitely the material pleasures and conveniences of life. When our fathers or grandfathers bought their first radio or first automobile, they did so with a genuine sense of adventure. But we seem to be reaching a point in which more diversity in material pleasures is becoming meaningless. As far as the middle classes are concerned, I am in agrement with those who say other types of diversity would be more valuable (for example, longer vacations, a greater contact with cultural activities, more frequent changes in jobs).

In fact, trying to keep up with the Joneses has cost the middle classes their freedom of choice. Many have the impression that as they grow richer they also grow poorer. For example, professional people often say they felt richer as graduate students or as members of the armed services than they now do making twenty or twenty-five thousand dollars a year. Why? Think of personal consumption expenditures as being divided into two types: discretionary and compulsory (the latter including, for example, expenditures for food, housing, and keeping up with the Joneses). As one's income increases, not only does the proportion spent on compulsory items increase; in most cases, the absolute amount available for discretionary purposes decreases. However, the increase in personal savings during the 1970s may indicate that the consumer is beginning to rebel against feeling that keeping up with the Joneses is necessary to leading a good life.

Nevertheless, while the reasons for continued progress may not be the same in the last quarter of this century as they were in the fourth quarter of the nineteenth century, progress is quite as important now as it was then. Why? Quite large, continuing advances in productivity will be required if the United States is to avoid a chronic inflation problem. To be sure, there are some who say workers should be satisfied with smaller increases in their real incomes. But people who preach this line are imposing newly acquired middle-class tastes on the working classes. Secondly, we might like to spend more on the underdeveloped countries, on education, or on better medical care. There is no incompatibility between a competitive society and one that cares about people. Quite the contrary. However, unless there is an upward trend in productivity increases, the United States simply will not be able to afford to be a more humanitarian country than it is today.

A third reason why progress, and all that it implies in adjusting to new circumstances, may be quite as important now as it was one hundred years ago involves the necessity of adapting to fuel shortages and environmental constraints. It would be relatively easy to improve productivity at the expense of the quality of the environment, for example, by using high-sulfur fuels. And it would be relatively easy to bring about improvements in environmental quality by sacrificing productivity gains. However, it is the necessity to make progress on both fronts simultaneously that will require quite as dynamic a society as we have ever had.

Much of the environmental legislation was passed in the belief that the environmental problems were temporary—as if cleaning up the environment were a once-and-for-all undertaking. But the appropriate analogy to keep in mind is not of a housewife who views cleaning her house as a fairly routine task, but rather of a housewife who discovers that, each time she cleans, the house becomes dirty in ways she could not have predicted. In other words, the essential nature of the problems of environmental degradation is that they are dynamic in nature. To be sure, much environmental legislation was premised on the assumption that it would be possible to make almost perfect predictions of not only the impact of environmental degradation on people's health, but also of the optimal measures required to deal with pollution. However, there is a great deal of uncertainty with respect to both costs and benefits. In other words, we know that, in the future, air and water will not be the free goods they were believed to be in the past. But inasmuch as we do not know just where and when new scarcities will develop, nor what measures will be required to deal with them, the problems of the environment must be regarded as dynamic issues.

What are the implications of environmental degradation for economic growth? The zero-growth people notwithstanding, not all forms of life are equally taxing on the environment. If economic growth were to occur in activities involving less environmental degradation per unit of output than the present pattern of growth there would be nothing wrong with it. In other words, dealing more effectively with environmental degradation need not mean the end of economic progress. On the other hand, it is also quite clear that achieving steady progress in productivity gains and lowering the rate of environmental degradation will require far more stringent energy conservation measures than have been adopted to date.

About two-thirds of the United States' energy is consumed outside of industry. Indeed, the use of energy to provide either a badge of social distinction (such as a long automobile) or a substitute for physical exertion (dishwashing machines and electric golf carts) or as a means of exercising (electric exercise machines) seems to know no limit. However, if the United States is to evolve in the face of current necessity, consumption habits will have to become less energy-intensive.

What, then, is wrong with a policy of microstability? If America is to remain a democracy in the Jeffersonian sense—a society that can adapt itself to new circumstances—risk-taking will be required in all sectors of society. And America today has as many risk-takers as it ever had. Yet the new stable-growth religion of the United States, which is steadily evolving toward a society with almost 100 percent microstability, is in fundamental conflict with the challenges facing this country.

To be sure, no one minds if someone else does the risk-taking. Indeed the demand for regulations stems from a desire to coerce one or another group to engage in risk-taking. But regulation cannot supply incentives to engage in risk-taking. Instead, it takes away our freedom for dealing with uncertainty. And as a consequence, we are likely to find that the effect of adopting additional regulations to make particular activities more certain will make the future viability of the United States more uncertain. In fact, without adding any new regulations we are already a much too constrained, bureaucratic society.

The politicians notwithstanding, in a world of strong uncertainties it is simply impossible for society as a whole to conserve its microstability. To be sure, in the short run it is possible to make some activities more predictable than they would have otherwise been. But the inevitable effect will be to introduce more uncertainty into other activities. The cities, for example, would like to reduce air pollution without any change in their way of life. And when a city like Los Angeles was persuaded to discourage individual driving by reserving a freeway lane for carpools and buses, its citizens acted as if one of their sacred freedoms had been taken away. Conversely, the leaders of American industry would like nothing better than to have mayors exercise a high degree of initiative, particularly if it were to spare them from risk-taking. But cities and industries cannot both conserve their microstability simultaneously. The more successful industry is in conserving its microstability, the more difficult will be the adjustment problem for the cities (and vice versa). For example, an alternative to the internal-combustion engine could play an important role in reducing smog. But it would make life in the automobile industry more unpredictable. Banning cars from downtown city areas could also help in reducing smog, but at the same time it would make local business fortunes more unpredictable.

Trying to conserve the microstability of some sectors of society not only shifts the burden for risk-taking to other sectors—in general those that have the least amount of political power—but by not coming to grips with problems now, such a policy makes future problems more difficult. For example, when air-quality standards are postponed, say, for two years, politicians assume they are delaying the cleaning of a room for two years. This is something like assuming that termites will postpone eating the foundation of a building if their extermination is postponed for two years. The fact of the matter is that the automobile population continues to grow. And as a consequence, the inevitable cost of avoiding minor revolutions now will be more serious revolutions later.

Or to consider another example. A new type of business fluctuation is developing in the United States: the administered business cycle. About two years before a national election, a major effort is undertaken to pump up the economy to give the appearance of prosperity without too much inflation, in order to convince the voters that the country is on the verge of a takeoff to perpetual stable growth. After which comes the post-election recession and the search for new measures to pump up the teetering economy. What is the cost to the economy of this kind of economic statesmanship? After each cycle the economy increasingly takes on the traits of a vegetable economy—an economy less and less able to cope with uncertainty—and it becomes more difficult to restore to prosperity. Unfortunately, however, politicians tend to define stability very narrowly, and seem not to be concerned about the cost of their actions, as measured in terms of the future stability of the economy. Nevertheless, the consequences of trying to pursue a policy of microstability are very clear. The burden of risk-taking is shifted from the protected to the unprotected sectors of the economy, and the economy as a whole is made less and less able to cope with uncertainty.

The Sacred Lessons of the Past

How is it that a country that led the world in dynamic behavior for sixty-five years accepted microstability as its policy goal? It is commonplace to observe that military organizations base their planning on the favorite lessons of the last war (in other words, those lessons that best match their preconceptions). Apparently, the same is true of economic policy. It is intended to take into account the so-called sacred lessons of the Great Depression. One of these lessons, according to Leon Keyserling (chairman of the President's Council of Economic Advisors, 1950-1952), was the need to demonstrate to the communist countries that the United States could enjoy the same degree of economic stability as they. Moreover, Keyserling also contended that stable growth was required to deal with the communist threat. In fact, the stable-growth theme first appeared in the National Security Council's famous *Study 68*.

But the reasons given by Keyserling for stable growth had little to do with its popularity among economists and politicians—particularly among those who were raised during the Great Depression. They saw in the theme of stable growth a means to fine-tune the economy to avoid even minor recessions. But few realized that by becoming less able to deal with uncertainty the economy would be made more vulnerable to a downturn.

To be sure, no one likes to see large numbers of unemployed. Yet it also must be acknowledged that in a dynamic society some unemployment is inevitable. In those industries featuring static efficiency people do become highly specialized; and through no fault of their own they can find themselves victims of the process of creative destruction. Conversely, an economy in which there was no technological unemployment would have no capability whatsoever to make adjustments to future circumstances.

This, of course, is of little consolation to those who become technologically unemployed or to minority groups. But trying to avoid even minor downturns not only makes the economy more vulnerable to a depression; as will be pointed out in the next chapter, a policy aimed at providing everyone with a job is by no means equivalent to a policy that equalizes opportunities. And as for our demonstrating to the Soviets that we can enjoy the same degree of stability as they, a policy of stable growth combines the worst features of capitalism and socialism: a highly unequal income distribution and inflexible business bureaucracies.

Another sacred lesson learned from the Great Depression is that a country should devalue the currency whenever it is threatened by a serious balance-of-payments deficit. According to this lesson, the Bruening government made a serious mistake by not devaluing the German mark more promptly—a mistake that helped bring Hitler to power. And it is true that in a deep depression the propensity to engage in risk-taking is so low that international competition can do little or nothing to revive it. Moreover, inasmuch as German firms in 1930 were among the most inflexibile in the world, devaluation undoubtedly generated more uncertainty than they could cope with.

Assume, however, that, because of a shortage of risk-taking, a country faces both chronic inflation and a chronic balance-of-payments problem. It faces chronic inflation because competition is not keeping wages in line with productivity gains. It faces a chronic balance-of-payments problem because its productivity is not rising rapidly enough, as compared with other countries, to provide goods at competitive prices. Under these assumptions the effect of devaluation will be simply to isolate business firms and labor unions in the devaluing country from negative feedback, thereby insuring the continuance of inflation and balance-of-payments problems (as in the case of Britain).

Strangely enough, the international trade theorists still believe, as Rousseau did, that the characteristics of nations are predetermined. Therefore, they generally take the position that a country with a balance-of-payments deficit is not in equilibrium.[10] But what if the country is suffering from a shortage of risk-taking? Devaluing promptly whenever faced with a balance-of-payments problem will make a shortage of risk-taking a permanent characteristic of the country. "Equilibrium" for the country in question will be an increasing rate of inflation!

The lesson? If policymakers want to conserve microstability, thereby ensuring that their inflation problems will remain with them indefinitely, they should devalue whenever a serious balance-of-payments problem arises. On the other hand, to make progress towards a less inflationary world, they ought to revalue the currency whenever a country's productivity performance declines relative to other countries, and they ought to do so in order to remedy the shortage of risk-taking. As a result of the accelerated decline in exports and the increase in imports, business firms and labor unions in the revaluing country must deal with more risk; and with incentives more favorable to risk-taking, the process of obtaining a balance-of-payments surplus will be speeded.

In short, inasmuch as it implicitly recognized the role of negative feedback, the argument for the gold standard did contain an important germ of truth that was discarded in the sacred lessons drawn from the Great Depression. Conversely, a central problem not only with international trade theory, but with economic theory in general, is that it ignores the role of negative feedback. Negative feedback is not included in classical equilibrium theory inasmuch as providing the entrepreneur with knowledge of the equilibrium price before trading occurs permits quantity adjustments to be made instantaneously. It is left out of Keynesian income-expenditure models inasmuch as it is assumed that wages and prices are completely inflexible with respect to making downward adjustments. To be sure, if economists pretend they can make classical predictions (the initial value predictions made by Newtonian celestial mechanics), negative feedback cannot be included in their models. However, the price paid for pretending economics can make such predictions is the complete inability to predict the character and speed of economic adjustment processes.

9. Internalization of Risk

If the United States is to escape from its current stagflationary predicament, risks must be internalized to provide the economy with a dynamic insurance policy: a policy directed toward insuring that the economy can more or less continuously adapt to new circumstances. At *best*, regulation can provide the economy with a short-term, static insurance policy (that is, a policy to reduce specific risks). As we have seen, however, the larger the degree of uncertainty, the greater the cost of regulation, in terms of a reduced rate of progress. Therefore, to obtain a more satisfactory economic performance, incentives must be changed to better favor the internalization of risks.

One way to internalize risks is through competition: by acting upon a technological risk to avoid losing a market to a competitor, a firm will make the future rate of progress more predictable. But the degree of uncertainty in the environment of business firms is not determined only by the degree of competition. As we already have seen, defining "stable growth" too narrowly can result in the promotion of microstability rather than macrostability. Likewise, a policy of devaluation, whenever a serious trade deficit develops, can promote microstability at the expense of macrostability. And as will be pointed out later in this chapter, many of the loopholes in the tax system an be regarded as measures to remove various special interests from risk-taking.

Understanding how the environment in which firms make decisions is affected by political factors has been the aim of "political economy" since the time of Adam Smith. However, the subject matter of political economy has been focused mainly on resource allocation questions, rather than on questions of the rate of progress.

How can more rapid progress be made in understanding the determinants of the degree of risk internalization, and how can a greater degree of risk-internalization be promoted in the American economy? The only way is to take our cue from Adam Smith, and make quite specific policy recommendations.

Promoting Competition

Antitrust policy has had two somewhat different objectives, as Carl Kaysen and Donald Turner have pointed out in detail. First, to prevent "unfair, unreasonable or coercive conduct," and second, to prevent "all powerful aggregations of capital."[1] Under the first objective, monopoly is not regarded as an evil in itself. In fact, some of the sponsors of the Sherman Act took the view that the Act was not applicable to those who established monopolies by virtue of "superior skill and intelligence."[2] The second objective is concerned not so much with conduct as it is with preventing the concentration of economic and political power.

These two objectives reflect quite different concepts of antitrust policy. The objective of preventing unfair, unreasonable, or coercive conduct can be regarded as a survival-of-the-fittest doctrine: as long as business firms engage in fair play, only the fittest will survive. The objective of preventing concentration of economic and political power can be defined in terms of two theories: one is classical economic theory and the other is a theory initially developed by Jefferson and Madison and later elaborated upon by Brandeis. The latter theory is often described as being aimed at protecting the small business man. But the underlying theory is quite as sophisticated as that which emerges from classical economic theory. It is that large concentrations of economic and political power can jeopardize the evolution of an entire civilization. And as far as Brandeis was concerned, this was the evil of bigness.[3]

Which particular objective the courts employ—emphasizing either specific wrongdoing or the dangers of large concentrations of power—has depended mainly on whether a government of Jeffersonian or Hamiltonian leanings is in power. To be sure, the courts, have never looked upon size as an evil in itself, inasmuch as there had to be some evidence of wrongdoing. Conversely, relatively few cases of wrongdoing have involved no concentration of market power. Nevertheless, there have been important differences in the degree to which the two objectives were emphasized. Thus, during the 1920s, when there occurred the second largest merger movement in the history of the United States, primary emphasis was placed upon specific wrongdoings. On the other hand, in a series of cases decided by the United States Supreme Court during the years 1946 to 1953, main emphasis was placed upon market power; indeed, many economists and lawyers regarded these cases as the beginning of a new era in antitrust. However, there is little doubt that during the 1960s the pendulum swung back to favor the narrow legalistic theory. Over the past fifteen years there have been no major cases that might have the effect of deterring the growth of mergers and conglomerates. And although there is a good deal of worry over foreign cartels, it seems to be taken for granted that, unless accompanied by collusion, price fixing is not bad. As the point is made in the 1975 *Economic Report of the President*: "With respect to price fixing, the most difficult problem is detection, and for this purpose antitrust authorities have relied primarily on informants."[4] The report does not say that, with or without collusion, "price fixing" is price fixing.

The problem with the legalistic concept of monopoly, which emphasizes specific wrongdoings, is that by failing to specify those characteristics of firms that enable them to survive, the doctrine comes close to proclaiming "the fittest is the fittest." For example, a firm may survive because it has the dynamic capability to find ways to cut costs or to increase the quality of its product (that is, because it has Type 1 or Type 2 rationality). Or it may survive because its leadership is gifted at finding ways to manipulate the environment to exempt the firm from risk-taking (Type 4 rationality). And in both of these cases the firm can be said to survive by virtue of its "superior skill and intelligence." But in the one case the firm has contributed to the macrostability of the economy, and in the other, the firm has protected its own security by jeopardizing the macrostability of the economy.

Marshall likened business firms to the "young, medium-sized and old trees in the forest."[5] And to put my proposition in terms of his analogy: when business firms compete by imposing risks upon each other they contribute not only to their own success but to the growth of the forest. On the other hand, when they fail to compete in deeds and seek the help of the government in exempting them from risk-taking, a few old trees can jeopardize the growth of an entire forest.

A further consequence of a narrow legalistic theory of monopoly is that it provides poor incentives for competition. Firms are provided incentives to avoid overt collusion, but no incentive to engage in risk-taking. This more basic problem goes back to the Sherman Act. The Sherman Act does not say that competition should be pursued as a positive goal. In fact, nowhere in the Sherman Act does the word "competition" appear. Instead, the buzz words are "monopolize" and "restraint of trade." And the penalty for violation can be either a large fine or a prison sentence. However, while it is often said such punishments are intended to deter violations, what they do instead is to make it more difficult to bring suits and narrow the incentives for competitive behavior: firms are not discouraged from engaging in parallel action with respect to products and prices; they are discouraged from engaging in overt collusion in order to accomplish this end.

One effect of the cycles of alternating narrow and broad interpretations of the antitrust laws has been to make the United States more vulnerable to serious depressions. The goal, if we want a dynamically stable society, is to have firms continuously take risks, and thereby conserve their ability to engage in dynamic behavior. To be sure, policies aimed at this goal cannot guarantee stability. But it is also clear that no matter what the cause of a depression, the less firms are able to deal with risk and uncertainty the more prolonged will be the recovery. For example, there is no doubt that, in most cases, mergers have the effect of making firms less able to take risks. And there is no doubt, therefore, that a broader interpretation of the antitrust laws during the 1920s would have made recovery from the Great Depression somewhat less difficult. Likewise, we in the United States are now paying a heavy price for not having had strong enforcement of the antitrust laws during the 1960s.

What should be done? Kaysen and Turner deserve a good deal of credit for having foreseen the necessity for making some fundamental changes in the antitrust laws. While most of the economic and legal fraternities were sleeping, in 1959 they saw the possibility of a trend towards weak enforcement such as occurred during the 1920s. And their chief recommendation was to make "undue market power" the criterion for antitrust action—even when such market power is unaccompanied by evidence of collusion. Firms would be permitted to have market power to the extent that such power would not jeopardize economies of scale; undue market power would be market power that could not be so justified.[6]

There are two standard objections to a policy of limiting market power. The first objection is that it would result in firms too small to mount an effective research-and-development effort. The second is that it would weaken incentives for growth. However, as Kaysen and Turner point out, the willingness of firms to mount an imaginative research-and-development program depends not only upon their size and financial ability, but also upon their incentives, that is, whether or not they are prodded by a competitor.[7] And if we could be sure that a policy of limiting market power would result in a significant improvement in the incentives for risk-taking there need be no concern. There are many examples of highly successful research-and-development programs conducted by firms smaller than those that would be allowed under the antitrust policy recommended by Kaysen and Turner.

It is true that limiting market power would weaken the incentives for growth. However, as was indicated in the last chapter, growth for its own sake is equivalent to microstability and does not result in economic stability, but rather in an economy that is less able to deal with uncertainty. So if limiting market power could increase the degree of dynamic behavior, the objection that it would weaken the incentives for growth would be irrelevant.

What is wrong with a market power (that is, concentration ratio) test is, first, that it is related to a relatively unimportant aspect of economic efficiency, namely, static efficiency; and second, in the real world in which progress can occur it is impossible to make good predictions of the relationship between market power and the rate of progress.

The aim in limiting market power is to more closely approximate the ideal of perfect competition in order to improve the allocative efficiency of the economy. However, the role competition can play in improving the allocative efficiency of the economy is of trivial importance as compared to the roles it can play in bringing about progress and as an economic stabilizer. In short, what is wanted is not a static, but a dynamic, test of performance.

To be fair to Kaysen and Turner it should be noted that they do consider both efficiency and progress, and that they would not apply the market-power test to firms engaged in introducing new processes, products, or marketing techniques.[8] However, whereas they seem to have in mind two types of firms—one that brings about progress and one that does not—in the real world no such dichotomy exists. Rather, there is an entire spectrum of cases ranging from infrequent improvements in products to frequent and superficial improvements to frequent and significant changes. And the price of refusing to face up to this reality could be the creation of a substantial loophole in antitrust enforcement. Moreover, incentives would be created to make superficial changes look like significant changes.

The more basic problem with a market-power test is that in a world in which progress can still be made it cannot make good predictions. An industry with only five firms ("a highly concentrated industry") might act as a trust with all firms offering the same products and prices, or the firms might engage in risk-taking, generate a wide diversity of ideas, and bring about an impressive rate of progress. And there is no way of predicting on the basis of a priori considerations how they will behave.

Neither is it possible to make good predictions of the behavior of large firms. Large firms can use their resources to manipulate their environments to enhance their own survival. And there can be no doubt that for firms with little ability to deal with uncertainty the real advantage of size is the ability to buy influence (through advertising, lobbying, and other measures). On the other hand, large firms containing a good deal of internal competition can, by pursuing parallel paths, accelerate the rate of progress. In short, it cannot be said that the courts were entirely wrong to insist that, in itself, size is not an offense.

Thus, the main objection to a market-power test is that it does not, and cannot, make good predictions. And the same objection applies to the "Brandeis-Jefferson" theory of monopoly. While large concentrations of economic and political power can jeopardize the evolution of a country, we cannot predict in advance how such power will be used. To be sure, as far as judges and juries are concerned, the Brandeis-Jefferson theory is probably more appealing than the pure competition argument. However, in the final analysis, any theory is likely to be regarded as so much philosophizing unless it can be backed up with evidence of its ability to make good predictions. Moreover, any theory must be translatable into everyday experiences that people can understand for themselves. And I suggest that, from these points of view, a dynamic test (changes in market shares) makes more sense than a static test (average market shares).

To say, however, that dynamic theory can make better predictions of performance than static theory is not to say that it can provide an unambiguous test of "good" or "bad" performance. And this brings us to a genuine dilemma. One side of the dilemma is this: if a program to promote competition is to be successful it must provide incentives for a wider interpretation of "competitive behavior" than is provided by present antitrust laws and the criteria employed in their enforcement. Success of any program to promote competition is not to be measured in terms of the number of actions brought, but rather in terms of the incentives provided and the behavior deterred. For example, there is no doubt that present antitrust laws have had an impact in deterring mergers. However, the main danger the United States faces now is not the danger it faced in 1890, when there had been a large increase in the concentration of economic power. Rather, the United States is now threatened with major industries displaying essentially the same behavior as the nineteenth-century trusts—but without any overt agreements to limit competition. Unfortunately, however, the antitrust laws do not provide a real deterrent to this type of behavior.

The other side of the dilemma arises from the narrow criteria required if the antitrust laws are to be enforced by existing institutions. Especially when the Supreme Court is packed with strict constitutionalists, the only way to assure that the antitrust laws will be enforced is to employ completely unequivocal criteria. In fact, the real appeal of a strict market power test is that, like a 55 mile per hour speed limit, it might supply an unequivocal test. This insistence upon unequivocal criteria stems, in turn, from the internal incentives of the legal profession. For the most part, the lawyers who become judges, especially nowadays, are not deep thinkers. Rather, they are what Jefferson termed "Blackstone lawyers," that is, people who go by the books.

In short, the dilemma facing the United States today arises from the fact that the incentives needed for the promotion of competition do not accord with those of the legal profession. A very good illustration of the dilemma is to be found in Senator Philip Hart's Bill:

To Supplement The Antitrust Laws, And To Protect Trade And Commerce Against Oligopoly Power Or Monopoly Power, And For Other Purposes.[9]

The preamble to Senator Hart's Bill makes clear that he did not think of competition in a narrow way:

> The Congress finds and declares that (1) the United States of America is committed to a private enterprise system and a free market economy, in the belief that competition spurs innovation, promotes productivity, preserves a democratic society; and provides an opportunity for a more equitable distribution of wealth while avoiding the undue concentration of economic, social, and political power; (2) the decline of competition in industries with oligopoly or monopoly power has contributed to unemployment, inflation, inefficiency, and underutilization of economic capacity, and the decline of exports, thereby rendering monetary and fiscal policies inadequate and necessitating Government market controls subverting our basic commitment to a free market economy . . .[10]

And yet, Hart's criteria for the possession of unlawful monopoly power tend to be narrow and unrelated to the broader goals. Monopoly, according to the Hart Bill, can exist under three circumstances: (1) a return on net worth in excess of 15 percent over a period of five consecutive years; (2) no price competition in an industry over a period of three years; and (3) four or fewer corporations accounting for 50 percent of sales in any industry.[11] The first and third of these circumstances are reasonably unequivocal, which from a legal point of view is good. Yet there is no assurance that these static criteria would contribute to the broader purposes of the bill. Limiting profits to 15 percent on net worth would impair risk-taking and productivity. Nor would the third test necessarily contribute to progress.

How to escape from this dilemma? Not only must the laws be changed, but so must the institutions engaged in enforcing the antitrust laws. Our more basic objective is a more rapid rate of progress. And to obtain a more rapid rate we need to create more uncertainty in the environments of business firms and labor unions. But how can we create more uncertainty without getting a greater diversity of people involved in the promotion of competition?

The type of behavior we would like to discourage is that associated with low risk-taking: consonance or near consonance of behavior with respect to products and prices. An industry that is not generating a diversity of ideas is to be regarded as an industry of slackers. The main test to be employed in deciding whether or not to be suspicious about any particular industry is constancy of market shares: constancy of market shares suggests that good use is not being made of human diversity.

But constancy of market shares does not result only from an unwillingness to take risks. It can also occur because the opportunities for further progress have been temporarily exhaused. How might we distinguish between these two situations? One test is the ability of firms to meet foreign competition. Generally speaking, American firms are at no disadvantage, compared to foreign firms, with respect to size of plants or expenditures on research and development. Therefore, if an industry is not doing well in meeting foreign competition it is reasonable to infer that its firms are not doing as good a job as they might in making good use of their existing potential. Moreover, it can also be inferred that the reason for their inability to compete is that they have become so highly structured they are inefficient from a dynamic point of view. To be sure, there will be exceptions in which foreign firms can be said to possess an advantage in scale economies. But unless there is genuine evidence that a firm is at a disadvantage in scale economies, the favored action should be dissolution. Of course, foreign firms can also have an advantage in terms of input prices. But such an advantage merely indicates that American wages and prices in an industry are too high. A policy of dissolving firms in an industry that exhibit nearly constant market shares and cannot meet foreign competition would perform two important functions. First, it would perform the function of a bankruptcy, that is, the reorganization of firms under new management. Second, it would create better incentives for risk-taking than now exist—particularly in the slow-history industries.

Unfortunately, however, the ability to meet foreign competition is a minimal test of performance—and not a test that can assure whether, in the longer run, the United States will be self-sufficient in ideas. Devising a test to determine whether or not both American and foreign firms are doing a good job in exploiting their technological potentials is crucial to a policy of promoting competition. As we saw in the last chapter, the basic problem with regulation is that it cannot generate a knowledge of current technological possibilities. But the same is true of a program to promote competition. It is not enough to proclaim an industry is doing a poor job in exploiting the technological potential available to it; there must be hard evidence.

How is such evidence to be provided? One possibility is to set up a government-supported research-and-development effort to compete with industry in those fields where, it is felt, more rapid improvements could be made in technology. For example, during World War II, the Office of Scientific Research and Development competed with the armed services in developing new military technology. And in principal, a strong argument can be made for a governmental effort aimed at discovering whether particular industries are doing a good job in advancing technology. For example, without a publicly conducted exploratory development program, how can it be known whether the automobile industry is doing a good job with respect to developing alternatives to the internal-combustion engine? Or how, without a competing effort, can it be known whether industry is doing a good job in searching for new sources of energy?

Unfortunately, however, bureaucratic incentives in public-supported research-and-development programs are not the same in peacetime as they are in wartime. During World War II, the Office of Scientific Research and Development was famous for sponsoring a wide diversity of approaches. But during peacetime, research-and-development organizations such as the Atomic Energy Commission or the National Science Foundation have been famous for concentrating upon a narrow menu of alternatives, because such a strategy minimizes bureaucratic risk. To be sure, a wide variety of research and of low-cost experiments is tolerated. But with respect to more expensive development projects, the best way a public agency can avoid making the "wrong" choices is by limiting its menu.

The only way around this dilemma is to create temporary ad hoc organizations to sponsor public research—organizations that would not exist for longer than two or three years, leaving little time to develop vested interests. Actually, a strong case can be made for motivating imaginative exploratory development projects by giving large cash prizes (five hundred thousand to five million dollars), because awarding prizes on the basis of accomplishments already made would minimize the need for an established bureaucracy. On the other hand, when development is constrained by a shortage of risk capital, a prize system may not stimulate an adequate number of projects. However, government-sponsored research-and-development projects should have "fixed commitment" contracts: contracts in which an organization is given a fixed sum to develop a crude test model. Such contracts were used with great success in radar development during World War II. And their essential rationale is that by preserving some degree of private risk-taking the degree of bureaucratic control is limited.

In any event, the purpose of a program for prizes or for fixed-commitment exploratory development projects is not necessarily to encourage private firms to do more in-house research and development. Rather, it is to encourage firms to become better borrowers, either by utilizing ideas arising from public-sponsored research or by encouraging them to contract for their own research. This is not to say, however, that all firms in an industry would be required to adopt advances more or less simultaneously. But if firms in a concentrated industry acted like a cartel by engaging in parallel actions with respect to products and prices, the presense of better alternatives would indicate that the behavior in question could not be ascribed to their having achieved perfection.

The basic purpose of this proposal is to change incentives to favor a higher degree of openness. The problem with government-supported research programs is that there is no Say's law for ideas—no law to assure that a greater supply of ideas will more or less automatically lead to a greater demand. The basic reason inventions made in British laboratories were often adopted by American firms before British firms made use of them is that the demand conditions were more favorable in America. On the other hand, to threaten dissolution of firms without being able to demonstrate that they are doing a poor job in exploiting a technological potential is a meaningless gesture. In other words, in order to increase the rate of progress, there must be favorable demand as well as favorable supply conditions. As in the famous example of Marshall's scissors, both blades are required to do the cutting.

In short, a "consonance of behavior plus" test is proposed: "plus" either the inability to meet foreign competition (when the failure cannot be ascribed to scale economies) or the unwillingness to make use of demonstrated ideas. And if firms failed to meet these tests, no evidence of conspiratorial behavior or other wrongdoing would be required. Failing to generate a diversity of ideas—no matter whether they were developed internally or borrowed elsewhere—would be regarded as evidence of a lack of competition.

It is also necessary to amend the antitrust laws to make it illegal for labor unions to impose constraints on productivity gains. In the public debate, high wage demands on the part of labor unions are often looked upon as the villain in causing inflation. However, it is difficult to keep wages high without restricting the introduction of labor-saving devices. For example, without constraints on the building of prefabricated houses, wages in building conventional houses would not be nearly as high as they are. Indeed, the fundamental reason labor unions impose constraints upon labor-saving devices is to keep wages artificially high.

There is no doubt that in the past the American labor force exhibited a greater flexibility than the British labor force. Even when we were relying mainly upon British technology, this flexibility often permitted us to obtain higher productivity than could be obtained with British labor and management practices. As an illustration of the payoff that can result from a flexible labor force, consider the following example taken from Elting T. Morison's excellent book *Men, Machines, and Modern Times:*

> In the years from 1864 to 1871 ten steel companies in this country began making steel by the new Bessemer process. All but one of them at the outset imported from Great Britain English workmen familiar with the process. One, the Cambria Company, did not. In the first few years those companies with British labor established an initial superiority. But by the end of the seventies Cambria had obtained a commanding lead over all competitors. The president of Cambria, R. W. Hunt, in seeking a cause for his company's success, assigned it almost exclusively to the labor policy. "We started the converter plant without a single man who had ever seen the outside of a Bessemer plant. We thus had willing pupils with no prejudices and no reminiscences of what they had done in the old country.[12]

On the other hand, there also can be little doubt that today American labor practices more and more resemble those of Cambria's competitors than those of Cambria. Therefore, unless labor union leaders are made to feel the risk of dissolution, there is little hope of reversing the trend.

If the United States is to ever again enjoy a high degree of macrostability, a policy to promote competition must have as its primary aim requiring that business and labor union leaders live with uncertainty and risk rather than use their power to transmit risks to others. Risk avoidance can result from restrictive labor practices. Whether in the steel industry, the petroleum industry, or the automobile industry, risk avoidance can also result from vertical integration, mergers, and conglomerates. Therefore, when organizations fail to internalize risk to a reasonable degree, they should be restructured in ways likely to result in more risk-taking.

In addition to defining competition more broadly, and acknowledging that labor unions can jeopardize dynamic workable competition, there is a need to change the institutions responsible for preserving competition. The Antitrust Division of the Justice Department and the Federal Trade Commission are reasonably satisfactory institutions when it comes to carrying out a program to promote competition, narrowly defined. But because the two agencies rely mainly upon lawyers, they are not the appropriate institutions to carry out a program to promote competition, broadly defined. A properly constituted organization responsible for bringing cases before the courts would be composed of not only lawyers and economists, but also engineers who had worked in highly competitive industries, plus entrepreneurs with no engineering training. In short, it would be composed of people who from their own experiences could understand why competition should be promoted as a positive goal. In fact, one of the most interesting features of the Hart Bill is the extent to which it recognizes that new antitrust methods and machinery are needed. It establishes an Industrial Reorganization Commission to determine whether monopoly power exists in major industries and to devise plans of reorganization. It also establishes a special court, the Industrial Reorganization Court, to try major cases. My main criticism of the Hart Bill: Why go this far to create new administrative machinery while defining competition in terms of the economics of 1890?

Advertising

Advertising can perform two quite different functions. It can provide relevant and reasonably truthful information about a product, that is, it can play an informative role. Or it can work on the psychology of the consumer—particularly on his fears and anxieties; that is, it can perform the same function in modern society as witch doctors do in primitive societies.

The most debated question about advertising is the effect it has on the consumer: Are advertising expenditures for competing products offsetting or do they increase the total demand for the products in question? A more interesting question, I submit, is the effect of the second type of advertising on the environment in which business decisions are made. As we already have seen, competition in deeds requires discriminating consumers who can distinguish between better and poorer alternatives. However, advertising directed towards manipulating their psychology assumes quite irrational consumers—consumers who, if they want to lead happy lives, will go along with the witch doctor's advice.

The extent to which consumers are irrational is an open question that need not be debated here. My point is that the assumptions made about the consumer, whether or not they are valid, certainly do have an impact on lessening the motivation of firms to search for better or less expensive products. Propagandistic advertising can be most successful when competition is promoted in terms of "style." And the effect of advertising is to cause the substitution of competition in style for competition in price or quality. In other words, advertising leads to an economy that generates a narrower rather than a wider diversity of ideas.

What should be done? According to one line of thinking, assuring more honesty in advertising is a government responsibility. However, with such involvement there is a genuine danger of government dictation of tastes. The other alternative, which has not received the attention it deserves, is to allow, for tax purposes, a modest deduction for informative advertising. This would make style competition more expensive and result in a substitution of price and quality competition.

The Tax System

According to conventional wisdom, an ideal tax system would have a neutral effect on incentives. However, in only one kind of world can an ideal tax system exist, namely, in an imaginary dilemma-less world optimized for a zero degree of openness. In the real world, tax systems may favor predictable or unpredictable behavior, but they cannot simultaneously favor both. Consider, for example, the collection of an equal amount of revenue by two tax systems. The first imposes high income taxes but low inheritance taxes, and the second imposes low income taxes but high inheritance taxes. The first admittedly provides an incentive to work hard in order to leave an estate for one's children, but the next generation is likely to be motivated to conserve the value of the estate rather than engage in risk-taking. So, whereas in the long run the first tax system favors an artificial aristocracy, the second favors a natural aristocracy.

The idea that tax systems can affect the degree to which risks are internalized is hardly new. The logic of increasing the degree of openness by increasing the internalization of risks is similar to the logic of the second law of thermodynamics. Sadi Carnot anticipated the concept of risk internalization in his writings on economics; consider his comparison of a tax on the rent of land versus a tax on land: "A tax on the rent of a farm would be much better than a tax on the land itself. Proprietors then could only avoid taxes by themselves improving their property. As it is, they merely collect the rents, and usually employ their surplus in unproductive expenditure, while the proprietary farmers devote theirs to the improvement of the land."[13]

Now, even though the concept of an open system had not been formalized as of the time Carnot wrote, it is apparent that he had in mind a tax that would increase the average degree of openness of French farmers by causing a wider search for new alternatives to improve productivity. Suppose that the average degree of openness of absentee landlords happens to be smaller than that of proprietary farmers who devote themselves to the land. And also suppose that whereas a tax on land is a tax on its raw value, a tax on the rent of land is a tax on its improved value. Then, a tax on the rent of land would at the same time increase the opportunity cost of land to absentee landlords and lower the opportunity cost to proprietary farmers (because the latter would not have to pay the tax). Therefore, a tax on rent would change the distribution of ownership to favor owners who display a higher degree of openness. Obviously, for Sadi Carnot to think in these terms he had to regard the human mind as an open system. In the Appendix it will be seen that he anticipated what I call the "leap before you look principle"—a principle which states that to make good use of clues an entrepreneur must *guess* at hypotheses.

To carry the argument one step further, let us consider a corporation that is owned by thousands of absentee landlords—the stockholders. Now there is no reason to assume that the stockholders personally have a lower degree of openness than the management. Nevertheless, in terms of the constraints imposed on management, the stockholders may not be altogether different from absentee landlords, inasmuch as they provide an incentive for the firm to concentrate on short-run objectives. So what can the government do to increase the rate of progress when it is very low—say, as it was during the first part of this century in the United States? As it did in 1916, it can impose a corporation income tax! If we assume that corporations "satisfice" in terms of profits after taxes, then the effect of a corporation income tax will be to increase the degree of openness; that is, if the corporations were satisfied with their earnings before the imposition of the tax, after the imposition of the tax they will act as if the degree of uncertainty in their environment had increased.

In other words, there were very good theoretical reasons for passing the corporation income tax. To be sure, in the long debate between economists over the corporation income tax, the main question pertained to the incidence of the tax: whether it was to be paid by the corporation or passed on to the consumer. However, the implicit assumption in this debate was that production functions were to be taken as givens; in other words, it was assumed that the economic system was closed to new ideas.

While it is no accident that the corporation income tax was passed when a progressive administration was in power, the effect of tax loopholes has been to nullify the basic purpose of the corporation income tax. Tax loopholes do not merely discriminate in favor of some types of risk-taking at the expense of others. The almost inevitable effect of tax loopholes is to discriminate in favor of relatively predictable activities and against relatively unpredictable activities. For example, while the oil depletion allowance discriminated in favor of a greater search for oil, it also discriminated against a search for new types of energy. In fact, the almost inevitable effect of removing the oil depletion allowance will be to induce a search for technological discoveries. Or to take another example: an investment credit provides an incentive for economic expansion; but by providing an incentive to this relative riskless activity, it discriminates against the discovery of ways to produce a given output with fewer inputs, because firms can satisfice in terms of particular profit levels on the basis of lower degrees of openness. Similarly, liberal depreciation allowances provide an incentive for large firms to acquire smaller ones as a tax write-off; however, they rob the corporation income tax of its initial rationale by discriminating in favor of expansion and against progress. However, it is no accident that the present tax system favors microstability rather than macrostability. Such a tax system is the logical complement of a policy of stable growth.

How the tax system should be changed to favor a more dynamic society than we have today is obviously a matter that will require a great deal of research. From the point of view of improving the performance of the economy, one matter requiring the urgent attention of economists is how to revise the corporation income tax so it will encourage productivity gains and discourage empire building. What is needed is the reciprocal of an excess profits tax: a tax with a high average rate (such as 50 percent) and a negative marginal rate with respect to cost savings from the previous year. With such a tax, a corporation could reduce its total tax burden by introducing a machine enabling it to produce an existing output with fewer inputs.

There is also an urgent need to consider environmental taxes, rather than regulation, as a means of encouraging more rapid progress in reducing environmental degradation. Of course, it is not necessary to convince economists that the costs of environmental degradation should be internalized. Moreover, there can be no question that if the costs and benefits were more or less known this would be the right approach. It would affect the decisions of entrepreneurs engaged in creating pollution by lowering their profits; and at the same time it would insure that the right amount was spent on environmental degradation. However, since neither the benefits nor the costs of reducing environmental degradation are known, the standard welfare approach is inapplicable, because it assumes a closed system. Physicians do not as yet know how various levels of contaminants in the air contribute to various diseases. On the other hand, the costs of reducing pollution will depend on the imaginativeness of business firms when searching for new alternatives. And their imaginativeness will depend on the degree of risk that is imposed upon them.

The basic reason environmental taxes are needed is not the traditional reason; that is, the tax is not intended to insure that the "right" amount will be spent on reducing pollution. Rather, it is intended to provide better incentives than can be provided with regulation. Up to a point, regulation will work; that is, if the regulations are stringent, sooner or later firms will reduce pollution to the lowest level that can be achieved using existing technology (such as the internal combustion engine). But with any technology, the difference in cost between reducing the first increment of pollution and the last is likely to be a factor of five or ten. Indeed, with respect to both air and water pollution, such cost differentials are now being found. However, regulation provides no incentive for firms to search for better alternatives; and for this reason it can only be regarded, at best, as a short-run measure.

To provide better incentives, risks must be internalized by making profits depend in part on improvements in reducing pollution. For example, new cars might be divided into four classes, according to how much they have reduced emissions, compared to the lowest-emitting car of the previous year. The bottom two classes could be required to pay excise taxes of $100 to $200, and the top two classes could receive rebates of $100 to $200.

What if firms refuse to play the game by engaging in consonant behavior? Failure to generate a diversity of ideas would be regarded as a failure of competition and the basis for a dissolution suit. People complain about the failure of firms to exercise "social responsibility." But no firm can be expected to take action when it does not know if its rivals will cooperate by competing. And under such circumstances, it is the responsibility of the government to take measures to insure that risks are internalized.

There are, of course, formidable problems involved in determining the initial tax rate and deciding when the rate should be raised or lowered. And under the very best of circumstances, a great deal of learning would have to take place after a system of incentives was put into effect. It must always be kept in mind, however, that the alternative to such incentives is not the automatic invisible hand. It is, rather, a system of direct regulation, which, with its perverse incentives, will produce worse results.

The necessity to conserve fuel will also require tax incentives. However, the ultimate purpose of conservation measures is not simply to reduce consumer demand, but to put pressure on business firms to change their menus of technology. For example, it is no accident that in Europe cars tend to be smaller than in the United States. The difference in fuel costs between driving an American compact car and a European subcompact can be up to twenty-five dollars a month—an income effect that can hardly be ignored.

There certainly must be a limit to how much taxes can be increased and to the overall tax burden that can be imposed upon a society. Some people may find themselves faced with more uncertainty than they can cope with. As far as the middle and lower income groups are concerned, personal taxes may already be too high. With respect to the upper income groups, it is often assumed that a highly unequal distribution of income and risk-taking go hand in hand and that a less progressive tax system would contribute to more risk-taking. However, in the managerial society in which we live, high rewards go not to those taking risks, but to those protecting firms from risks. And if this is true, a personal income tax that is more progressive, because it contains fewer loopholes, will favor the natural aristocracy and contribute to risk-taking.

The main purpose of taxing business firms should be the encouragement of a greater degree of dynamic behavior. To do this, tax rates must bear a close relationship to economic performance, whether the performance is measured in terms of reducing inputs per unit of output, or in terms of reducing environmental degradation per unit of output. Many people believe that the encouragement can be provided by more favorable tax treatment of research-and-development expenditures. Research and development, however, is an input, not an output. And more favorable tax treatment may have no noticeable impact on the rate of progress, because it only provides an incentive to define research-and-development activities more broadly. Admittedly, the measurement problems are more difficult if taxes designed to favor a greater degree of dynamic behavior are related to outputs (productivity advances) rather than inputs (research-and-development expenditures). However, if the tax provides the right kind of incentives, a tax that can be only roughly measured is infinitely better than a tax that can be precisely measured yet provides no incentives for better performance.

Equal Opportunity Policies versus Full Employment Policies

When the Full Employment Act was passed in 1946, the general aim was an economy free of major depressions. This goal was entirely consistent with a policy featuring a high degree of macrostability: a policy to make good use of human diversity by assuring that people with more or less equal abilities would have more or less equal opportunites. In fact, many liberals were enthusiastic about a "full employment, stable growth" policy because they saw in it a means to provide better opportunities for minorities.

An equal opportunities policy would assure that, while everyone is given an equal chance to be a success, no one is denied the right to be a failure. And by not seeking to guarantee people the right to a job, the general aim of such a policy is a society featuring a good deal of risk-taking. In fact, inasmuch as it recognizes the reciprocal relationship between individuals and society as a whole, such a policy comes close to capturing the very essence of a Jeffersonian democracy, wherein the development of the individual is emphasized: if individual development is to occur, people must be faced with risks and be required to use their imaginations. The development of a society to deal with new challenges is stressed: if societies are to evolve in the face of dilemmas, a great deal of highly decentralized risk-taking will be necessary in order to bring about smooth progress directed toward increasing output per unit of input and reducing environmental degradation.

Conversely, a country that attempts to protect everyone's right to a job cannot hope to equalize job opportunities. On the contrary, those countries whose aim is to protect people's rights to jobs are sooner or later destined to become highly stratified societies in which the differences between those engaged in various occupations tend to be regarded as God-given. In other words, the protection of everyone's right to a job would make America an altogether different society than it was in the past.

And, paradoxical as it may seem, a country that attempts to guarantee jobs, rather than to equalize opportunities, is destined to become a country in which unemployment is always a serious problem. Which industries have provided the most new job opportunities? Look at the experience of almost any industry, and you will find that when job opportunities are expanding most rapidly, competitive rivalry, as measured by changes in market shares, is greatest. However, a country that attempts to guarantee jobs is devoted to microstability, and a country devoted to microstability is one in which competition cannot flourish.

In thinking about their future careers, college students now have a much smaller propensity to take risks than they did fifteen years ago. Their professors may think youth is being wasted on the youth. But the students would like nothing more than having a job guaranteed to them. And the reason is not hard to find: job opportunities are scarcer, because there are not many industries in which competition is still thriving. In short, the lack of competition becomes a self-aggravating force; that is, it produces a society with more anxiety, and the more anxiety in a society, the more difficult it is to pursue a policy that would equalize opportunities.

It must be emphasized, however, that for an equal-opportunities policy to be widely supported, there cannot be large inequalities in income and wealth unrelated to the willingness and ability of individuals and firms to engage in risk-taking. For example, without closing the loopholes in the tax system, it would be politically impossible for any president to ask the American public in general to engage in more risk-taking.

By contrast, a full-employment program, narrowly defined, is almost guaranteed to create perverse incentives for the internalization of risks. While the government can undertake to prevent major downtowns with no serious affect on private incentives, the goal of fine-tuning the economy to prevent all fluctuations in economic activites will sooner or later lead to the gradual elimination of private risk-taking: with such a policy, every group in society has an incentive to intervene in the political process to shift the burden of risk-taking to some other group. And the further the government goes toward guaranteeing everyone's right to a job—the further it moves toward eliminating uncertainty from the environment—the more it dulls the propensity to engage in risk-taking. In other words, the further a government goes in guaranteeing jobs, the more uncertain it makes job opportunities. A land of opportunity is, almost by definition, a land with favorable incentives for risk-taking.

As a result of the change in incentives, the relationship between voters and elected officials becomes a client/lawyer relationship. The position taken on the various issues is no longer an important criterion for deciding between public officials, except when voting for one rather than another candidate is likely to result in a distribution of income more favorable to the voter. And as a further result of the change in incentives, the relationship between the various groups in society becomes that of a zero-sum game: whether or not defended in such terms, all issues are regarded as distributional issues.

It is ironic that, while each group in society is motivated by the desire to make its future more certain, the effect of viewing policy decisions in terms of a zero-sum game is to make the future of the country more and more uncertain. Progress can come about only when there is risk-taking. The avoidance of risk-taking not only shifts responsibility to someone else, it fosters the development of people who are obsessed by the desire for security; and by attempting to eliminate challenges from peoples' lives, it minimizes the possibility of all types of progress.

In short, a full-employment policy, narrowly defined, is almost certain to create a prisoners' dilemma situation: a situation in which, by virtue of their unwillingness to take risks, all the prisoners are made worse off than they might otherwise be. And if risks are not internalized, the only real alternative available to such societies is one based upon using the powers of the government to coerce individuals and business firms. And it is no accident that those countries not favoring the internalization of risks feature instead highly coercive societies.

Therefore, if the United States is to acquire the degree of macrostability it once possessed, it is imperative to substitute equal opportunities for a full employment policy. The question facing the country is not whether a 4 percent or 6 percent unemployment rate is the "right" figure. It is, rather, whether full employment is the "right" objective.

This is not to say, of course, that the problems of the unemployed should be ignored. To be sure, a significant proportion of the unemployed is represented by people who have been out of work for less than two months. As far as the minority groups are concerned, however, unemployment is a much longer-run problem. And insofar as it often involves learning new skills, technological unemployment can also be a longer-run problem. Moreover, because of a declining birth rate and an older population, it is to be expected that the pressures to prevent technological unemployment from occurring will increase.

It would be nice if the unemployment problems of the minority groups could be solved by providing equal educational opportunities. But according to people who have been directly involved in working with the children of minority groups, the problem is not that simple. They say that more often than not the basic problems result from values created in the home. They also report that dealing more effectively with these problems will call for specially trained teachers, a special program of training beginning in kindergarten, and a good deal of work with parents.

There are, of course, many unresolved social issues—and they probably will remain unresolved until a major effort has been made to set up experimental schools. However, while there are substantial differences among informed people with respect to the particular measures that will be necessary, one thing seems to be very clear: it is naive to believe that the problems of unemployment among the minority groups can be dealt with by a full employment policy.

Likewise, it is not easy to find effective solutions for the problems of technological unemployment. Neither unemployment insurance nor the negative income tax represent a reasonable answer to the needs of a highly skilled worker who, through no fault of his own, has become technologically unemployed. Perhaps, as in Japan, people should be encouraged to retire at the age of fifty-five. Certainly, an early retirement program would have been a less expensive way to deal with the farm problem than using price supports to keep farmers at their jobs. According to the Protestant Ethic, however, people must be kept on their jobs until retirement—no matter how expensive it is to society as a whole.

Or perhaps what is needed is a retraining program, combined with technological unemployment insurance, which would maintain the person's income for a specified period, say, two years. Either this kind of measure or early retirement would be consistent with an equal opportunities objective.

My main purpose, however, is not to make specific policy recommendations. It is, rather, to point out possible ways of dealing with unemployment problems that, on the one hand, are consistent with an equal opportunities objective, and, on the other, would preserve the scope for private risk-taking. The government can help equalize opportunities, thereby promoting a dynamic society. But it cannot undertake to guarantee full employment, narrowly defined, without ultimately destroying the incentives for risk-taking and the opportunity of individuals to deal with new challenges.

Responsiveness of Organizations to Increased Risk

Fairly good predictions can be made of the internal changes required in organizations if they are to deal with higher or lower degrees of risk and uncertainty. To be sure, it would be nice to have better ways to measure the internal characteristics of organizations and improvements in the performance of a technology. But better measurements would not necessarily contribute to better theory.

On the other hand, an understanding of the dynamics involved in becoming adjusted to dealing with a higher degree of risk and uncertainty would contribute to better theory. For example, today we can only guess about the responsiveness of the United States' automobile industry to foreign competition. What we would like to know is how much of a crisis is really required before a significant increase in the degree of openness can be discerned? From the standpoint of devising more sensible public policies, it would also be desirable to know more about the dynamics of becoming adjusted to dealing with a higher degree of risk. For example, from the point of view of devising environmental taxes, it would be necessary to make rough predictions of the impact of alternative tax measures upon behavior. Indeed, a better understanding of the dynamics involved in dealing with a greater degree of uncertainty may be the single most important issue to be resolved in the social sciences.

To raise the issue in a somewhat different form, how poignant does a crisis have to be for politicians and policymakers to understand that over the past ten years profound changes have occurred in the American economy? How great does an economic crisis have to be before they are willing to concede that trying to avoid minor economic fluctuations can increase the vulnerability of the economy to major fluctuations? How widespread does a crisis have to be for politicians to understand that by trying to spare everyone from risk-taking they are making the future of the United States more unpredictable?

However, it is not only the extent of the crisis that will determine how long this country will continue to base its policies on the sacred lessons of the Great Depression. A good deal will depend on people's tolerance of an economy that cannot escape from stagflation and on their perception of the alternatives. Many people feel that having to decide between a policy of restraint and a policy of regulation is like trying to decide whether they prefer to be bombed by day or by night. Moreover, their common sense tells them that the real issue facing the United States is not how little or how much the government does, but what the government does, and how it affects economic performance. The choice facing the country cannot be posed in terms such as "what can you do for country?" or "what can your country do for you?" Rather, it is a choice between developing a more coercive society than now exists or recognizing, as Jefferson and Madison long ago recognized, that for democracies to survive the relationship between individual and government must be reciprocal: highly interactive societies that feature a good deal of risk-taking foster the development of the individual; and societies that foster the development of the individual are best when it comes to adapting to new circumstances.

Appendix

Notes

Index

Appendix: Two Types of Rationality

Middle-class rationality is the rationality associated with a given, or a very slowly changing, environment. In other words, it is the rationality described in Marshallian economics. By contrast, happy-warrior rationality is the rationality associated with a rapidly changing environment. And the essential difference between these two types of rationality is that whereas the former is constructed on the basis of a look-before-you-leap principle, the latter is constructed on the basis of a leap-before-you-look principle.

There are two reasons for starting this discussion with a brief overview of Bayesian probability theory. In the first place, it provides the most realistic statement of middle-class rationality that has been developed to date. Bayesian probability theory implicitly assumes a semiclosed system paradigm, the same paradigm upon which Marshallian economics is based. It is more realistic than Marshallian theory in that it explicitly deals with the uncertainty involved in adapting to a given environment. Or, to put the point another way, inasmuch as it allows some learning to take place (as a result of modifying prior probability distributions), but does not permit the entrepreneur to use his imagination, it can be regarded as the best attempt to date to patch up classical economic theory.

The second reason it is useful to start with Bayesian probability theory is that once a semiclosed system is regarded as the limiting case of an open system it is relatively easy to understand how open-system logic is related to semiclosed-system logic.

Since there are Bayesians and Bayesians, I have chosen to rely mainly on the writings of L. J. Savage, a Bayesian generally looked upon as having thought most deeply about the fundamental assumptions of Bayesian probability theory.[1] On three general propositions, all Bayesians seem to be in agreement. First, uncertainty is subjective and measurable in probabilistic terms; that is, one's confidence in a hypothesis (belief, opinion, hunch, or theory) or parameter can be measured by the bet he would be willing to place upon it. Thus, whereas Marshallian man knows what he knows, Bayesian man, at least in probabilistic terms, knows what he does not know: the branches on the decision-making tree are taken as givens, and Bayesian man weeds out the less attractive branches by experimenting. Second, it almost goes without saying that Bayesian man is a risk averter: he buys information to minimize the risk of making wrong choices; that is, he "looks before he leaps." Third, there is general agreement among all Bayesians for determining how hypotheses or parameters (represented in prior probabilities) should be modified in the light of experimental evidence to obtain posterior distributions. Bayes' theorem is:

$$P(H/D) = \frac{P(D/H)\,P(H)}{P(D)}$$

P is the conditional probability (the preliminary probability estimate) on the assumption that *H* is a reasonable hypothesis (that is, on the assumption there is genuine statistical uncertainty); and *D* is the actual probability, estimated on the basis of data obtained from experiments.

If a person had to bet whether a coin were "fair" or "unfair," that would be the prior probability, after which the hypothesis would be tested by conducting experiments—by repeatedly tossing the coin. And the formula indicates how the prior opinions would be modified in the light of data obtained from the experiments. The initial bet may have been that the odds of the coin coming up heads or tails (a fair coin) were about fifty-fifty; or that an "unfair" coin would be likely to come up heads in two out of three tosses. But it does not really matter what guess had been made initially because, as Savage has shown, a "large" number of experiments will yield identical results no matter what prior probability is selected.[2] As Savage notes: "If observations are precise, in a certain sense, relative to the prior distributions on which they bear, then the form and properties of the prior distribution have negligible influence on the posterior distribution."[3]

What is the fundamental assumption upon which Bayesian theory is based? Savage was quite specific in acknowledging that "Reformulations of Bayes' theorem apply to continuous parameters or data."[4] Or, as he later modified this assumption: "Prior distributions need not be and never really are completely uniform. To ignore the departures from uniformity, it suffices that your actual prior distribution change gently in the region favored by the data."[5] "Rare events do occur," Savage acknowledges, "although rarely, and should not be permitted to confound us utterly."[6]

It can be seen, therefore, that Bayesian probability theory is based upon the logic of a semiclosed system. A semiclosed system paradigm assumes a relatively predictable type of evolution in terms of a given or a very slowly changing environment. And so does Bayesian probability theory. By virtue of the fact that knowledge improves gradually Bayesian man need not use his imagination to construct new hypotheses.

Or to put the point another way: Bayesian man can look before he leaps because the world around him changes so slowly he can afford to ignore the interactions between his world and the larger world. Does this mean that he can be expected to know everything about the outer world and never have cause for regrets? To his credit, Savage freely acknowledges that, when carried to the extreme, the look-before-you-leap principle breaks down:

> Carried to its logical extreme, the "Look before you leap" principle demands that one envisage every conceivable policy for the government of his whole life (at least from now on) in its most minute details, in the light of the vast number of unknown states of the world, and decide here and now on one policy. This is utterly ridiculous, not—as some might think—because there might later be cause for regret, if things did not turn out as had been anticipated, but because the task implied in making such a decision is not even remotely resembled by human possibility. It is even utterly beyond our power to plan a picnic or to play a game of chess in accordance with the principle, even when the world of states and the set of available acts to be envisaged are artificially reduced to the narrowest reasonable limits.

> Though the "Look before you leap" principle is preposterous if carried to extremes, I would nonetheless argue that it is the proper subject of our further discussion, because to cross one's bridges when one comes to them means to attack relatively simple problems of decision by artificially confining attention to so small a world that the "Look before you leap" principle can be applied there. I am unable to formulate criteria for selecting these small worlds and indeed believe that their selection may be a matter of judgment and experience about which it is impossible to enunciate complete and sharply defined general principles . . . On the other hand, it is an operation in which we all necessarily have much experience, and one in which there is in practice considerable agreement.[7]

Granting that the look-before-you-leap principle breaks down when carried to the extreme, is it a universal principle? If the environment is changing very slowly, then it is a sound principle. For example, it is a sound principle for the Swiss chocolate industry. So is it for middle-class merchants who have little or no imagination. To be sure, minor dilemmas are almost always encountered when borrowing ideas from one environment to be used in another. But if one enters an occupation or a profession in which knowledge changes very slowly, the risk of encountering major dilemmas can be minimized.

On the other hand, when there are genuine advantages to be realized from changing an environment, and when entrepreneurs with a real sense of adventure are willing to devote themselves to this task, it hardly can be claimed that the look-before-you-leap principle is appropriate. For example, Einstein certainly did not take his environment as a given: to resolve some major dilemmas in the field of physics he changed physics in a major way. Can it be said that he was irrational? By developing the DC-3, the Douglas Corporation interacted with its environment to change it. Can this be described as an irrational act? Abraham Lincoln saw in slavery an institution that created a major dilemma for society as a whole because it was incompatible with the preservation of a democratic society. Can it be said that by acting to change this institution he was acting irrationally?

Every day we are forced to take serious risks in order to avoid more serious risks. For example, a good part of medical care comes under this heading, as do most divorces. And in changing occupations, people are often involved in comparing two risks: the risk of accomplishing little more in their present occupation versus the risk of trying something new. Are they irrational if they assume that the latter risk is the lesser?

Obviously there are many situations in life in which the rational strategy is to "leap before you look"; that is, on the basis of relatively scanty evidence, the entrepreneur must be willing to fall in love with a hypothesis. To be sure, there are genuine risks involved in impetuous behavior: a person can become so attached to a hypothesis he will never change his mind no matter what additional evidence is forthcoming. But if people are unwilling to use their intuitions to suggest new hypotheses, how can they compare alternatives? For example, there can be dozens of experiments that serve to confirm a new hypothesis. But unless the entrepreneur is willing to fall in love with the hypothesis, how can he uncover the evidence? A person who simply daydreams about changing his occupation may certainly be engaged in self-deception. But unless willing to seriously entertain the proposition that a change will benefit him, how can he acquire the relevant information?

In fact, if people could never interact with their environments to change both their ideas and their environments, they would have no means of acting as their own psychiatrists in preventing themselves from having serious mental disorders. And can anyone say that by acting as one's own psychiatrist, rather than hiring one, one is acting irrationally?

As an illustration of the mental attitudes required for happy-warrior rationality, consider the following aphorisms:

> Form resolutions in advance in order not to reflect during action.
> Then obey thyself blindly.
> The promptitude of resolutions most frequently accords with their justice.
> Yield frequently to the first inspiration. Too much meditation on the same subject ends by suggesting the worst part, or at least causes loss of precious time.[8]

These leap-before-you-look recommendations are to be found in the diary of Sadi Carnot, an early nineteenth-century engineer now credited with having discovered the key ideas for the second law of thermodynamics. Moreover, Carnot's arguments were so carefully drawn that they remain valid to this day, even though in his time the first law of thermodynamics had not been stated![9] No doubt, Sadi Carnot's message was that a person can be so filled with self-doubt that he can never construct a new hypothesis.

How might we utilize these ideas to construct a leap-before-you-look principle? According to the Bayesian look-before-you-leap principle, if an entrepreneur can afford it, an infinite number of experiments will lead to the same answer—no matter what prior probability estimate is initially selected. However, the logic associated with an open system paradigm is not nearly so deterministic. Even if he has the resource to conduct an infinite number of experiments, there is no guarantee that an entrepreneur will come up with a satisfactory resolution of a dilemma. What can be said is that, if the entrepreneur wants to give himself the best chance of putting the law of large numbers on his side, he will use his intuition to leap to new hypotheses. The entrepreneur's riches are his hints. But if his hints are not to be squandered the entrepreneur must trust his intuition.

Notes

1. Three Mysteries

1. Moses Abramovitz, "Resource and Output Trends in the United States since 1870," *American Economic Review* 46:5-23 (May 1956).

2. Robert M. Solow, "Technical Change and the Aggregate Production Function," *Review of Economics and Statistics* 39:312 (1957).

3. Wassily Leontief, "Factor Proportions and the Structure of American Trade: Further Theoretical and Empirical Analysis," *Review of Economics and Statistics* 38:386-407 (November 1956).

4. Raymond Vernon, "International Investment and International Trade in the Product Cycle," *Quarterly Journal of Economics* 80:190-207 (May 1966).

5. Simon Kuznets, *Economic Growth and Structure* (New York: Norton, 1965), p. 313.

6. Ibid., pp. 306-307.

7. Edward F. Denison, *Why Growth Rates Differ* (Washington, D.C.: Brookings Institution, 1967), pp. 305-308, 314-315.

8. The technology-intensive industries include chemicals, pharmaceuticals, electric and nonelectric machinery, and aircraft. For further discussion see Michael Boretsky, *U.S. Technology: Trends and Policy Issues,* National Technical Information Service, U.S. Department of Commerce, PB-227930 (October 1973).

9. Ibid., pp. 117-141.

10. Denison, *Why Growth Rates Differ,* p. 298.

11. William H. Gruber and Raymond Vernon, "The R&D Factor in the World Trade Matrix," in *Technology and Competition in International Trade* (New York: National Bureau of Economic Research, 1968), p. 266.

12. Alfred Marshall, *Principles of Economics* (London: Macmillan, 1922); see particularly his statement on "Economic evolution is gradual," p. xiii.

13. Merton Peck, "Science and Technology," in *Britain's Economic Prospects,* ed. Richard E. Caves et al. (Washington, D.C.: Brookings Institution, 1968), p. 449.

2. A Dynamic Process

1. See, for example, Jacob Schmookler, *Invention and Economic Growth* (Cambridge, Mass.: Harvard University Press, 1966).

2. For discussion of the S-shaped curve phenomenon, see Simon Kuznets, *Six Lectures on Economic Growth* (New York: Free Press-Macmillan, 1959); John L. Enos, *Petroleum Progress and Profits: A History of Process Innovation* (Cambridge, Mass.: MIT Press, 1962); R. Miller and D. Sawers, *The Technical Development of Modern Aviation* (London: Routledge, 1968); Abbott Payson Usher, *A History of Mechanical Inventions* (Boston: Beacon Press, 1929); and especially "Technical Change and Capital Formation," *Capital Formation and Economic Growth, National Bureau of Economic Research Conference,* vol. 6 (Princeton, N.J.: Princeton University Press, 1955).

3. Frank M. Knight, *Risk, Uncertainty and Profit* (Boston: Houghton Mifflin, 1921), p. 19.

4. Frank M. Knight, "Diminishing Returns from Investment," *Journal of Political Economy* 52:26-47 (March 1944).

5. Putting one's imagination to work means guessing on the basis of hints. And if it were impossible to use one's intuition to guess, it would be impossible to change the initial conditions.

6. N.L.S. Carnot, *Reflections on the Motive Power of Heat,* tr. R. H. Thurston (New York: Wiley, 1890).

7. The relative cost of developing these two airplanes was provided by Arthur Raymond, a former vice-president of Douglas.

8. Based on a RAND study on radar development by B. Klein and E. Sharkey.

9. John Jewkes, David Sawers, and Richard Stillerman, *The Sources of Invention,* 2nd ed. (London: Macmillan, 1959).

10. Joseph A. Schumpeter, *Capitalism, Socialism, and Democracy* (New York: Harper & Brothers, 1942), pp. 153-163.

11. See, for example, James P. Quirk, *Intermediate Microeconomics* (Chicago: Science Research Associates, 1976), pp. 308-312.

12. The fundamental assumptions of Bayesian probability statistics are discussed in the appendix.

13. John Maynard Keynes, *Essays in Biography* (New York: Macmillan, 1933), p. 107.

14. John Maynard Keynes, *The General Theory of Employment, Interest and Money* (New York: Harcourt, Brace, 1936), p. 245.

15. John Kenneth Galbraith, *The New Industrial State* (Boston: Houghton Mifflin, 1967), pp. 10-34.

16. George Gaylord Simpson, *Biology and Man* (New York: Harcourt, Brace, 1964).

17. Alfred Marshall, *Principles of Economics,* 8th ed. (London: Macmillan, 1920), pp. 247-249, 315-316, 323, 421, 461, 843-844.

18. Leon Walras, *Elements of Pure Economics,* tr. William Jaffe (London: Allen and Unwin for the Royal Economic Society, 1954; Homewood Ill.: Richard D. Irwin for the American Economic Association, 1954), p. 1.

19. This point is discussed in detail in Chapter 6.

20. Joseph A. Schumpeter, *Theory of Economic Development* (Cambridge, Mass.: Harvard University Press, 1936).

21. Schumpeter, *Capitalism, Socialism, and Democracy;* Galbraith, *New Industrial State.*

3. Static Efficiency versus Dynamic Efficiency

1. Joseph A. Schumpeter, *Capitalism, Socialism, and Democracy* (New York: Harper & Brothers, 1942), p. 83.

2. Frank H. Knight, *Risk, Uncertainty and Profit* (Boston: Houghton Mifflin, 1921), p. 233.

3. Ibid., p. 249.

4. Ibid.

5. Kenneth J. Arrow, "Uncertainty and the Welfare Economics of Medical Care," *American Economic Review* 3:941 (December 1963).

6. Simon Kuznets, *Economic Growth and Structure* (New York: Norton, 1965), p. 313.

7. B. F. Skinner, *Science and Human Behavior* (New York: Macmillan, 1953).

8. George Gaylord Simpson, *Biology and Man* (New York: Harcourt Brace, 1964), ch. 7.

9. Lawrence J. White, *The Automobile Industry since 1945* (Cambridge, Mass.: Harvard University Press, 1971), ch. 13.

10. Simon Kuznets, *Modern Economic Growth: Findings and Reflections* (Stockholm: Nobel Foundation, 1972).

11. Based on studies made at RAND and data obtained from Eli Devons' study on British aircraft-engine development for the Air Ministry, 1958.

12. Ibid.

13. H. J. Habakkuk, *American and British Technology in the Nineteenth Century* (Cambridge: Cambridge University Press, 1967). p. 58.

14. Ronald Miller and David Sawers, *The Technical Development of Modern Aviation* (New York: Praeger, 1970), pp. 32-45.

15. Ibid., p. 99.

4. Dynamic Competition

1. George J. Stigler, "Perfect Competition, Historically Contemplated," in *Essays in the History of Economics* (Chicago: University of Chicago Press, 1965), pp. 234-268.

2. Ibid., p. 235.

3. Adam Smith, *Wealth of Nations* (New York: Dutton, 1947), vol. 1, pp. 88-107.

4. Ibid., p. 117.

5. Stigler, "Perfect Competition."

6. Ibid., p. 266.

7. R. P. Feynman, R. B. Leighton, and M. Sands, *The Feynman Lectures on Physics* (Reading, Mass.: Addison-Wesley, 1963), p. 1-1.

8. Richard P. Feynman, *The Character of Physical Law* (London: British Broadcasting Corp., 1965), p. 147.

9. Feynman, *Lectures on Physics,* p. 1-1.

10. See, for example, Sir George Thompson, *The Inspiration of Science* (London: Oxford University Press, 1961), p. 126.

11. Stigler, *Essays in the History of Economics,* p. 22.

12. See Smith, "Of Colonies," *Wealth of Nations,* vol. 4, ch. 7.

13. Wallace Klippert Ferguson, *Renaissance Studies* (New York: Harper & Row, 1970).

14. Alfred Marshall, *Principles of Economics,* 8th ed. (London: Macmillan, 1920), p. 7.

15. Ibid., p. 748.

16. John Maynard Keynes, *The General Theory* (New York: Harcourt, Brace, 1958), p. 381.

17. See John Gallager and Ronald Robinson, "The Imperialism of Free Trade," *Economic History Review* 6 (1):1-15 (1953).

18. D. C. M. Plott, "Economic Factors in British Policy During the New Imperialism," *Past and Present* 7:120-138 (April 1968).

19. Ibid., p. 123.

20. Keynes, *General Theory,* p. 380.

21. Frederic M. Scherer, "Market Structure and the Employment of Scientists and Engineers," *American Economic Review* 57:524-531 (June 1967).

22. Frederick T. Knickerbocker, *Oligopolistic Reaction and Multinational Enterprise* (Cambridge, Mass.: Harvard University Press, 1973).

23. George Woodwell, *Diversity and Stability in Ecological Systems* (Upton, N.Y.: Brookhaven National Laboratory, 1969).

24. Claude Shannon and Warren Weaver, *The Mathematical Theory of Communication* (Urbana: University of Illinois Press, 1964).

25. Sir Eric Ashby, *Technology and the Academics* (London: Macmillan, 1958), p. 15.

26. Smith, *Wealth of Nations,* vol. 1, p. 111-112.

27. Ibid., p. 9.

28. Ibid., p. 5.

29. C. D. Darlington, *The Evolution of Man and Society* (New York: Simon and Schuster, 1969), pp. 674-675; see also George Gaylord Simpson, *Behavior and Evolution* (New Haven: Yale University Press, 1958), pp. 512-515.

30. Jonathan Hughes, *Industrialization and Economic History* (New York: McGraw-Hill, 1958), ch. 5.

31. John Stuart Mill, *Principles of Political Economy,* vol. 2 (New York: Appleton, 1877), p. 340.

5. Case Studies of Dynamic Competition

1. Ralph C. Epstein, *The Automobile Industry* (New York: A. W. Shaw, 1928), p. 320.

2. Ibid., p. 49.

3. Ibid., pp. 47-48.

4. Allan Nevins and Frank Hill, *Ford,* vol. 1, *The Times, the Man, the Company* (New York: Scribner's, 1954), p. 194.

5. Ibid., pp. 193-194.

6. Ibid.

7. *Should We Have a New Engine?* (Pasadena: Jet Propulsion Laboratory, California Institute of Technology, 1975), ch. 6.

8. Epstein, *The Automobile Industry,* p. 182.

9. John B. Rae, *The American Automobile* (Chicago: University of Chicago Press, 1965), p. 59.

10. Nevins and Hill, *Ford,* vol. 1, chs. 12, 14-16.

11. Allan Nevins and Frank Hill, *Ford,* vol. 2, *Expansion and Challenge, 1915-1933* (New York: Scribner's, 1957), p. 12.

12. Ibid., p. 245.

13. Ibid., p. 269.

14. Ibid., p. 390.

15. Ibid., ch. 12.

16. Rae, *The American Automobile,* p. 61.

17. Nevins and Hill, *Ford,* vol. 1, ch. 18.

18. Ibid., p. 474.

19. Rae, *The American Automobile,* p. 61.

20. Epstein, *The Automobile Industry,* pp. 353-354.

21. T. A. Boyd, *The Professional Amateur* (New York: Dutton, 1957), pp. 117-123.

22. Epstein, *The Automobile Industry,* p. 242.

23. Ibid., p. 168.

24. Ibid., Appendix B.

25. Nevins and Hill, *Ford,* vol. 2, p. 170.

26. Alfred P. Sloan, Jr., *My Years with General Motors* (New York: Doubleday, 1964), p. 174.

27. Almarin Phillips, *Technology and Market Structure* (Lexington, Mass.: Heath, 1971), see particularly ch. 1.

28. R. R. Nelson, M.J. Peck, and E. D. Kalachek, *Technology, Economic Growth and Public Policy* (Washington, D.C.: Brookings Institution, 1967).

29. Paul A. Samuelson, *Economics* (New York: McGraw-Hill, 1976), pp. 734-735.

30. Phillips, *Technology and Market Structure,* p. 51.

31. A. E. Raymond, "The Well-Tempered Aircraft" (the 39th Wilbur Wright Memorial Lecture), *Journal of the Royal Aeronautical Society* 31:12 (October 1951).

32. Phillips, *Technology and Market Structure,* p. 50.

33. Ibid.

34. Ibid.

35. Ibid.

36. Robert Schlaifer and S. D. Heron, *Development of Aircraft Engines and Fuels* (Cambridge, Mass.: Harvard University Press, 1950).

37. Raymond, "The Well-Tempered Aircraft," p. 13.

38. Ibid., p. 28.
39. Ibid.
40. Ibid., p. 16.
41. Ibid., p. 17.
42. Arthur E. Raymond, "The Origins of the DC-3" (unpublished memorandum, 1938), p. 6.
43. Phillips, *Technology and Market Structure,* pp. 50-51.
44. Ibid., p. 40.
45. Arthur E. Raymond, *Who? Me? Autobiography of Arthur E. Raymond* (Arthur Raymond, 1974), p. IV-1-2.
46. Ibid., p. IV-1-4.
47. Ibid., p. V-1-3.
48. John E. Tilton, *International Diffusion of Technology: The Case of Semiconductors* (Washington, D.C.: Brookings Institution, 1971).
49. Ibid., pp. 161-163.
50. Joseph A. Schumpeter, *Capitalism, Socialism, and Democracy* (New York: Harper & Brothers, 1942).
51. John Kenneth Galbraith, *The New Industrial State* (Boston: Houghton Mifflin, 1967).
52. Joseph A. Schumpeter, *Theory of Economic Development* (Cambridge, Mass.: Harvard University Press, 1936), p. 86.
53. Schumpeter, *Capitalism, Socialism, and Democracy,* p. 84.
54. Ibid.
55. Ibid., p. 132.
56. Ibid., p. 133.
57. Galbraith, *The New Industrial State,* p. 16.
58. Ibid., p. 219.
59. Joseph A. Schumpeter, *Business Cycles* (New York and London: McGraw-Hill, 1939), pp. 87-102.

6. Microbehavior and Macroperformance

1. A. H. Maslow, *Motivation and Personality* (New York: Harper & Row, 1954), pp. 205-206. See also Erich Fromm, *The Anatomy of Human Destructiveness* (New York: Holt, Rinehart and Winston, 1973), p. 370.
2. Thomas S. Kuhn, *The Structure of Scientific Revolutions* (Chicago: University of Chicago Press, 1970), pp. 66-77.
3. C. D. Darlington, *The Evolution of Man and Society* (New York: Simon and Schuster, 1969), pp. 674-675; see also George Gaylord Simpson, *Behavior and Evolution* (New Haven: Yale University Press, 1958).
4. Adam Smith, *Wealth of Nations,* vol 1 (New York: Dutton, 1947), p. 115.
5. *Encyclopedia Britannica,* 1968 ed., vol. 12, p. 989.
6. "Letter from Jefferson to Madison, September 6, 1789," in Adrienne Koch, *Jefferson and Madison: The Great Collaboration* (New York: Knopf, 1946), p. 86.
7. Ibid.
8. Thomas A. Marschak, "Strategy and Organization in a System Development Project," in *The Rate and Direction of Inventive Activity: Economic and Social*

Factors, A Report of the National Bureau of Economic Research (Princeton, N.J.: Princeton University Press, 1962).

9. Alvin J. Harman and Susan Henrichson, *A Methodology for Cost Factor Comparison and Prediction,* RAND Report RM-6269-ARPA (Santa Monica, Calif.: RAND Corp., August 1970).

10. Ibid.

11. Thomas Marschak et al., *Strategy for R&D: Studies in the Microeconomics of Development,* Econometrics and Operations Research, vol. 8 (New York: Springer-Verlag, 1967).

12. For two very interesting articles see Robert Perry, *Comparisons of Soviet and U.S. Technology,* RAND Report R-827-PR (Santa Monica, Calif.: Rand Corp., 1973); and Arthur J. Alexander, *Weapons Acquisition in the Soviet Union: The United States and France,* RAND Report P-4989 (Santa Monica, Calif.: Rand Corp., 1973).

13. Werner Heisenberg, *Physics and Beyond* (New York: Harper & Row, 1971), p. 56.

14. Donald W. MacKinnon, "The Characteristics of Creative Architects" (American Institute of Architects-Association of Collegiate Schools of Architecture Teacher Seminar, 1963); and Edward B. Roberts, "Entrepreneurship of Technology," in William H. Gruber and Donald G. Marquis, eds., *Factors in the Transfer of Technology* (Cambridge, Mass.: MIT Press, 1969).

15. Richard M. Cyert and James G. March, *A Behavorial Theory of the Firm* (Englewood Cliffs, N.J.: Prentice-Hall, 1963).

16. Ibid., p. 109.

17. Ibid., p. 120.

18. Ibid., p. 121.

19. Max Weber, *The Theory of Social and Economic Organizations* (New York: Oxford University Press, 1947).

20. Tom Burns and G. M. Stalker, *The Management of Innovation* (London: Tavistock, 1961).

21. Ibid., p. 5.

22. Ibid.

23. Ibid.

24. Ibid., pp. 5-6.

25. Ibid.

26. Ibid.

27. Paul R. Lawrence and Jay W. Lorsch, *Organization and Environment* (Cambridge, Mass.: Harvard University Press, 1967).

28. Ibid., p. 157.

29. Ibid., pp. 157-158.

30. Ibid., p. 155.

31. Alfred Chandler, *Strategy and Structure: Chapter in the History of Industrial Enterprise* (Cambridge, Mass.: MIT Press, 1962).

7. An Explanation of the Mysteries

1. J.-J. Servan-Schreiber, *The American Challenge* (New York: Atheneum, 1968).

2. Louis D. Brandeis, *The Curse of Bigness* (New York: Viking, 1939), p. 115.
3. Ibid., p. 35.
4. Harvey Libenstein, *Beyond Economic Man* (Cambridge, Mass.: Harvard University Press, 1976), p. 30.
5. Abraham Bergson, "On Monopoly Welfare Losses," *American Economic Review* 63:853-871 (December 1973).
6. Frank Hyneman Knight, *The Ethics of Competition* (New York and London: Harper & Brothers, 1936), p. 66.
7. Edwin Mansfield et al., *Research and Innovation in the Modern Corporation* (New York: Norton, 1971), pp. 48-50.
8. Ibid., p. 206.
9. Ibid., pp. 88-109.
10. Ibid., pp. 108-109.
11. Edwin Mansfield and Samuel Wagner, "Organizational and Strategic Factors Associated with Probabilities of Success in Industrial R&D," *Journal of Business* 48 (April 1975).
12. Mansfield et al., *Modern Corporation,* p. 207.
13. Lawrence J. White, *The Automobile Industry Since 1945* (Cambridge, Mass.: Harvard Universiy Press, 1971).
14. Ibid., pp. 126-133.
15. Alfred P. Sloan, Jr., *My Years with General Motors* (Garden City, N. Y.: Doubleday, 1964), p. 265.
16. George J. Stigler, "Production and Distribution in the Short Run," *Journal of Political Economy* 47:305-327 (1939).
17. Jet Propulsion Laboratory Report.
18. White, *Automobile Industry Since 1945,* pp. 284-285.
19. *Should We have New Engine?* (Pasadena: Jet Propulsion Laboratory, California Institute of Technology, 1975).
20. Joseph A. Schumpeter, *Capitalism, Socialism, and Democracy* (New York: Harper & Brothers, 1942); Thorsten Veblen, *The Engineers and the Price System* (New York: Viking Press, 1933).
21. Schumpeter, *Capitalism, Socialism, and Democracy,* see particularly chapter 13, "The Crumbling Walls."
22. Simon Kuznets, *Economic Growth and Structure* (New York: Norton, 1965), p. 313.
23. Veblen, *Engineers and the Price System,* p. 12.
24. Ibid., p. 278.
25. R. J. Ball and T. Burns, "The Inflationary Mechanism in the U. K. Economy," *American Economic Review* 66:467-485 (September 1976).
26. Milton Friedman, "The Role of Monetary Policy," *American Economic Review* 58: 11-17 (March 1968).
27. Milton Friedman, "A Theoretical Framework for Monetary Analysis," *Journal of Political Economy* 79: 323-337 (March 1971).

8. Public Policy Trade-offs

1. *Economic Report of the President, January 1976* (Washington, D.C.: U.S. Government Printing Office, 1976), see particularly pp. 30-39.

2. George J. Stigler, "The Theory of Economic Regulation," *Bell Journal of Economics* 2:3-21 (Spring 1971).

3. Alfred Marshall, *Principles of Economics*, 8th ed. (London: Macmillan, 1920), p. 8.

4. H. Averch and L. Johnson, "Behavior of the Firm under Regulatory Constraint," *American Economic Review* 52:1052-1069 (December 1962).

5. Stigler, "Theory of Economic Regulation," pp. 3-5.

6. Glen Cass, "Air Pollution Control Agency Behavior: Implementing Legal Mandates in an Uncertain World" (Pasadena: Environmental Quality Laboratory, California Institute of Technology, 1976).

7. Morris P. Fiorina, "Is There a Washington Establishment?" (unpublished manuscript, 1976).

8. For a similar point of view, see Paul L. Joskow, "Inflation and Environmental Concern: Structural Changes in the Process of Public Utility Price Regulation," *Journal of Law and Economics* 17:291-327 (1974).

9. Louis D. Brandeis, *The Curse of Bigness* (New York: Viking Press, 1934).

10. See, for example, Richard E. Caves and Ronald W. Jones, *World Trade and Payments: An Introduction* (Boston: Little, Brown, 1973).

9. Internalization of Risk

1. Carl Kaysen and Donald Turner, *Antitrust Policy: An Economic and Legal Analysis* (Cambridge, Mass.: Harvard University Press, 1959), p. 18.

2. Ibid., p. 19.

3. Louis D. Brandeis, *The Curse of Bigness* (New York: Viking Press, 1934).

4. *Economic Report of the President, February 1975* (Washington, D.C.: U.S. Government Printing Office, 1975), p. 1949.

5. Alfred Marshall, *Principles of Economics* (London: Macmillan, 1922), p. 315.

6. Kaysen and Turner, *Antitrust Policy*, pp. 25-89.

7. Ibid., pp. 84-85.

8. Ibid., p. 58.

9. S. 1167, A Bill, "To supplement the antitrust laws, and to protect trade and commerce against oligopoly power or monopoly power, and for other purposes" (93rd Congress, 1st Session, March 19, 1973), pp. 1-2.

10. Ibid., pp. 2-3.

11. N. L. S. Carnot, *Reflections on the Motive Power of Heat*, tr. R. H. Thurston (New York: Wiley, 1890), pp. 206-208.

12. Elting E. Morison, *Men, Machines, and Modern Times* (Cambridge, Mass.: MIT Press, 1966), p. 40.

Appendix

1. Leonard J. Savage, *The Foundations of Statistics* (New York: Dover, 1972). For a more concise statement, see Ward Edwards, Harold Lindman, and Leonard J. Savage, "Bayesian Statistical Inference for Psychological Research," *Psychological Review* 70:193-241 (May 1963).

2. Savage, *Foundations of Statistics*, pp. 46-50.

3. Edwards et al., "Bayesian Statistical Inference," p. 202.

4. Ibid., p. 198.

5. Ibid., p. 202.

6. Ibid.

7. *The Foundations of Statistics,* pp. 16-17.

8. N.L.S. Carnot, *Reflections on the Motive Power of Heat,* tr. R.H. Thurston (New York: Wiley, 1890), p. 208.

9. R. P. Feynman, R. B. Leighton, and M. Sands, *The Feynman Lectures on Physics* (Reading, Mass.: Addison-Wesley, 1963), p. 44-2.

Index

Bei Fragen zur Produktsicherheit wenden Sie sich bitte an:
If you have any questions regarding product safety,
please contact:

Walter de Gruyter GmbH
Genthiner Straße 13
10785 Berlin
productsafety@degruyterbrill.com